The Romance Zone

Relationship, Travel, Cultural and Marriage Guidebook to Latin American Ladies

James N. McLeod
Bruce T. White

T.L.C WORLDWIDE, INC.
P.O. Box 924994
Houston Texas 77292-4994
(713) 896-9993
www.tlcworldwide.com

First edition, 1999.

©1998 copyright by James N. McLeod and Bruce T. White. All rights reserved. No part of this book may be reproduced in any form or by any means, without permission in writing from the publisher.

Visit our website at www.foreignromance.com

Printed in the United States of America.

The Romance Zone: Relationship, Travel, Cultural and Marriage Guidebook to Latin American Ladies published by:
In One Ear Publications
P. O. Box 637
Campo CA 91906-0637

ISBN 1-881791-05-X

C.I.P.

McLeod, James N. and Bruce T. White.
The romance zone: relationship, travel & cultural guidebook to latin american ladies /
James N. McLeod and Bruce T. White. —
p. cm.
Index.
1. Latin America—Description and travel—
1999 - I. Title.

Table of Contents

Dedication

To all single people seeking happiness through unconventional methods and who will successfully find it.

Authors' Note

This book is about Hispanic culture. More specifically, it is about Latin American women and the cultural forces which affect them, and it has been written to address a very specific need. Every year more and more American men are marrying women from Latin American countries. Sometimes they have no problems at all at any stage of the process, but occasionally they do run into trouble because of misconceptions arising from cultural differences or from a lack of awareness of the nature of the countries themselves. If you are one of the men who has married, or who is hoping to marry, a Latin American woman, then this book is for you.

In Latin America, rudeness, or failure to observe basic good manners is viewed much more critically than in North America. Society is more restrained, conservative, and traditional, with more attention paid to conventions of behavior. People are much more concerned with appearances, "proper" behavior, dress, and social convention than we are in the United States. There are far more "don'ts" in Hispanic culture than in ours, and violations of the rules of behavior are much more frowned upon. Unconventional and individualistic behavior may be acceptable under some circumstances, especially since you are a

3

foreigner and are not expected to know all of the rules, but it will help you a great deal if you know enough to be able to show respect for the Latin way of doing things.

Generally, behavior in public places is not as casual as it can be in our culture. For instance, people do not put their feet on a desk; they don't lean back in a chair in a stretched position; they do not sit or perch on a desk or table. In a crowded airport or bus station, no one sits on the floor. Men do not stand or walk with their hands in their pockets. In restaurants, people do not figure up and pay their portion of the check.

Customs can be learned in time, though, simply through observation. What can't be observed are cultural expectations and beliefs...those internal guidance systems that cause people to act as they do. More than anything, this is what cultural anthropologists focus upon to gain knowledge of a culture. People can't usually tell you about them, because they are not consciously aware that they exist; only that it feels "right" when it's done that way, and "wrong" when it isn't. If you are seriously interested in understanding a Latin woman, and getting along well with her and her family, you have to know about those unseen forces which motivate her and control her feelings and actions. Your internal guidance systems are not the same as hers. I would like very much to see the problems that often show up in inter-cultural marriages reduced to an absolute minimum, and that is my objective with this book. The man in search of a Latin American wife needs to know about her culture, because when he knows her culture, he knows a great deal of what he needs to know about her.

There is one issue that I would particularly like to clarify before getting into the book. I frequently refer to the United States and Americans. I have done that because I

4

expect the vast majority of the readers to be from that country, but the book will be just about as useful to anyone else who is a foreigner in Latin America. Comparisons are frequently made between Latin American culture and American culture, and that is the main reason I restrict my considerations to Latin America and the United States.

Some people may object to my frequent use of the term "American" when discussing citizens of the United States. Writers of travel books usually advise you not to call yourself an American while in Latin America, because Latin Americans are also Americans. My response to that is "hogwash!" In all of my years in Latin America, and there have been quite a few, I have never encountered an objection to my referring to myself as an American, and I am almost always referred to as an "American" or as a *"Gringo"* (*Gringo* is a neutral term in every country except Mexico, and denotes nothing more than a person of Anglo or European descent). Several years back I followed a hot debate over the use of the term in the "Letters to the Editor" section of the *Tico Times,* an English language newspaper published in Costa Rica. Most writers agreed with those who think that we shouldn't call ourselves *"Americanos,"* and suggested instead such terms as *"Norteamericanos"* (forgetting that North America also includes Canada and Mexico) or *"Estadounidenses"* (United Statesians), overlooking the fact that there is also another United States in the Western Hemisphere (*Estados Unidos Mexicanos*) who are also *"estadounidenses."*

What everyone seems to forget (except for the Latin Americans themselves) is that the proper name for our country is "The United States of America." Our country is the only country in the world that actually has the word "America" as part of its official name. That is why I use the word and that is why its use is justified. I am not being ethnocentric or nationalistic. I simply would like for our usage of the word to conform to usage in the rest of the world and for us not attempt to appear shamefaced about using that name. I don't bandy the word about, though. I frequently get asked if I am American. I either say yes, or I say *"Soy Texano."* They like that even better. It gives us something else to talk about. I am rarely asked **what** my nationality is, leaving me to come up with the name. Usually people simply ask me where I am from. When that happens, I just simply say *"de los Estados Unidos."* To say "I am from America" is inappropriate.

I approach the writing of this book as if you can speak Spanish. Perhaps you can, but it is most likely, I realize, that you probably cannot, and if you do know some Spanish, your vocabulary may well be limited. This is not an oversight on my part. Many things that you will need to communicate can best be done in Spanish, and my assumption is that you are seriously considering seeking a Latina as a mate. This being the case, my hope is that you will go about your business in Latin America with a small English-Spanish dictionary in your pocket or an electronic translator in your hand. You will learn basic Spanish more quickly than you expect. But please remember this: **Don't be afraid to talk with people,** no matter what kind of mixture of Spanish and English you might be able to put together. The people will be delighted, and will do what-ever they can to communicate with you.

My guess is that the vast majority of American men who marry Latinas locate their spouses through one of the introduction agencies or marriage agencies currently doing business in both the United States and in several Latin American countries. One of the very best of the introduction agencies, T.L.C. Worldwide, Inc., is in Houston, Texas. Bruce White, the president of T.L.C., and I met some years ago while I still owned my own introduction agency, based in Costa Rica, which I had begun after retiring from some 25 years of working in Latin America as a cultural anthropologist. We became good friends, and while I no longer have an introduction agency (nor want to do the hard work it requires) nor work professionally as an anthropologist, Bruce White and James Smith, vice-president of T.L.C., and I work together on a number of matters related to their efforts to introduce North Americans and Latinas. I highly recommend them. Feel free to express your opinion regarding this book at any time by fax at 713-681-0950. Thanks for the feedback & best wishes.

☐ *James N. McLeod, Ph.D.*
Anthropologist

There is a surprising current interest in foreign ladies, and especially Latinas (Latin Ladies) from Western men. Since founding T.L.C. Worldwide, Inc. in 1992, I am constantly amazed at the popularity of "International Dating" (and the subsequent marriages). Personally, I've always been physically attracted to women with dark hair and eyes, but I found that I was even more refreshed by the personalities, beliefs and backgrounds of Latinas. I had dated several Latinas in the Houston area, but I was even more impressed after visiting Latin America. For years I had seen the advertisements to meet foreign ladies of Asia and Russia, but I decided that this same concept should work even better with the ladies of Latin America, based on their compatibility, proximity and, of course, their beauty.

International Romance is a great option for gentleman unhappy with their current dating environment. The vast majority of participating American men are serious and sincere regarding the selection of their best friend and future spouse. Because of the time, work, and expense involved, most insincere thrill-seekers are simply not interested in a courtship abroad. It's much easier for these guys to meet women through conventional means such as a local nightclub. But then, maybe that's why we have a domestic divorce rate of 50-70%. Hundreds, possibly thousands of our gentleman clients have dated and married Latinas who are happier, younger, and more attractive (with fewer complications) than could be found locally.

Latin American ladies also benefit from International Dating programs. Often these ladies find American gentleman willing to accept them regardless of social class, children (if any), or their economic status. Even professional Latin women find foreign Introductory Services and American men more suitable for the type of future spouse that they desire. American men are often preferred because of their honesty, faithfulness and ability to express love. We present Latinas from all social classes, from single mothers or factory workers to dentists, doctors, and attorneys. Once a Latina commits to an American gentleman she often sacrifices her homeland and the closeness of family and friends. Thus, the Latinas are genuinely just as sincere as our gentleman clients. Our six year record of success shatters the negative and outdated stereotypes of dating abroad and foreign marriages. Our program is not for everyone. But, for those individuals who are positive, realistic and willing to try, international romance offers great opportunities in finding a suitable life-mate. The only limitations to overcome are skepticism, complacency and a closed mind.

I believe that this new method of meeting people and establishing relationships with those of different cultures and countries is only in it's infancy. Through technological

8

advancements, freedom to travel, and global political improvements our world is becoming an increasingly smaller
planet. This fact is evident in the news everyday. From
experience I know that once most men embark on foreign
relationships, they rarely return to traditional domestic
dating. Both the women and men in our programs are
seeking the same system of values. The primary components include faithfulness, devotion, family-orientation,
and a secure future with overall happiness. I hope that by
reading our book you will understand why many men are
finding compatible, loving, and sincere ladies in Latin
America to be their spouses. Maybe a Latin Lady is in your
future too.

☐ *Bruce T. White*
   President, T.L.C. Worldwide, Inc.

Introduction

Trouble at Home

You can pick up almost any magazine that carries ads for international introduction services and you will find quite a few advertisements for companies specializing in various Asian countries, Eastern Europe, Russia, the Caribbean, and Latin America. Why the demand?

I've talked with hundreds of men who were clients of my own company, or some whom I simply met on the street in Latin America, or who participated in T.L.C. tours, and the now predictable answer to my question about why they prefer Latin women is that they simply cannot tolerate the American woman's behavior and attitude anymore, and that they don't have these problems with Latinas. I believe that there is a lot of truth to this, but I also suspect that it is a simple answer to a much more complex issue.

Lets deal with that particular issue for a moment. There really have been some major shake-ups in American family structure and sex role behavior during the last 30 years. The stable family of the 1950's largely became a relic of the past as American women entered the job market and found that they could be economically independent and

11

responsible for themselves and not have to depend on a man to take care of those things. The wide-spread women's liberation movement of the 1980's demanded a change in men's behavior at home, at work, in the street, and everywhere else that men and women had contact with each other. Men had to step back, take a deep collective breath, and try to figure out what to do next.

Different men have dealt with the situation in different ways. Most have adapted a great deal, and many are, in fact, finding that not having to consistently play the traditional male role is a bit of a relief. I wonder, though, if perhaps the baby wasn't accidentally dumped along with the bath water as the women's liberation movement changed the patterns of relationships between the sexes. Those men who have been willing to discuss with me the issue of American women, beyond a superficial level, generally express a kind of sadness that comes from missing something important in life; as if the hopes they had nourished earlier for intimacy, sharing, and building a future with someone they could depend upon, had been dashed with no chance of recovery.

About the Men

A *Woman's Day* article published in 1984 reported the results of a sociological study conducted with some 250 men who had utilized an Asian introduction service to attempt to locate a wife. The average age was 37, the majority had at least two years of college, they had been married at least once, most were white, and 63% earned over $20,000 (1983 dollars) per year. It would have been simple enough to have kept my own records, because quite a lot of this information was provided on my application forms. But

I didn't, and I no longer have the forms. The above describes fairly well the clients I did have, however, and I think also fairly closely fits the general profile of T.L.C. clients that participate in tours. I would estimate, however, that the average age is a bit higher, probably closer to 40-45. Clients have ranged from their early twenties to mid-sixties, and most are successful in locating mates if they make the effort to do so. Aside from the fact that men who are looking for a Latin American wife feel pretty empty inside when they contemplate life with an American woman, what are the other motivations?

A Younger, Prettier Woman

Bruce White and I have discussed this issue many times, and it has also been a topic of discussion with a number of clients. The truth is that Latin American women are frequently willing to marry a man 10 to 30 years older than she is. And, other than in Latin America or Asia, where can a man marry a beautiful lady that many years younger than he? The immediate temptation is to suggest that a young woman is looking to an older man for financial security (please see next section), but there really is a lot more to it than that. Maturity is highly respected in Latin America, and a woman realizes that she can have a more stable marriage with a mature man. Most of my applications from the ladies stressed their desire for a stable and mature man. However, do not assume that I am recommending a wide age spread. I am not. You will, as you read further, discover that I recommend common sense.

Marriage Stability

The United States has an extraordinarily high divorce rate: approximately 50% of all marriages end in divorce (higher in some areas and lower in others). It's not only expensive, but it is bad for the morale. I do not know what the divorce rate in Latin America is as a whole, but it's a lot less than that, and not just because of the strength of the Catholic Church. Marriages between Latin American women and North American men have the low divorce rate of only about 12%. That's a major improvement. Latin American women are reared to see marriage as a permanent thing, and they will go to great lengths to see that the bonds remain strong. Interestingly enough, by the time an introduction service's clients get to them, the men are ready for a stable marriage, too. They have either been through a divorce or two or have enough mature insight to know that a growing and lasting marriage is the only kind of marriage worth having.

Marital Fidelity

Over the years I have read a number of surveys published by both women's and men's magazines showing the percentages of married women who have had affairs during their marriage. These include *Woman's Day, Cosmopolitan, Playboy,* and a number of others. The percentages of infidelity among American Women ranged from about 35% to about 60%, with the readers of the more racy magazines having a higher rate of infidelity. Several years ago I read a survey, done by a government agency, and published in a national Costa

Rican newspaper. The survey reported infidelity rates among lovers and married people, by ages, gender, and other factors. The analysis comparable to those published by the American magazines showed a marital infidelity rate of 14%. And Costa Rica, incidentally, is reputed to have the most flexible moral standards regarding sexual behavior, in all of Latin America. Latin American women sincerely believe in sexual fidelity.

Traditional Role Behavior

Quite a few American men have had problems because their wives have chosen to work outside the home. I think that it's not generally because they want a submissive and dependent wife, but that when two married people pursue two separate careers a number of conflicts can arise, including the ever-present specter of infidelity. Most of the women that you will be meeting through an introduction service are middle-class girls and will, in all probability be employed because of the necessity of earning an income. Some will be professionals who have spent a number of years preparing for their careers. In general, though, the absolutely most important goal for a Latin American woman is to have a husband, family, and her own home. I have yet to receive an application that didn't express this ultimate desire. She wants to be a wife and all that is implied by the term, provided that she is treated well. If she is already involved in a professional career and wants to continue it, it will probably be considered less important than her role in the home.

About the Women

Most are middle-class girls, most are in their 20's and 30's, most have never been married, and most do not have children. Those who have gone to the trouble of having a photograph made (and they are expensive in Latin America), filling out an application form and mailing it in, are specifically interested in meeting a North American man. Some very few are looking only for a pen pal or friendship, but the vast majority want a husband. Why do they want a foreign husband?

A More Reliable Husband

A common theme running through applications from the girls is that American men are considered to make better husbands, and that they are sick and tired of Latin American Don Juans who don't know the Spanish word for responsibility. The problems usually revolve around drinking and infidelity. Unfortunately, heavy weekend drinking is a favorite male pastime in Latin America, especially within the lower class, but also common in the middle class. The complaint is that money spent in bars could be better spent if used for the family. Sexual infidelity has long been part of the Latin American male's culture, who frequently have mistresses (middle and upper classes) or who visit prostitutes (lower class). Although women accepted it in the past, they never liked it, and the more modern Latin American woman simply won't put up with it.

Economic & Social Gain

It would amount to ignoring reality if I were to say that most didn't hope to improve their situation in life. Every Latin American country is third world, and no matter how hard someone works, it is very difficult to earn enough money to make any real gains. But is there anything wrong with wanting to make some net gains in life? Don't you yourself do whatever you can to improve your situation in life? Doesn't an American woman also hope to marry well? Why, then, should it be any different with a Latin American woman? The truth is that there is an economic component, but I do not believe that it is as important as other considerations.

More Sexual Equality

As they are in Spain, Latin American women have always been second class citizens and they still are...both at home and on the job (although this is gradually changing). Latin American women don't want to be like American women, but they are aware that American men will treat them more as equals, and they do most definitely want their basic humanity to be recognized. Married Latin American women are frequently confined to the home, allowed out only for shopping or to visit her relatives. Physical abuse is common. The modern Latin American woman is tired of it. She wants to be respected, and she believes that the American man will respect her.

17

A Balanced Equation

Examining the above, it doesn't require a genius to recognize that American men generally represent what the women are looking for and vice-versa. This isn't to say that every Latina will be good for every American man, but the needs are there on both sides, and there seems to be an adequate supply on both sides. I hope to see more and more international couples getting together.

Part I

The Cultural Overview

19

Chapter 1

What Is Latin America?

The term "*Latin* Countries" doesn't refer to Latin America, but rather to those Mediterranean countries that were heavily influenced by the early Romans (who spoke Latin) and by the early Catholic church. Specifically, they are Italy, Portugal, and Spain (some geographers also include France and/or Greece). "Latin America" consists of those areas in the Americas that were colonized by Spain and Portugal, and settled by people from those two countries. Due to a treaty between Spain and Portugal back in 1494, just two years after Columbus arrived, and before anyone knew just how far east South America extended, Portugal accidentally wound up with a large chunk of South America, which later became Brazil–the purpose of the treaty was to give Africa and Asia to Portugal and the New World to Spain. Except for Brazil, which was settled by the Portuguese, and where the Portuguese language is still spoken, all the rest of Latin America has a Spanish heritage. There are some countries in Central and South America that are not considered to be part of Latin America. Belize, nestled in between Mexico and Guatemala, and fronting on the Caribbean Sea, was controlled by England, and was settled by former English owned slaves from the Caribbean Islands. Guyana, Suriname, and French Guiana, three small countries on the northern edge of South America, are also not considered to be part of Latin America. All three were used by European countries for agricultural purposes, and were primarily populated by slaves from Africa. Guyana was British, Suriname, Dutch, and French Guiana (home of the infamous Devil's Island penal colony), French.

Specifically, the twenty Latin American countries are (Caribbean, then north to south through Central America and counterclockwise in South America):

» Cuba (Caribbean)
» Dominican Republic (Caribbean), site of Columbus' first settlement.
» Puerto Rico (Caribbean), U.S. Territory
» Mexico (North America)
» Guatemala (Central America)
» El Salvador (Central America)
» Honduras (Central America)
» Nicaragua (Central America)
» Costa Rica (Central America)
» Panama (Central America? Many Panamanians consider themselves to be part of neither Central nor South America, although geologically and geographically it is clearly in Central America.)
» Colombia (South America)
» Venezuela (South America)
» Ecuador (South America)
» Peru (South America)
» Bolivia (South America)
» Chile (South America)
» Argentina (South America)
» Paraguay (South America)
» Uruguay (South America)
» Brazil (South America)

Chapter 2

A Short History

Contact

Everyone knows that Christopher Columbus, an Italian captain sailing with a Spanish and Portuguese crew under the flag of Spain, discovered the tropical portion of the New World in 1492 (the Vikings beat him to North America), possibly landing first at Watling's Island (there is still some disagreement about which island it was) in the eastern Bahamas. He sailed south and west, discovered Cuba, and wound up at Hispaniola (a large island which is now made up of Haiti and the Dominican Republic), where he established a small settlement. The Caribbean Islands were dominated at that time by a fierce, warlike seagoing tribe, the Caribs (although many other tribes lived in the Caribbean), and by the time he returned on his second voyage the village was no more. Although Columbus most likely encountered Indians in the Bahamas and in Cuba, the events that occurred between that small settlement and the Indians already living on Hispaniola became what were probably the first intensive contacts between Europeans and American Indians.

What is not generally known, and what I would like to discuss briefly, is the nature of the Indian populations existing at the time of early Spanish settlement of the Americas. It is important to the extent that, while Spanish culture certainly dominates in all of the Latin American countries (except for Brazil), most of the people themselves are the result of genetic mixtures between Spaniards and Indians (commonly called "mestizos"), and many of the cultural and racial differences between Latin American countries are due to differences between the early pre-existing Indian cultures and populations.

Indian Settlement of the New World

Anthropologists are in firm agreement that American Indians have an Asian origin, and that their ancestors entered into what is now Alaska from what is now Siberia by way of the Bering Strait. This came at a time when vast quantities of water was stored in glaciers throughout much of the northern part of the world, lowering world-wide sea levels 300 feet. At that time the Bering Strait was nothing more than relatively flat, forested land, resembling the lands on either side, and probably well filled with game, as Alaska is now. The saber-toothed tiger was long gone, but the woolly mammoth was still around, as was most of the wildlife found today. No one suggests that the early Indians knew that they were moving into a new world, uninhabited by humans. They were merely following game as they slowly moved their camps across the Bering Strait and into North America.

Anthropologists, however, are not at all in agreement as to when this slow migration took place. Obviously it had to take place during a time of heavy glaciation so that the sea level would be low enough to permit passage, and a corridor had to be open along the plains of northern Alaska and west central Canada (to the east of the Rocky Mountains) between the areas of glaciation. However, during the Pleistocene Epoch (the "Ice Ages") there were four major glaciations, and although their time spans are pretty well documented, nobody really knows during which glaciation the first entry was made. During the last 40,000 years the Bering Strait has been dry land only twice: Once from about 32,000 years ago to 36,000 years ago, and again between 13,000 years ago and 28,000 years ago. However, during the latter glaciation much of the corridor was closed, and most of Canada was covered by glaciation. This leaves the most likely period as being somewhere between 32,000 and 36,000 years ago.

The problem is that it is very difficult to get accurate dates of early sites, even with radiocarbon dating. Some fairly accurate dates have shown human occupation near the southern tip of South America (as well as several other areas in South America) as early as 9,000 years ago, and a few North American sites appear to be older than 25,000 years. Although there is nothing resembling a consensus, the majority of anthropologists seem to agree on an entry of roughly 30,000 to 35,000 years ago.

However long ago it happened, there has been enough time for the evolutionary process to produce distinct racial differences between modern day Indians living in different areas. If you could take an Indian from northern Mexico, one from highland Guatemala, one from the jungles of Panama, one from highland Peru, and another from the Amazon Basin, dress them all the same, and put them in a police line-up, it would be remarkably easy to identify from where they came. Time and adaptation to living in their different environments have made them physically distinctive.

Indian Cultures

It is an anthropological axiom that cultures are, for the most part, adapted to the environment in which they exist. Present day Indian populations exist in hot deserts in northern Mexico, cold deserts in the Andes, temperate climates throughout Latin America, mountain rain forest in Central and South America, and hot, humid, jungle rain forest in eastern Panama and the Amazon Basin. Most of them rely on simple horticulture or agriculture of one kind or another. Most are in some way tied into the urban economy in the sense that some of their products are sold for cash. Cities and towns throughout Latin America have public markets to which Indians go to sell handicrafts and agricultural products.

When Columbus and his intrepid crew stumbled upon the New World, that pattern already existed. Simple hunter/gatherers lived in Mexican deserts, the Amazon Basin, and in Patagonia (southern South America). Simple horticulturists lived throughout Latin America. But most important to the future of the New World, two areas had already developed intensive agriculture with irrigation, lived in concentrated cities, and were politically and militarily well organized. These were the Aztecs of Central Mexico, living where Mexico City eventually developed, and the Incas, with a far ranging empire stretching along the Andes mountain range across what is now Ecuador, Peru, Bolivia, and Chile (although large numbers of Mayan Indians still live in southern Mexico and in Guatemala, the

Mayan civilization, as such, had fallen into ruin some 400 years before Columbus arrived). It was important to the future because these were the Indians who had the gold and silver coveted by the Spaniards, whose actions shaped what Latin America was to become.

The Spanish Adventure

To put the Spanish conquest of Middle and South America into perspective, consider that it happened between 1492 and 1532, 40 years from the time of Columbus' arrival to the subjugation of the last major civilization, the Incas. To put that 40 years into perspective , consider that it has been the amount of time that passed between 1956 and 1996. Dwight D. Eisenhower was president of the United States in 1956, and it was during his administration that the U.S. Interstate Highway program was begun. That highway system is still not complete. So, when you consider the immense task of conquering by force almost an entire continent and part of another one, the Spaniards moved rather quickly. Considering how slowly things seem to move in present day Latin America, this comes as a surprise to some people.

Actually, the *conquistadores* had some help from unexpected quarters. That help came in the form of intense rivalry and active warfare between neighboring Indian tribes and political conflict within the two existing civilizations. Another, more subtle, form of help came in the form of smallpox and several other European diseases, which the Spaniards had so generously brought with them. Europeans had developed resistance to the diseases over the centuries, but the indigenous Americans had none. Epidemic after epidemic weakened Indian populations, many to the extent that they could not resist the Spaniards, and some to the point of extinction. In many areas of Latin America, the missionaries had to abandon their efforts simply because there were not enough Indians left to support their missions.

To add more perspective, it helps to consider what was, in general, going on in other parts of the world with other European powers. This had a lot to do with why Spain was able to get away with some 200 years of exploitation of Indian slave labor in the gold and silver mines, and another 100 years of colonial control. At the time of Columbus' first voyage, Africa was already being colonized. Portugal had established a foothold in West Africa (from which they and the Dutch later developed a lucrative slave trade), the Dutch were making regular spice runs down the west coast of Africa, around the Cape of Good Hope, and across the Indian Ocean to the Malayan Archipelago (the "Spice Islands"). England was beginning to explore East Africa and India, and were just a short time away from establishing trade relations along the coast of China. Those countries with traditions of maritime trade were, in effect, staking out their claims in every piece of land in the world that was being newly discovered.

Columbus' four voyages were, however, nothing more than attempts to find a shorter, more efficient route to the "Spice Islands" so that they could beat other shippers in the spice trade. Columbus had no idea of the riches in gold and silver available in the New World. He never made it to areas where there was much of it, and the Indians he met had very little. By the time of Columbus' fourth voyage it was obvious to everyone that a whole new world had been discovered, and that while it clearly offered some possibilities, it was still a nuisance standing in the way of a shortcut to the spice trade, and they were still looking for a way to get to the Pacific Ocean. The shortcut was not found until 1914 when the Panama Canal was opened.

Europeans in the 15th and 16th centuries approached the rest of the world and its cultures from a highly ethnocentric point of view. It was considered quite normal and right for "civilized" people to establish dominance and control over the "savages" of the world (however, one of the problems that Europeans had with the Chinese and Japanese is that the Europeans themselves were considered to be the unwashed savages). It really wasn't until the early 1800's that these ideas began to change, and they didn't change until the locals became difficult to handle and started throwing out the colonial governments.

During Columbus' second voyage, by which time it had become obvious that Spain had the potential of controlling a great deal of new territory, the royalty of Spain and Portugal got together with the Catholic Pope to work out an arrangement to reduce the possibility of conflict with each other (they are neighbors on the Iberian Peninsula). Spain wanted all of the New World, and Portugal didn't want Spain messing around with Africa and Asia, and was even objecting to their presence in the New World. In the Treaty of Tordesillas, signed in 1494, only a year or so after Columbus got back with the news, Portugal agreed to let Spain have all newly discovered lands west of longitude 48 degrees, (which so far as anyone knew at the time, ran right down the middle of the Atlantic Ocean), and Spain agreed not to bother Portugal in their attempts to colonize Africa and Asia. No other European power acknowledged the treaty, and none of the indigenous people living in the affected areas had any knowledge of their fate. This approach seems rather arrogant in today, but that's what they did, and that's why Brazilians speak Portuguese today.

What the Spaniards didn't know (nor the Portuguese either) is that 48 degrees west longitude passes right through South America and lops off most of what is now Brazil. Had Spain known that South America stuck out so far to the east, they might have insisted on 38 degrees west longitude, which would have given them all of the South American continent. As it turned out, Brazil's eastern coastline wasn't discovered until 1500 when Pedro Cabral, a Portuguese trader, sailing from Lisbon down the coast of Africa, on his way to India, veered west across the Atlantic Ocean and landed on Brazil. They only stayed nine days, then went back across the Atlantic Ocean. To this day, since he was ostensibly bound for a trip around Africa to the spice islands, nobody actually knows for sure why he wandered so far off course. The probable answer is that the Portuguese government wanted him to check out whether they may have gotten something from the treaty. It wasn't until 1519 that Ferdinand Magellan, a Portuguese captain with a Spanish crew, explored the coast of South America, including Brazil, on his round-the-world trip.

The Spanish Conquest

Columbus, during his four voyages, explored Hispaniola, Cuba, Jamaica, the Leeward Islands, Trinidad, the coasts of what are now Venezuela and Colombia, and the coast of Central America. In addition to Hispaniola, small settlements were established on the Caribbean coasts of Colombia and Panama by other explorers who had been excited by Columbus' discoveries. A gent by the name of Vasco Nuñez de Balboa had been poking around the coasts of Colombia and Panama for some twelve years and had heard stories from Indians of a vast sea which lay to the south and west of Panama, and about a great civilization with large quantities of gold, obviously what we now know as the Incas. In 1513 he and a small group of men braved 50 miles of dense jungle to cross the Isthmus of Panama to become the first Europeans to see the Pacific Ocean from the west coast of the Americas.

At that time not much could be done about getting ships into the Pacific Ocean, because a passage still had not been found. After Magellan's circumnavigation of the world, the situation changed. The southern tip of South America extends almost into Antarctica. The weather is cold and miserable, with some of the worst winds in the world. Cape Horn, the absolute southern tip, is known to sailors to have the most dangerous seas that exist, with waves often exceeding 50 feet in height (and which have been recorded higher than 100 feet), frequently capsizing and destroying sailing vessels. Magellan, however, didn't actually have to go around Cape Horn because there is a passage inside the cape leading from one ocean to the other, allowing for a calmer and safer trip, but still with some very tricky weather. Magellan found the passage, crossed it, and it was named after him: the Straits of Magellan. Of course, this didn't happen until 1520, and it took several years for his one remaining ship to make it back to Europe. Magellan himself was killed by natives in the Philippines. His crew let the rest of the Europe know about the passage and the fact that no other passage existed between the Atlantic and Pacific Oceans.

Spanish ships finally started going into the Pacific, exploring the west coast of South America, eventually basing themselves in Panama where a settlement had been established near the site of present day Panama City. In 1524 and 1526, Francisco Pizarro confirmed some of the rumors regarding the Inca civilization during two explora-tory expeditions, and in 1532 mounted an armed invasion with about 200 men. The Inca government was quickly subdued (although guerrilla resistance continued for another 40 years and the mountain city of Machu Picchu was never found by the Spaniards).

Thirteen years earlier, in 1519, Hernán Cortés had invaded Mexico, landing near what is now Veracruz, and made his way to the center of Aztec civilization, Lake Tenochtitlán (whose filled-in lake bed now supports Mexico City). Astounded by the amount of gold possessed by the Aztecs, the Spaniards systematically set about undermining the government, and had complete control within two years.

For the next 300 years Spain very tightly controlled what happened in the colonies. Colonial governments were structured by Spain, and colonial governors and governmental functionaries were strictly accountable to Spain. Three ports were established to ship gold and silver to Spain. These were Veracruz in Mexico, Cartagena in Colombia, and Portobello in Panama. Shipping of gold or silver from any other port was not allowed. The riches shipped out of Portobello mostly came from the Inca Empire, and had been moved by ship up the Pacific coast to what was to become Panama City, and then carried by mule train to the Caribbean port of Portobello.

In the early 1800's Spain began to lose control of all of it's American colonies, except for Cuba and Puerto Rico, and revolutionary wars for independence occurred in Mexico, Central America, and South America. By 1823 Spain no longer had any American colonies outside of the Caribbean, and a period of adjustment followed in which the colonies shifted borders and alliances until eventually the present day countries emerged (with the exception of Panama, which was part of Colombia until 1903).

The Physical Result

There is no country of Latin America in which there has not been racial mixing. Most notable, of course, is the "mestizo" result of Indian and Spaniard mixing, and in later years, in some countries, mixing of former African slaves with mestizos.

Large Indian (defined both culturally and racially) populations still remain in southern Mexico and the Yucatan Peninsula, Guatemala, Panama, the Amazon Basin, Ecuador, Peru, and Bolivia. In other areas the populations are predominately mestizo. Several areas have concentrations of populations that are primarily of European descent. These are Costa Rica, parts of Colombia, Chile, Argentina, Paraguay, and Uruguay. Costa Rica's Indian population was largely wiped out by European diseases, and with only a small amount of gold, remained a backwater country until tourists recently discovered it. As a consequence, Costa Rican people are comparatively light-skinned, having descended mostly from Spanish settlers. Highland Colombia is similar in this regard, having had large numbers of Spanish settlers, and an Indian population largely destroyed by disease. Chile, Argentina, Paraguay, and Uruguay, in addition to Spanish settlers, had large numbers of immigrants from other European countries during the 19th and 20th centuries, particularly from Italy and Germany. These four countries still have distinct sub-populations and cultures derived from Europe.

All of the Caribbean Basin countries have distinct black populations along their coastal areas, descendants of African slaves brought to work in plantations on the Caribbean islands. These countries are Honduras, Nicaragua, Costa Rica, Panama, Colombia, and Venezuela. Unlike the

United States, there has never been institutionalized racial segregation in any part of Latin American, and genetic mixing has commonly occurred between mestizo and black populations.

Chinese immigrants have arrived in great numbers to all of the Latin American countries. You will have no problem finding Chinese restaurants in any Latin American city. Generally, the Chinese populations tend to remain apart, but there has been some mixing. There are, in addition, immigrants from the Middle East and India, most of whom are thoroughly integrated into the economic system, but who have not done a great deal of intermarrying.

Part II

Facts about Latin American Women

Chapter 3

Individual Differences

They Are Not All the Same

Until you get to know the people of any given society well, you really have no choice other than to generalize about them, and this mostly takes the form of stereotypes. We have our stereotypes about the Germans, French, Italians, English, Japanese, etc., and, in general, there is some truth to stereotypes. But, a stereotype, no matter how accurately applied to a population at large, will not be accurate when applied to an individual in that population.

It is commonly said that Latin American women are gentle, caring, supportive, faithful, and home loving. That is true...in general. But, I've known some first-class bitches in Latin America who get a real charge out of tearing down men, and who like nothing better than to find a squeeze on the side. Does this fit with the stereotype? Not at all.

Beyond individual differences, there are also general behavioral differences between the inhabitants of different Latin American countries. Again, these are stereotypes, but still reflect a portion of the truth. For instance, it is said that Costa Rican women tend to be very friendly, but cannot be depended upon to be faithful. Panamanians are said to be hard-working, down-to-earth, and honest. Colombians are stereotyped similar to Panamanians, except that they are considered to be more beautiful. Venezuelans are said to be more sophisticated. Hondurans are considered to be the most home-loving of all.

How can one look realistically at such stereotyping? You simply have to take it with a grain of salt, and instead of relying on a stereotype, spend your time taking a real close look at the lady that interests you.

Yours Will Be Special

As much as I hesitate to do so, it is necessary for me to use, to a large extent, generalities in this book. What I am describing are cultural patterns. Cultural patterns apply to the population as a whole, but more to some people than to others, in that some people fit the model more closely than do others. There will always be a great deal of variation with respect to any cultural trait. Latin American women vary from "somewhat attentive" to "always attentive," with the largest number of women falling in the middle, an area that we can "regularly attentive."

A lot of women from the U.S. and Latin America show the same degree of attentiveness to their husbands. However, generally speaking, Latin American women are more attentive to their husbands. What it boils down to is that you can't **expect** any particular individual in any given culture to fit a stereotype, although the stereotype may have some truth to it, and your best bet, as always, is to take a close personal look at the lady that interests you.

Then you must base your decisions on what you have learned in the past and where your awareness leads you today.

Chapter 4

Social Class

Spanish Inheritance, New World Style

Social class is being dealt with in this book, not because it's just something to write about, but because it is so very important in Latin America; much more so than in the United States. In defines behavior in many ways, large and small.

It determines who can marry whom, and it has a definite bearing on which women will be available for marriage to you, as well as the kind of wife she is likely to make for you after marriage. Bear with the discussion, if you will, because it could be important to you. Rigid social class structure was brought over by the settling Spaniards, and was made perhaps even more rigid because of the relationship between Spanish settlers and the indigenous people. Wherever Indians exist in Latin America, they are always at the bottom of the heap, and only through adopting Western style behavior, dressing as a *Mestizo* (mixed Spanish and Indian), and fully participating in the

41

market economy, can they hope to become an accepted member of even the lower class, although very few of them would want to lose their cultural identity in that manner.

The United States, Canada, Australia, and some European countries have the most egalitarian societies in the world. We accept it as a given that it is normal to be able to, through hard work, move up the social class ladder. Don't we repeat it as a truth that even the poorest man has a chance to be president of the United States? It actually isn't possible, of course, except through some huge accident of fate. However, social class boundary permeability is a fact of life in the U.S. We are not totally stuck. Education, hard work, a decent job, and a measure of luck can move a person from one social class to a higher one. Conversely, an absence of the above can move a person down a notch, too.

This is not generally true in Latin America. Throughout most of the history of Latin America there has been a rigid two-class system. This originally started out as a division between Spanish settlers and Indians. Since there were no Spanish women available during the early years of the conquest, the Spaniards quickly bred with Indian women. Most of the early adventurers can be best described as low-lives, and the women were usually taken by force or purchased. The resulting offspring were the genetically mixed *mestizos*. Over the years, as genuine Spanish settlers arrived to make their permanent homes in the New World, often with wives and children, and often sending later for members of their families, an actual upper class began to emerge. As this process developed, both the adventurers and the *mestizo* became the lower class. Indians were still quite apart, with their own cultures, and not really part of the class system.

Because of the nature of the Spanish system of political administration in the New World, Spanish settlers, especially those who were involved in some manner in government activities, were awarded free land grants in partial exchange for their duties or for the simple fact that they were arriving as settlers. This is somewhat reminiscent of the early U.S. homestead policy for getting settlers to move into the midwest, with the offer of a free 40 acres and a mule. Spanish land grants, however, were a whole lot larger than 40 acres. They were normally many thousands of acres (my grandfathers's farm in Texas was part of an early Spanish land grant which was originally 60,000 acres). This resulted in families who had a lot of land and those who had none.

It is not at all difficult to see the results of this policy in modern Latin America. Those who had the land had the ability to produce whatever product was in demand at the time, and which could be produced on the land available. Land ownership produced wealth, wealth produced power, and power produced, in many cases, corruption.

The Emerging Middle Class

Latin America is still solidly dominated by a small, but immensely powerful upper class.

This is true in absolutely every country in Latin America regardless of how they might insist differently (Costa Ricans, for example, say that it is not true for them, but I can assure you that it is. Every president they have ever had has come from the coffee producing gentry).

Modern day commerce, however, and its resultant need for lawyers, secretaries, salesmen, and desk jockeys, has contributed to a major change. So has growing governmental sizes, with its need for bureaucrats. Bureaucrats, lawyers, and desk jockeys of all types have to be educated, and because of this, school systems have been enlarged, producing a need for more and more teachers.

Those countries whose economies are more deeply involved in world trade are moving more quickly in this direction than are others, and this is the direction that produces the middle class. The middle class seems to be emerging most rapidly in Mexico (which now ranks 4th worldwide in number of billionaires, many of whom got that way through corruption and drug trade), Costa Rica, Panama, Colombia, Venezuela, and Brazil. Those most behind in this process of change are Guatemala, Ecuador, and Bolivia, not coincidentally the areas with the highest percentage of Indian populations and with the most centralized control by the upper class.

The Upper-Class Lifestyle

The upper classes of Latin America live very much like the upper classes in any other part of the world. In fact, there are more similarities between the upper classes of Europe and Latin America than there are between Latin American middle and upper classes. Most upper class people are educated abroad, speak either (or both) English or French as well as Spanish, and learn the proper skills for social interaction within the upper class, no matter what the country. Friends and associates tend to be within the same class, and marriage is almost always within the class.

You are not going to get a detailed description of how the upper class single girl lives. This is partly because I don't know a great deal about it, but also because even if you are upper class yourself, she is not likely to be available to you.

She usually marries in her late teens or early twenties and stays married, even if for decorum and to maintain family ties. Divorce is usually not an option for her, because her marriage will have been sanctioned by the state and performed in a Catholic ceremony (most of the upper class in Latin America are Catholic). Her husband, if not selected by her parents, will be from a family well-known to her family, and who has an equal upper class social standing. So sorry sir, but you will not, barring some unique twist of fate (such as widowhood), be able to marry an upper class Latin American girl. She simply is not likely to be available.

The Middle-Class Lifestyle

It might be tempting to consider the American middle class to be on roughly the same level as the Latin American upper class since income in Latin America is generally lower than in the United States. That is absolutely not so. The upper classes in the United States, Europe, and Latin America are basically comparable. They are all wealthy and come from long lines of established family. Wealth itself does not guarantee, and is usually not enough, to gain admission to the upper class. A long line of family history needs to be there first.

As would be expected, upper class Latin Americans live just as well as upper class people anywhere, except that they usually have more power and control on a national level, and there is a much larger gap between upper levels of the middle class and themselves. As far as I can tell, it is virtually impossible for a middle class person to move into the upper class.

The middle classes of Latin America are comprised of people with essentially the same kinds of occupations as those in the United States, with perhaps the exception of doctors, who often come from the upper class and are frequently educated abroad. Basically, middle-class people are white collar workers. In the United States, blue collar workers are normally part of the middle class, but in Latin America the income for manual workers of any kind does not produce the kind of life style that could be considered middle class. Back when I was a college professor, any plumber, electrician, or carpenter was earning a great deal more money than I was and they were certainly living better than I was. Yet they were considered blue collar and I was considered white collar. The differential is reversed in Latin America.

North American middle-class families generally live more comfortably than do their counterparts in Latin America. Allow me to present an hypothetical example as an illustration by presenting a couple of fictional mid-level bank officers. Let's place our American bank officer in a medium sized town in the Midwest, and we'll put our Latin American bank officer in David, Panama, where I live. It's also a medium sized town. Our American bank officer has a gross income of $50,000 per year, out of which he is able to take home roughly $35,000 per year, or $2,800 per month. His home is in the suburbs, and he has a monthly mortgage payment of $800. It is likely to be fenced, have a neatly manicured lawn, and be nicely finished, trimmed with wood, well constructed. His floor will be covered with carpeting, and the entire house will be air conditioned and tastefully furnished with color coordinated furniture. He will own two late model automobiles of a make and model suitable for bankers. He will belong to at least one service club (such as the Lions Club, also widespread in Latin America), and perhaps a mid-level country club. I won't try to predict what he will be eating for his meals, but we can be sure that he has a wide range of options. He also has a wide range of options when it comes to social activities.

Our hypothetical Panamanian bank officer earns $800 per month, which comes to $9600 per year. Out of this he pays no taxes, but a small amount is deducted for social security, which allows him to have virtually free medical care at government hospitals with government doctors. He also has no mortgage on his house or land, because the land was given to him by his parents, and he started building his house himself while he was a young man and still working as a teller in the bank. He does, however, have a bank loan payment of $70 per month against a home improvement loan that he took out last year to build an additional room onto his house because of his growing family. His house is built of cinder block, the floor is uncovered cement. He doesn't use carpet, partly because of mildew problems, but also because it's too expensive. His house doesn't have wood trim because of the relative scarcity of wood and it's expense. His house covers approximately 1400 square feet, giving him enough room for two bedrooms for the children, and a small one for he and his wife. The lawn is small, and since he doesn't own a lawnmower, he has a man come in once every two weeks during the rainy season to cut the grass with a machete. As for an automobile, he has one, but it's a ten year old Toyota. He would like to get a new one, but since they cost about 20% more than they do in the U.S., he can't afford one just yet. Actually, he's only had this one for two years. Before that he took the bus to work.

He belongs to the Lion's Club, and enjoys the monthly meetings, especially because his wife understands the necessity of restaurant eating at that time and doesn't insist that he brown-bag it or go home for lunch. He has four children, and the older two are in a bilingual private school that sets him back $90 per month because he and his wife understand the importance of learning English in order to get a well-paying job. It's not too difficult to predict what he will be eating for dinner. Most likely it will be stewed chicken (more expensive than in the U.S.) or beef (slightly less expensive than in the U.S.), or grilled beef with onions, along with the inevitable rice (slightly more expensive than in the U.S.), perhaps accompanied with beans (more expensive than in the U.S.), and most likely a Coca Cola (cheaper than in the U.S.). They occasionally visit family and friends, and occasionally take in a movie, which costs $2 for adults and $1 for children. Their leisure time is mostly spent watching TV.

Both of these men occupy comparable middle-class positions. The differential in income is something to be expected considering the general differences in income between Latin America and the United States. What might not be expected, though, is that it is not a whole lot cheaper to live in Latin America. Housing is definitely less expensive, either to rent or to purchase. But interest rates for home loans are exceedingly high in most of the countries. For example, a home loan in Panama costs 8% to 10% per year; in Costa Rica, 30% to 40% per year. That is why most people build their own homes, cinder block by cinder block, as the cash is available. Generally, eating in restaurants is less expensive than in the U.S., but individual food items, purchased at a supermarket, usually cost a little more. In some countries, at the present time, food is much more expensive than in the United States. Nicaragua and Argentina come to mind.

The main point of this illustration is to show the vast difference in disposable income and the uses to which it is put. Our Panamanian banker is spending a large percentage for his children's schooling, and this is not uncommon because private schools are usually chosen by middle-class families because of their superior educational facilities. In the U.S. an equivalent education would be free (not counting the taxes). His family has plenty food, but they have to be very careful with their choices. Entertainment is strictly limited to inexpensive activities. He is not, in general, living nearly as well as is his middle-class counterpart in the United States.

The Single Middle-Class Girl

Most unmarried middle-class Latin American women work and live at home with their parents. Some few who work in the city and do not have relatives nearby may room with other girls in the same situation. This is uncommon, though, because most will have cousins, aunts and uncles, grandparents, or brothers and sisters with whom they can live and contribute some of their income to the household. Some will be divorced or never-married, but will have children who will be left with her parents while she is out earning a living. Normally they will also contribute money to their parents or to whichever relative is caring for her children.

While it is usual for the unmarried single American girl to have her own apartment and automobile, which she supports through her job, this is not a significant pattern in Latin America. Part of this is cultural, part is economic, and part is just plain demographics. Latin American women have much closer ties to their families than do women in the U.S., and they also receive much more social support from them. She not only usually has a place to live, but it would be somewhat of an insult to her family should she choose to live on her own. Her independence would raise certain social questions, as well, which would not be issues in the United States. "Nice girls" just usually don't live on their own in Latin America and would likely to be seen as a reflection of her moral character.

Another factor is that the large, well protected apartment complexes so common in American cities are really quite rare in Latin American cities. They are beginning to appear in some of the more modern cities in Venezuela, Colombia, Panama, Argentina, and Brazil, but they are still rare, and they are very expensive.

The major controlling factor is economics. As I showed in the illustration with our Panamanian banker, costs of living are rather high in relation to income, and this is true throughout Latin America. Secretaries in Central America, for instance, depending on the country, will usually earn the equivalent in dollars from $150 to $450 per month (the lower incomes are in Guatemala, Honduras, and Nicaragua), more if she is a legal secretary or is bilingual. How can she possibly support a $300 apartment and a car? A store clerk will usually earn somewhere between $75 and $300 per month. In David, Panama, the going rate is about $200 per month (this gives you a chance to compare her situation to our hypothetical banker). Here a school teacher will earn about $500 per month, a secretary $300 to $400 per month.

Most of the girls in the T.L.C. program are middle class, as they are in other programs. They are the ones that read the ads placed by introduction companies in the newspapers, and they are the ones looking for foreign husbands. Much more will be said about them in other chapters, because they are the subject of this book, but for now, the issue is social class.

The Lower Class

Again, because it is not especially likely that you will be meeting many lower class girls, I am going to limit my discussion of them to a personal vignette. It will be of some value to you to learn a little about the Latin American lower class. In discussing the lower class, I am not writing of the homeless street people, so sadly common in cities throughout Latin America. I am speaking instead of the residents of the barrios on the hillsides, living in cardboard and tin shacks (some of wood or cinder block) above Lima, Peru, San José, Costa Rica, and Río de Janeiro, and every other Latin American capitol that has hillsides, as well as those who live in the high rise tenements of Panama City and in the shanty towns surrounding Mexico City. Frequently, rural farmers are just as poor, and many are also considered to be lower class, but their situations are different, and they are not being considered at this point.

Perhaps the most clearly identifiable characteristic of a lower-class family is that no one person in the family has regular employment with a dependable salary. There may, in fact, be several breadwinners in the household, but work is likely to be sporadic for each of them and at a very low income. Allow me to illustrate from a very personal point of view: I was married to a lovely Costa Rican lady from a lower-class family, and frankly did not want the divorce when it became inevitable (I don't mean to imply that all such marriages inevitably end in divorce. She simply refused to leave her family and I refused to live in

San Jose. We are still good friends). When we first met, she and her young daughter lived in a haphazardly built shack of galvanized sheet roofing and used lumber in the mountains above San Jose. Her brother had begun the house several years earlier on some public right-of-way alongside a dirt street. The city did not object, and eventually gave him squatter's rights. The electric company didn't object either when he strung some lines from their uninsulated wires to the house, nor did the water company complain when he tapped into the public water system.

When we first met, her brother and his wife had four young children, all of them living together in two small bedrooms. Her father and mother had moved in from the country and were living in another small add-on room, and she, her daughter, and a 16 year-old niece were in yet another tiny add-on room. In spite of the congestion and lack of privacy, everything was clean and well-ordered. As mentioned, there was running water, but there was no toilet. Everyone used the outhouse, which was just a few feet from the regular house because of lack of space. It could get odoriferous if the wind blew from the wrong direction.

The family's only apparent problem was one of economics. My wife's brother worked, whenever he could find work, as a day laborer, and being fairly skilled as a carpenter, he did that whenever the opportunity came up, which wasn't too often, and he made approximately $2 per hour. My wife worked regularly as a sales clerk, but always earned less than $200 per month. The two of them were the only income producers for the family, which numbered eleven people. Coffee picking season, which lasts about three months each year, was always welcome because it meant extra income. My wife's niece, father, brother's wife (and brother too, if he didn't have a job going), and their three oldest children, left at about 5 AM every day except Sunday to pick coffee. Exhausting work, but a comparatively good source of income.

They never went hungry, but the variety of food was very limited. Rice, beans, and eggs for breakfast, rice and beans for lunch, rice, beans, and perhaps a little chicken or beef for dinner. Day after day after day, except for Sundays. Sundays produced a big pot of soup with beef and a variety of vegetables.

I have told you about this to give you some idea as to how one particular mid-level lower-class family lives in this particular part of Latin America. They are poor, but are much better off than many other poverty level families in Latin America.

My wife was motivated to get a basic education, and while she had to work during the day, and was unable to finish regular high school, she did attend night school whenever possible, and finally received her diploma. One of the unfortunate results of poverty in Latin America is that so many of the poor are never able to receive what we would consider even a basic education. Some of the countries have a literacy rate of about 50% (which means that only about half the adult population can read and write), while others claim a literacy rate of up to 98%. However, literacy can be achieved by the end of fifth grade, and in itself, doesn't indicate much of an education.

Almost all of you who are reading this book have finished high school, most of you have some college education, and many of you have advanced or specialized educations. When I stated at the beginning that it is unlikely that you will be meeting many lower-class girls, it is mostly because not that many lower-class girls wind up in introduction programs, because most don't read newspapers where the ads appear. If you do, however, have the chance to meet an attractive and intelligent girl who just happens to be poor, don't let it discourage you that she is. Mine was most definitely a jewel in the rough.

One thing that you need to consider, though, is what you are going to talk about after you've been married for a while. In the United States you would most likely choose a girl with an educational level similar to yours, or at least close enough that you have similar interests. You would consider whether you have mutual goals and aspirations, and would think of the long-range responsibilities you have towards each other. It will be to your advantage to keep in mind the same criteria when you consider marriage with a Latina. Even though your wife may be from a different culture, once you've bridged those differences and no longer have to struggle with them, you are still faced with a day-to-day existence together, and it makes some sense to look in advance for interest in and capability for a mutually agreed upon lifestyle. You need to be sure that she's thinking in the same terms that you are.

Chapter 5

Rural vs Urban

The Rural Life

In a lot of ways urban life in Latin America is comparable to urban life in the United States. That's where the jobs are and that's where the excitement is. And, in a lot of ways rural life in Latin America is comparable to rural life in the United States...if you move it back 50 years.

Farming in the U.S. has gone the way of big business, and the agricultural endeavors now earning a profit are large operations. They are no longer family enterprises. In fact, it is mainly through government agricultural support programs that family farmers continue to exist in the U.S. While there are also many very large agricultural enterprises in Latin America (coffee, bananas, tomatoes, rice, etc.) which grow their products for both domestic consumption and for export, the vast majority of agriculturalists are family farmers. Most live like American farmers of 50 years ago, planting a variety of crops for home use and selling whatever surplus they can produce. Most have hens for eggs and meat, and enough roosters to keep them fertilized. Some have a cow or two for milk, and a few have hogs for meat. Most depend on small stores in nearby towns for staples such as coffee, sugar, flour, and rice. Most grow their own corn for grinding and for livestock and chicken feed (this is especially true in Mexico, where corn is depended upon as heavily as rice is in countries further south).

Most Latin American countries have what might be called "outreach programs," in which teachers are sent on a rotating basis to even the smallest rural villages to provide basic education. In the smaller villages, this rarely extends beyond 6th grade (if even that far), and "higher education" has to be obtained in larger towns, providing that there are family members with which the child can live while going to school. Panama, at least (I'm not aware of how the other countries handle it), tries to see that every rural settlement, no matter how deep in the jungle, has at least one teacher. And, if the settlement is Indian, they attempt to get a teacher who was originally from that particular tribe, and who speaks the native language.

Medical attention is handled in much the same manner, with at least a nurse making the rounds and holding a clinic every couple of weeks, and with a government doctor visiting every month. Actually, there are very few rural villages completely cut off from civilization. Most are accessible by road because of the simple necessity of bringing in supplies and transporting surplus to the outside for sale, and someone needing medical attention can be evacuated if necessary. I have been evacuated on a couple of occasions, in Mexico, stretched out in the back of supply trucks. On one occasion, when the supply truck wasn't due in for a week, my Indian friends brought in the local medicine man to cure me of a severe infection. Don't ask my why it worked, but it did, and it saved me a bumpy ride into town.

Rural-Urban Migration

Every major Latin American city has been facing severe problems of overcrowding and urban poverty for the last 30 years, and some of them for much longer than that. Farm families tend to be large, and limited amounts of family land can only be cut into so many pieces until there is not enough land left to support the family cultivating it. What happens at that point is that some members of the family have to start looking for paying jobs, and about the only places employment can be found are in the cities. Thus, as populations grow, the growth is not evenly distributed around the country, but winds up in the cities. Rates of population growth in Latin American countries range from 0.07% per year (Cuba) to 3.1% per year (Guatemala). Aside from those two, the average annual rate of increase in Latin America as a whole is 2.1% per year, with the lower rates occurring in the more economically developed countries.

Rates of rural-urban migration are not evenly divided between the sexes, however. All of Latin America is highly agricultural. Men are far more useful on farms than are women, and there is a much higher percentage of women moving from rural areas to the cities than men. We frequently hear of such absurdly high ratios as twelve women to every one man in Latin American countries. It simply isn't so. I once read in *La Nación,* Costa Rica's leading newspaper, that Costa Rica had ratio of six women to one man. Not believing it, I checked with the Census Bureau. Costa Rica's overall ratio was 1.1 women to 1 man. However, San José's ratio was indeed 6 to 1. This skewed ratio is common throughout major cities in Latin America because of the sex differential in rural-urban migration. There are jobs as secretaries, waitresses, cashiers, clerks, prostitutes, etc., for women in cities, but virtually nothing in rural areas. So that is where they go.

Rural Social Values

I have been told many times, especially by older women, that the girls who make the very best wives are those that grew up in the country. What they mean, of course, is that country girls tend to be more conservative, and the old ladies who told me that are themselves conservative. There is a certain amount of truth to what they are saying, though. Country girls do tend to have more traditional values and give more importance to husband, home and family than do city girls. There is even a great deal of difference between the residents of small towns and big cities. The girls of David, Panama, a city of about 120,000, are considerably more traditional, in general, than the girls of Panama City. Frankly, I like them better. But then, I'm a bit traditional myself.

But you don't have to go to the country to find a country girl. Most of the country girls now live in the city, a result of rural-urban migration.

Chapter 6

Social Expectations

A short discussion of social expectations is being brought in at this point because, just as it still is in Spain, almost every social situation has some fairly tightly proscribed behavioral patterns related to it, and these are some of the things that you will need to learn if you are to be well accepted and avoid offending people (details of the expectations are described in following chapters).

Latin American culture places value on group conformity, social appearance (including dress and behavior), family loyalty, fatalism (that things cannot be controlled), obligation, deference to authority, and paternalism (having someone in power looking out for you). Family relations are characterized by hierarchical roles, deference to maturity, strict control of emotions (especially anger), and sex-linked characteristics favoring the male. Americans value individualism, personal achievement, efficiency, rationality, optimism, pragmatism, freedom, and rejection of authority. Latin American culture focuses upon group cohesiveness while American culture focuses upon the individual and individual rights and freedoms.

As you can see, there are some built-in sources of conflict, and it will require not only your awareness of the rules for behavior, but a constant attentiveness to them until they become natural for you. Specific rules are dealt with in Part 3 of the book, but as you read the chapters between here and there, please keep in mind the social values listed above which ultimately control social structure, behavior, and emotions.

Chapter 7

Family Structure

The Extended Family

For the American man, family usually means his wife and children and his parents and siblings; a total of two nuclear families encompassing three generations. For the Latin American girl, family goes much farther than that, usually encompassing four generations, with close ties extending out to several degrees of aunts, uncles, and cousins. This "extended y" is the most important social unit in Hispanic culture.

Extended family ties are very strong. Families are very open in their daily lives and people easily welcome family members and friends of family members into their homes. When someone travels to another town or city to study or to look for work, or for a shorter stay, such as for medical treatment or shopping, the common practice is for that person to stay with relatives, or even with friends of relatives.

Many members of a family may live together in one household for social, practical, and economic reasons. The family is a shelter for younger members, even married ones, until they are economically established, and for girls, until

61

they are married. This is not considered a lack of independence on the part of the young people nor an imposition on the others. In the same manner, the family is also a refuge and place of care for the older members.

Starting at the beginning of the process, neither males nor females are expected to set up a separate residence from their parents until marriage. Frequently, a male who has married will bring his new wife to live with him in his parent's home until he can afford his own residence. Females are usually expected to leave home upon marriage and live with her husband wherever he may be (although occasionally her husband will move in with her family.

As time passes, as sons have children, and as parents age, the parents are likely to move in with one of the children, either male or female, taking along with them any daughters who have not yet married. It may strike you as a peculiar way to handle things, but since they may live together, you might very well meet her grandparents along with her brother's family at the same time you meet her parents.

Birth Control

Families in third world countries tend to be large. There are economic situations in which large families can be valuable, especially with agriculture, where an individual's labor contribution can more than offset the drain caused by an additional mouth to feed. That has long been the situation in Latin America, although it is rapidly changing in urban areas. The Catholic Church has never condoned birth control in any artificial form, and this attitude has contributed a great deal to large families in Latin America. However, I am not aware of any countries in Latin America where basic birth control is not readily available, at least in the form of condoms, and, so far as I know, birth control pills and monthly injections are available in all of the countries. Modern Latin American families, at least in urban areas, are taking birth control seriously and are limiting the size of their families for economic reasons.

Family Ties

Given the fact that families tend to be large in the first place, and that family unity is culturally desirable in the second place, any one person is going to have widely spread close family ties. I can remember family reunions from my childhood, on both my mother's side and my father's side that usually involved from 50 to 100 people. That happened only once a year, though, and the events were planned a year in advance. Such family get-togethers can happen on any given Sunday in Latin America. I'm still not sure how it was set up and organized, or even if it was, since so few people had telephones, but several times a year my Costa Rican wife and I would go to visit relatives of hers, where, during the course of a Sunday afternoon, at least 50 people would drop by. Sundays are family days throughout Latin America. In some shape, form, or fashion, almost everyone is going to be visiting a relative or be visited by a relative. If visiting relatives isn't on the agenda for the day, then the family is expected to go somewhere and do something together.

What are the responsibilities of relatives? It basically depends on how close the family relationship is. The closer the relationship the more that can be expected and the more that has to be given. Parents are expected to feed, protect, and in every way support their children when necessary. Children are expected to care for their parents when they are old and give them money when it is needed. Brothers are expected to lend money when necessary, and sisters are expected to care for their siblings when they are sick, and baby-sit when necessary. More distant relatives are expected to use their connections to help obtain jobs and favors. Perhaps most importantly, a person's closest friendships are usually with family members, perhaps with a sibling, or with a cousin.

Growing Up

There is no doubt whatsoever that boys in Latin America have the favored position, but all children are highly valued. While Christmas is probably the most important celebration of the year, children's birthdays are not far behind. Even the poorest of families manage to put together some kind of celebration, inviting dozens of other children, buying or making *piñatas,* serving food and drink, and giving gifts to all. For some families, the annual birthday celebrations are major items for the budget and are carefully planned and saved for many months in advance.

To a North American, who is accustomed to seeing self-discipline systematically instilled in growing children, Latin American children appear to be pampered. Very rarely does one see spanking or any other kind of negative reinforcement. Positive reinforcement, though, for desired behavior, is common. What seems to control children's behavior more than anything else is that a sense of belonging, being an important part of a large family, is instilled early and they are constantly encouraged to behave properly in order to maintain harmony.

Boys generally have very few responsibilities as they are growing up. Girls, on the other hand, are expected to be mother's helpers and they learn early to handle household duties and take care of younger siblings. They are expected to be subservient to their male siblings unless the boys are younger than she, in which case she plays a mothering role. These expectations are, of course, what maintains the *machismo* complex in Latin American men, but it also tends to result in women who are more responsible and who are more emotionally mature at an earlier age than their counterparts in the United States.

Chapter 8

Interpersonal Conflicts

When it comes to dealing with problems, Americans remind me of a bulldozer, pushing the rocks out of the way with force. Latins remind me of a river, flowing around, between, and over the rocks. In spite of the stereotype about the Latin American woman's fiery hot temper, I never have seen much of it. In fact, the only times I have seen it has been as a result of jealousy or suspected infidelity (I have been prosecuted a few times, but never convicted). Generally, when there is a conflict, a Latin prefers to avoid direct confrontation, and if at all possible, just let the problem go away by itself. This is especially true of the Latin female. Anger is an extremely difficult emotion for many Latinas to deal with in a positive manner, and to direct their anger against men is not acceptable. They are expected to live, without complaint, with whatever is causing the problem.

One important characteristic of the culture is emphasis on harmony in social relations, especially within the family, and Latins will usually go out of the way to keep the peace. Generally, you can get red-in-the-face-angry at a clerk, mechanic, or whatever, and he will then calmly proceed to tell you whatever it is that he thinks it is that you want to hear. It's hard to stay mad when people respond that way. It doesn't really resolve anything, but it at least defuses the situation.

Americans are accustomed to dealing very directly and overtly with other people when differences arise. Usually we like to talk about what is bothering us and then look for a pragmatic solution. That is not the Latin way of doing it. If the subject can be avoided, it will be avoided, and if it can't, your Latina will probably prefer to talk around the subject rather than confront it directly. It can be frustrating, especially when you know that the problem needs to be solved, but can't be solved without discussing it.

When it comes to problems in the home, there are two things that you absolutely must not do. You must not yell at her and you must not criticize her. Now the yelling most of us can control with a little willpower, but what do you do when she is doing something that annoys you and you want her to change her behavior? Well, you do not tell her that you don't like it, you don't tell her that she's wrong, and you don't tell her that she doesn't know what she's doing. In fact, you don't say anything that sounds like criticism. If she's putting too much salt in her cooking, don't tell her that she's using too much salt. Simply tell her that you would like a little less salt. Can you see the difference? With the first statement you're putting her down, and with the second statement you are saying what you want. I have never run into trouble by saying what I wanted, but I have never failed to have problems when I complained about something. Another example: I am a world-class champion snorer, and my ex-wife is a light sleeper. She never complained about my snoring, but she did mention on a few occasions that she had a little trouble sleeping. I got the meaning, but it didn't insult me because of the way she put it.

One thing that never ceases to amaze me is the Latin American's capacity for forgiving and forgetting. I have done things to people, accidentally, carelessly, or deliberately, that, had it been done to me I would have forever held a grudge. But yet, I could see those same people several months later, and it would be as if nothing had ever happened. Even if they were the guilty party, it would be as if the offense hadn't happened. I was expected to be like any other Latin, and it was assumed that I had forgiven and forgotten the event. My ex-wife and several girlfriends have also forgiven me for a remarkable range of offenses. I am sure that this capacity is rooted in the Latin way of bringing up children to live in harmony. Carrying grudges certainly doesn't contribute to smooth social relations.

The only situations that I am aware of that frequently do result in long-term hard feelings is when a man's sense of honor has been violated or his stance of machismo has been insulted. These are serious offenses and can result in a hostility that can last for a lifetime or can result in immediate violence. There are some differences between countries, too, regarding what is considered to be a violation of sense of honor and the amount of violence that is acceptable, or even required, as a result of it. I haven't spent enough time in most of the Latin American countries to be able to compare them all in this regard, but there are distinct differences in two of the countries in which I have spent many years. Mexican men, for example, seem to live on the edge of violence and at the same time, wear their honor on their shirtsleeves. Woe be to the other man who dares to challenge his sense of machismo. Costa Rican men, on the other hand, have a live-and-let-live attitude, and it is difficult to provoke them to overt anger, regardless of the nature of insults sent their way. I have managed to do it on a few occasions, though.

My suggestion for getting along in Latin America is to leave your bulldozer parked in the U.S., and try to be as much like a river as possible.

Chapter 9

Attitudes Toward Men

Machismo: Latin Male Chauvinism

Most Latin American women are brought up in homes that are male dominated. She may or may not have a father living in the home, but she probably has brothers, uncles, and grandfathers around to exert some control upon her. The general expectation is that she, as a girl, is supposed to obey and attend the male's every need. Males are not expected to assist with housework, cooking, cleaning, washing, or anything else that has to do with the home except for lifting heavier things or taking out the garbage (and that's not real common). They are simply expected to bring home the paycheck if they are adults, or play with their buddies if they are children.

Most of the men grow up with attitudes leading to "masculine" behavior around other men and dominating and controlling behavior towards women (with the exception of mother, who is usually idolized as a saint and suspected of being a virgin). This phenomenon is called

71

"machismo." The man who shows this kind of behavior is called *"machista,"* and the behavior itself is called *"macho"* behavior. The girls don't like it.

The girls don't like it because it makes them into second-class citizens and puts them at a disadvantage in life. They have to work harder because of it and get fewer rewards. It leaves them in the house while husband is out partying with his buddies or spending money on a prostitute or his other woman. They also don't like it because it effectively deprives them of emotional intimacy with a man. A *machista* has little use for emotional indulgence and has little to share with his wife except for sex. *Machismo* leads them to be very self-centered, possessive, jealous, and demanding. Still, unless a woman is fortunate enough to marry a Latin man with a more modern outlook, or a North American or European, she is stuck in the system.

There is, however, a desirable side to *machismo,* and this shows up in the form of the *"caballero,"* or gentleman, whose behavior is much like that of the American gentleman of the old days. He protects his wife and family from all dangers and provides them with the necessary security in life. He stands up to give a woman his seat, opens the door for a lady, carries heavy packages, and helps with the heavy household chores. The girls do like that. The current popularity of introduction services among Latinas suggests that they believe that many American men have this latter trait. If this isn't already a part of your behavioral repertoire (or if it has been pounded out of you by American feminists), it might be a good idea to start practicing. You'll need it.

Marianismo:
The Female Corollary

In a 1996 published book, *The Maria Paradox,* two Latina psychologists analyzed what they call "*marianismo,*" the female equivalent of *machismo* (the word *marianismo* is not part of the normal Spanish vocabulary, but *machismo* is). They consider it to be the other side of the coin, by which female roles are defined, just as male roles are defined by *machismo.* Although modern Latinas have changed a great deal, and are no longer the same as their mothers or grandmothers, a great deal of the Hispanic heritage has been passed on to them as "*marianismo.*" Drs. Gil and Vazquez list what they call the "Ten Commandments of Marianismo:"

» 1. Do not forget a woman's place.
» 2. Do not forsake tradition.
» 3. Do not be single, self-supporting, or independent minded.
» 4. Do not put your own needs first.
» 5. Do not wish for more in life than being a housewife.
» 6. Do not forget that sex is for making babies...not for pleasure.
» 7. Do not be unhappy with your man or criticize him for infidelity, gambling, verbal and physical abuse, alcohol or drug abuse.
» 8. Do not ask for help.
» 9. Do not discuss personal problems outside the home.
» 10. Do not change those things which make you unhappy that you can realistically change.

The ten commandments are, as the authors put it, "*marianismo* in its purest and darkest form." But, just as the modern Latina is rejecting *machismo*, she is also rejecting *marianismo*. Even so, it still affects her, just as many of the values handed down from our grandparents still affect us.

At the roots of *marianismo* is the expectation that women be selfless in their behavior towards others. Latinas tend to define themselves in terms of how well they do things for others rather than in terms of any other personal characteristics or in terms of occupational or professional competence. Unless you can convince your Latina that she really is doing very well by you, she will not be likely to be satisfied with herself as a woman. Passivity is one result of this cultural heritage, and Latinas tend to be more comfortable with men making the decisions. You may believe that this is exactly what you want, especially if you are angry with American women for challenging your decisions. I can tell you from experience, however, that it can become very boring when your mate refuses to express opinions or desires, even to the extent of not wanting to say what dinner she wants to order from the menu. As a man reared in North America, you are probably going to need some of the give-and-take that comes when a woman is willing to express some degree of individuality. I suggest that you strongly encourage your Latina to be free to express herself as a person with her own individual needs and desires. It will make your life more of a pleasure.

In Latin America (but more especially when a Latina moves to the United States), *marianismo* is losing its hold on younger women. If it were not, there would be no women available for the introduction programs, because this approach to locating a husband is most definitely unacceptable under the old system. For instance, women, in cities at least, usually work at paying jobs if they are not married. This can't help but make them more independent.

Attitudes towards sex have changed, as well, and women now expect to enjoy sex and be sexually satisfied. *Cosmopolitan* magazine, which we all know is a magazine targeted at the modern, urban, sophisticated woman, has a Spanish language version which is distributed throughout Spanish-speaking Latin America and is very popular. And, the modern Latina has learned to look for change whenever change is needed, and this is a departure from the old ways. This willingness to change is seen in the large numbers of Latinas now participating in introduction programs. It is very much a departure from tradition and would have been completely unacceptable a generation ago.

Vices

The Spanish word *"vicios"* simply means vices, but it is the most commonly used word in the ladies' application forms. They always want a man *"sin vicios."* Actually, what it means more than anything else is that they want a man who doesn't drink, smoke, do drugs, or run around with other women. Latin American women **really** don't like smoking and drinking. To some extent it is related to health concerns, but it also has social significance and is identified with the lower class.

Taking Care of the Man

Most Latin American women have grown up taking care of men and seeing to it that they are happy and satisfied. It is so normal to them, so completely ingrained, that they really don't even have to think about it. She will see it as her responsibility to make things good for you, and she will probably enjoy doing it. It will make her feel even better if you actively show appreciation for her efforts. I used to disappoint my wife occasionally by refusing some offering that she was making to me, and she was genuinely saddened by it. But, honestly, I wasn't hungry all the time.

How She Wants You to Take Care of Her

I see two components to this...emotional and financial. Let's deal with the emotional first. If she has her choice about it, she will be put on a pedestal and worshipped as a goddess. But isn't that true of women everywhere? Actually most Latinas go to a great deal of trouble and expense to maintain their bodies in good condition and to dress attractively. By doing so they are putting together a very nice package which they hope will please you and which will continue to attract you. I haven't seen many modern Latin American women go to seed after marriage just because she had already caught her husband. Being attractive to her man seems to be a continuing effort. But, she does expect her man to appreciate her efforts, and it doesn't hurt anything at all to encourage her to stand on that pedestal from time to time. It's not likely to become habit forming.

When I first began my introduction service, I was very surprised at how many women expressed a deep loneliness and desire to share emotionally with a man. And I'm talking about some very good-looking ladies...some that you would expect to have male attention coming from every side. I'm sure that they did receive plenty attention, but what they were missing was a sense of sharing with a special man. Emotional closeness and sharing was what they wanted and weren't getting. She will want you to take care of her in that manner.

If there is any one thing that can be identified as being most important to a Latina, it is security. She wants the security of knowing that you will always be there. She wants to know that you will protect her under any circumstances, and that you will respect and take care of her. She also wants the security of a home...her own home. And this is where the financial aspect comes in. I have actually met very few gold-diggers in Latin America. A few, but not many. All women (and men too, for that matter) want the security of not having to worry about where the next meal is coming from or about getting evicted from the house. If possible, she wants the home to be owned, not rented. There were a few months during the time I was married to my Costa Rican wife (Remember? The one from the poor y) that business took a downturn and money was so scarce that I had to buy food on credit from a local store. It was uncomfortable at the time, but I wasn't particularly worried because I knew that it was a temporary situation. It frightened my wife a lot, though, because she had grown up living on the edge without having had the security of knowing that things would improve. I still feel bad about those few months, because at that time I was unable to offer her the security that she so very much needed.

Another reason the women need security is because of her children. You may or may not marry a woman with children, and you may or may not have children of your own with her, but if children are involved, she will absolutely demand that those children are protected and fed. Children are very important to Latin American women. They come before everything else, including you.

Age Differences

I have only mentioned my last wife, but I have actually been married twice to Latin American women. The first was Panamanian. We were together for a very short time, and I lost her for reasons that neither of us could control. I mention her now because both of my wives were 26 years younger than I. My current girlfriend is 21 years younger. I don't think that age differences are particularly important in marriages with Latin American women. The main reason is that they mature differently and earlier than American women. As you remember from the discussion of growing up in the family, the whole process of maturing is one usually involving a great deal of responsibility, and that has its affect on the adult woman.

Although not all Latinas are the same in this regard, age differences are certainly not as important to the Latin American woman as it is to her counterpart in the United States. Actually, as long as a man keeps himself fairly healthy, she's not likely to be particularly concerned about either his age or his looks. What is going to count for her is how he treats her, and if he's smart he will treat her very well, especially if that is about all he has to offer.

There is something that you need to be concerned about, though, and it's something that I think about as I get older. I do expect to marry again, and it is most definitely going to be to a Latina (I wouldn't have it any other way). At the age of 56, I can still marry someone in her early 20's. But is it fair? Either to her or to me? Although things are still going fairly strongly, at some point in time I'm going to lose some, if not all, of my sexual potency. What's going to happen then? The chances are that she would remain faithful to me, but it certainly wouldn't be fair to her. And, unless I die suddenly, the young woman would be stuck with caring for a sick old man. The other side of the coin is, how much will I get of what I need from her. There is a special kind of maturity that only time, or perhaps having children, gives a woman. It may very well be that this kind of peaceful maturity is of more value to an old fart like me than the excitement of being with a young beauty.

The point that I'm making is that a fairly young woman is available, regardless of your age. But is that something you really want? If you do marry someone a great deal younger than yourself, please arrange for her security after your death. Widows rarely remarry in Latin America (although, if she remains in the United States her prospects wouldn't be totally bleak). Please see to it that you have adequate life insurance. And it will be best if you can leave her a house, too.

I would also like to impress upon you that it is not necessary to pay a great deal of attention to the age range that the ladies give a preference for in the T.L.C. publications and videotapes. The applications have a space for age range preference, and most of them fill it out. I have noticed over and over again, however, that men both older and younger than the specified range have perfectly good success with the ladies. Don't let it hold you back if you don't seem to fit her ideal. The chances are that she's not even sure what fits her until she sees what options she has.

Jealousy

Jealousy is a fact of life for most Latin American women. I didn't have problems with jealousy (most of the time) with either of my Latin wives because both of them trusted me (most of the time), but I have heard frequent complaints about jealousy from Anglo friends who married to Latinas. They actually do have some very legitimate reasons for growing up with a tendency towards jealousy, in that Latin men have a well-earned reputation for infidelity (in all fairness to my Latin male friends, I do know a few who are completely true to their wives, or so they say).

Even though American men have the reputation for fidelity, she will still be looking for signs that you either want to play around or are already doing it. So walk the straight and narrow until you really get her trust. It may take a while. Then she might let you look if you don't touch.

Personal Habits at Home

Latinas throughout Latin America are good housekeepers. Houses may be small and over-crowded, but they are clean. Cleanliness is seen as an important virtue. This also applies to their personal hygiene. Even in the higher altitudes with cool climates, not that many homes have hot water, and most people take cold water showers. It is something that I have never gotten accustomed to, and I sincerely dread taking showers. The only way I can handle them is by thinking about the worst problem I have just long enough to take my mind off of the shower. Cold water or not, Latinas stay clean, and it is important to them.

Many households have small top-loading Japanese-made washing machines (none are automatic) that can hold a few pounds of laundry, then spin dry them in a separate compartment garment at a time. They are comparatively inexpensive, but as part of a limited overall budget, can often be unaffordable. In many other households, laundry is done by hand. As time consuming as either method is, clothing is still washed weekly and Latinas always wear clean clothing. Dry cleaning establishments are not very common in Latin America, are non-existent outside of cities, and are expensive. Consequently, few people except men who need to wear suits for business have clothing that requires dry cleaning.

The cleanliness I have been impressed with...but the cooking leaves a lot to be desired. Of course there's not a whole lot that one can do with corn, beans, rice, range beef, and yard hens. I am sure that there are some very good cooks in Latin America. I just haven't been married to one yet, and I keep hoping to find one that knows how to use a cookbook and is willing to cook from it. Actually, having good food to eat at home is not likely to be a problem if you are living in the United States. From what I have heard from American men who have married Latin Americans, the ladies were delighted to learn new dishes and to have such a wide variety of fresh and frozen foods to cook with.

Budgeting

Budgeting money is frequently a source of conflict between American men and their Latina wives. Actually, it can be between any husband and wife. Most of the problems that I have heard about occurred between the periods of engagement and marriage, and after marriage, while she was still waiting to get her visa and arrange to fly to the U.S. Frequently what happens is that the man will encourage her to quit working in order to prepare for everything, and he will send her money to make up for the lost salary. The complaint is that the month's compensatory salary he sent will be spent during the first week, and she is suddenly needing more, as if her expenses had doubled or tripled once he started footing the bill. I think that this is mostly a matter of being forced to budget earlier, and now that she is in better economic circumstances, she feels a little more free about spending. She will have to learn how to handle money better, but my suggestion is that instead of giving her large lump sums, send the money weekly and don't send any more until the appointed weekly time. Western Union is especially useful for this.

Chapter 10

Relationships and Sex

Friendships

Outside of the family, most of a girl's social relationships are with other girls of about the same age.

The closest and most intimate friends are likely to be family, such as with cousins. Actually, even friendships outside the family don't really begin to take on much significance until she is a teenager. During high school (seventh grade on) she will begin to form friendships which continue through high school and beyond. It is a common sight to see groups of a half-dozen or so teenagers happily strolling along, chatting with one another. Usually a special relationship forms with several other girls, which can persist as friendship throughout a lifetime. Friendship changes significantly upon marriage, though, for at this time a woman is expected to make her husband and children the absolute center of her life. Casual going out with the girls comes to an abrupt end and she will most likely only see her friends at social get-togethers.

An old custom, derived from Spain, is the Sunday evening "*paseo*" (derived from the verb "*pasear*," which means "to walk," "to parade," or "to pass"). It is becoming less and less common as cities become larger and more impersonal, and dangerous at night, but still exists in some of the more traditional small towns. When I first went to live in Mexico in 1957, it was still common and was a delightful experience, and a wonderful way to meet girls. Most towns and cities of Latin America have a park in the center of town (usually called the *Parque Central*, or in Mexico, the *Zócalo*), usually in front of the oldest cathedral in town, and always a city block in size. Normally there are trees and park benches, and the park is surrounded by a sidewalk. Usually around seven in the evening (where the custom is still practiced) you will see women (of all ages, married and single) walking around the park in small groups talking with each other and sharing gossip. Their husbands are likely to be in a bar across the street talking with their buddies, or perhaps sitting on a park bench. Walking in the opposite direction, passing the girls in a sort of parade (thus the *"paseo"*) will be small groups of boys and young men, glancing out of the corners of their eyes, occasionally making eye contact and sharing a smile with some particular girl.

This old custom gave boys and girls the opportunity to look over potential marriage partners without ever having to get into a compromising situation which could have occurred had they been alone. After several months, even years, perhaps several boys and several girls might begin to sit together on a park bench, talk, and get to know one another better. Eventually, as a group, they might even begin to go out together at other times, perhaps to parties, or to a movie.

While it's true that this custom is no longer common in Latin America, the fundamental motivations behind it still exist. Courtship for the young is a slow and tedious process. Even today, teen-agers don't usually date alone until they have become very well acquainted, their families approve of the match, and they have made some sort of exclusive commitment to each other. Ordinarily, boys and girls will go out in groups until they are old enough to start pairing off.

Courtship tends to be a formal process even today, and the presence of a chaperon, perhaps the girl's sister or a cousin, is still accepted as being fairly normal at the beginning of a courtship, especially among the middle and upper classes. It is also still normal that the girl's parents must approve of the boy and it is still considered good form that the boy ask for her father's permission to marry her.

There is a special celebration that frequently accompanies a girl's coming of age and signals to the rest of the community that she is now a young lady and no longer a child. It is her "*quinceaños*" party, given by her parents at the time of her 15th birthday. It is usually a large and elaborate affair, and can involve several hundred people, including all of her friends, male and female, and frequently their parents as well. It is not always done because it's expensive. Most girls are not expected to start pairing off with boyfriends until after that 15th birthday celebration.

The process involved in courting a woman who has been first contacted through an introduction service is, of course, very different from the normal Latin American courting patterns. First, the chances are that she will be an adult and at least in her early twenties. Second, the process of correspondence (even if they first met during a tour) serves as an alternative for a normally lengthy courtship process, because it also usually takes a while to accomplish (I have known Americans to marry Latinas within a week of meeting them, but I don't recommend it). In some cases it will still be important to ask her father's approval for marriage, especially if she is young and still a virgin (and the family usually knows if she is), and in all cases the prospective husband needs to be introduced to the extended family as a matter of courtesy to them.

The Madonna/Whore Complex

Traditional Hispanic culture has it that a girl should be a virgin until after her wedding ceremony. This was a reasonably practical expectation back in the days when girls consistently married between the ages of 15 and 18. If a girl wasn't married before the age of 20 she was generally considered to be an old maid and had the options of having illicit sex, thus forever ruining her chances for marriage (which didn't matter much anyway, since she wasn't likely to get married after 20), or die an old maid virgin. This expectation wasn't really contrary to her wishes anyway since sex was traditionally considered to be distasteful to the woman and done only for economic reasons or to accommodate her husband.

Even now, when a girl crosses the line and has sex before marriage and doesn't marry the boy she has sex with, she is not considered to be as desirable for marriage by other men, and even the boy she had sex with now considers her to be less desirable as a wife. Her options are reduced even more if she has a child.

In the context of traditional Hispanic culture, a girl who has sex (and enjoys it) without being married is considered a bad woman (whore), and one who waits until marriage for sex and who doesn't enjoy it, is a good girl (madonna). Thus the Madonna/Whore dichotomy, which is basically the same thing that I remember from my high school days as the Good girl/Bad girl dichotomy, something strongly impressed upon me by my mother. Mothers, incidentally, throughout Latin America, are seen as madonnas by their sons even if they work as prostitutes.

But these same sons are the ones causing most of the girls' problems. Just about any Latina will tell you that men's only interest is in sex. Having been an incorrigible repeat offender in my youth, as well, I can appreciate their complaint. However, in Latin America, where prostitutes (many of whom are very attractive) are available in even the smallest of towns, I think another dynamic is at work. Certainly challenge and conquest are part of the interest in seducing a virgin, but the deeper motivation may be that of testing the girl, and if she doesn't stand up to the madonna test, disgracing her for her failure.

Thankfully, the situation has changed a great deal and is still changing rapidly. Now it is reasonably well understood that it is perfectly normal for women to enjoy sex. However, virginity is still considered by many women to be a highly valued thing to bring to her marriage, especially among the middle and upper classes. A number of the girls joining my introduction service made the point that they were virgins and expected to remain so until marriage. Quite of few of these were in their mid- to late twenties, and some were even in their thirties.

Unmarried Mothers

Figures provided by the Costa Rican public health hospitals and clinics in 1992 showed that 49.7% of all babies born during the previous year in that country had been born to unmarried mothers. Wow! What's going on here if chastity is such an important issue? Almost half of all babies were born out of wedlock!

Perhaps hypocrisy is part of it, but there are several other factors at work, too. Let's begin by eliminating one variable. Costa Rican women are, as a whole, not as traditional when it comes to sex as are those in other countries. Making love is frequently said to be the national pastime (this statement was even made in a major Costa Rican newspaper). While unmarried mothers are common in all of the Latin American countries, as far as I know, none of them have a rate of illegitimacy as high as Costa Rica (I don't have the figures for Brazil, but suspect that it might possibly be as high or higher).

Leaving Costa Rica behind as an atypical example, poverty has a lot to do with illegitimacy, just as it does in the United States and other developed countries. Both the urban poor and the rural poor suffer from the problem. Part of it comes from lack of education, part from lack of hope, and part from the culture of poverty.

I'm not qualified to discuss the lifestyle of the urban poor girl who becomes pregnant, except to say that this is where a high percentage of prostitutes come from. I can tell you about the rural poor, though, because I spent a lot of time living with them. First off, the Hispanic cultural tradition of virginity until marriage is not as strong among the rural poor as among the middle and upper classes, nor is supervision and control as strong. A middle-class girl in town is readily observable by others if she dares to go places alone with her boyfriend. Very few have cars and they have to take public transportation or walk. Perhaps most limiting, however, is where they can go to have sex unobserved. Where can they go except to a park or hotel? One is public and the other is a pretty big step for first time sex.

The situation is quite a bit different out in the country. A popular activity in the evenings, especially on Saturday and Sunday, is for groups of young people just to hang around a park or perhaps in front of a country store, drinking Cokes and making small talk. As a boy and girl grow to know one another, its a fairly simple matter to slip off by themselves for some kissing and hugging. Eventually this develops into slipping off a little farther away for some serious petting and eventually, sex. People frequently joke about "the bushes that shake in the night."

Usually in rural areas this kind of relationship tends to be stable and may very well endure for a lifetime without the benefit of a legal marriage. However, it is unusual for a rural girl to be promiscuous while still living at home. It would be known about and bring shame to the family.

It isn't at all uncommon for a girl to become sexually active at the age of 14 and give birth at the age of 15. Obviously, she is too young to marry the father, even if they could afford the money, which they probably can't; and he isn't likely to be much older than she. The usual solution is for her to continue to live with her extended family. Her having had the child does not bring shame on the family, because it is more or less accepted in rural areas, and the child is simply integrated into the existing family.

The event can even enhance the girl's social status, both within the family and within the community. Now she is a mother, and mothers enjoy that special status conferred by Hispanic tradition.

When she is old enough, and if it is mutually agreeable, she and the boy may eventually set up their own household or she may move to his family's house. In any case they will be considered to be "married" by the community, and will probably refer to each other as "husband"

and "wife." Actually, they are probably as married as anyone else, but this type of union is less stable simply because it is so easy to terminate. So, rather than reflecting promiscuity, a portion of the high national figures on illegitimacy actually reflect this kind of union.

My Costa Rican wife had a 2 year-old daughter when we met. She had never been married. And, she is about as far away from being promiscuous as one can get. I asked her if the pregnancy was an accident, and she said that it was most definitely planned. Since she was unmarried at the time she became pregnant, I was curious to know what kind of motivation would cause her to deliberately take on the responsibility of a child as an unmarried mother. Her answer was simple, and she seemed to consider me a dunce because it wasn't obvious to me. She was 23 years old at the time she got pregnant, didn't consider it likely that she would ever get married, and she wanted a child. Such a simple, obvious answer: She wanted a baby.

I wonder just how common this situation is in Latin America. Having and raising children are so very important to the Latina. What are her options if there is not a satisfactory man available to marry? She quite obviously has to make a choice between chastity and motherhood.

In all of the Latin American countries bachelorhood is an attractive alternative to marriage. It allows one to continue the *machista* lifestyle without being saddled with the responsibility of marriage and fatherhood (although most of the countries nominally require child-support payments, it is rarely asked for in the case of illegitimate children, and even if asked for it is not awarded unless he has signed papers to the effect that he is the father and is giving the child his surname). He will be able to live with his mother or another family member for as long as he wishes, spend his money on whatever he likes, and date as many women as he can obtain and afford. That is another problem faced by the Latina. Not only does a bad ratio of men to women in the cities reduce her choices, but quite a few of those who appear to be available actually aren't. This, I think, also contributes to the number of unwed mothers in Latin America. If they are going to have a child, they may have to do it on their own. In all of the Latin American introduction programs you will find a number of unmarried mothers. Some of them may have gotten that way by accident, others may have had an informal marriage as described above, but I suspect that quite a few of them got pregnant for the same reason my ex-wife did.

Sexual Stereotypes

The red-hot "Latin lover." How many times have you heard that expression? There's really not a lot of truth to it, either for men or women, but they both believe it about themselves.

Studies done of Hispanic males in New York City (as cited by Gil and Vazquez, *The Maria Paradox*) show that their sexual behavior is just about the same as the Anglo male, except that the Anglo may be a little bit more concerned about his wife's pleasure (perhaps because she insists on it). They have sex with the same frequency, for just about the same length of time, and do pretty much the same things. So, the famous "Latin lover" is a fiction when it comes to sex. He is not a fiction, however, with regard to the ardent manner he pursues the object of his attention. He pulls out all the romantic stops, at least until he marries her or gets her into bed. Latinas constantly complain about how men lose interest after marriage. Does that sound familiar?

What about the "hot Latina" stereotype? Is it true? I don't know of any studies that have been done on this subject. From my own experience, which I can't claim is extensive, but which I would consider to be a scientifically acceptable sample for statistical analysis, I would call this stereotype just as fictional as the one for men. I really can't see a lot of difference in bed between *Latinas* and *Anglas*, and I have spent a lot of time (and money) seriously exploring and looking for those differences. Perhaps I would consider the North American woman to be a little better in bed, because, if anything, the *Latina* is not as likely to have had as much experience. But it's a whole different matter when it comes to romantic behavior. The *Latina* excels in that department, just as does the *Latino*.

Unfortunately, the North American and European male doesn't fare well in the stereotype department. We are considered to be somewhat cold in personal relations, not particularly romantic, and not as hot in bed. I personally don't believe it to be true. I normally don't get more than one complaint per week, and some weeks none at all. So, I would suggest that you do as I do. Take the matter firmly into hand, put your very best into it, and just keep plugging away.

Chapter 11

Friendship & Romance

Latina Friendliness

Single men in the United States frequently see overt friendliness on the part of a single woman as being romantic interest, because that's usually what it is. An American woman who has no romantic interest is usually only going to display a limited amount of friendliness, and it is readily distinguishable for what it is. She may even be rude, making it more readily distinguishable.

Latina friendliness is open and communicative. The problem is that are no real apparent differences between simple interest in a new friend or the possible beginning of a romantic relationship. It looks the about same in either case. What in the United States would be interpreted as a romantic interest is likely to be nothing more than the same kind of friendliness that she would display toward any other friendly person. A married *Latina* is not likely to show much open friendliness at all, other than to say hello, unless her husband is present or unless she is with a group of her friends. The obvious reason is to discourage any unwanted advances.

Sincerity

I usually return to the United States to visit family twice a year. It is inevitable that during those visits I read newspapers, watch some television, and talk with people. I don't have cable TV in Panama (although I could get it), and normally get news of what is going on in the world from Panamanian newspapers and the international editions of weekly news magazines. I am always shocked by what I find taking place in American culture. Had I been in the U.S. all along, I probably would not notice the changes, and were I not so thoroughly part of Latin culture now, I probably wouldn't notice the basic differences between Latin American and North American ways of dealing with life.

What always strikes me with some force is that American culture is moving so quickly towards an addiction to hyperbole and exaggeration in everyday life. It is as if the simple things that people do and have happen to them as they go about living day-to-day hold little value, and that excitement has to come from the spectacular rather than from the ordinary. It also seems that in communication with other people, Americans just don't seem to hold themselves in high esteem unless they can appear to be larger than life, and have some major achievement to hold out for presentation.

One of the problems that comes from living in this manner is that it is particularly difficult to just simply be oneself, and communicate with and relate to others in a simple, honest, straightforward manner. Latins don't like direct confrontation and will obfuscate rather than talk directly about something that troubles them. They will, however, be direct, open, simple, and totally sincere in normal relations with other people. It is not part of the culture to put on a front and attempt to appear to be anything that one isn't. This leads to an easy and comfortable interaction with others, leaving the door wide open to friendship without pretense. This is true with men (except where *machismo* plays a part) as well as with women. I don't know what to call this other than just plain sincerity. I like it very much.

How to Tell If It's Romance

I wish that I could provide you with some specific clue that would enable you to determine the difference between romantic interest and simple friendliness, but I can't. Sometimes a cue is there, but usually it isn't. Just don't assume, because a woman shows interest, that it's romance. By the same token, don't assume that because it appears to be just friendship, that doesn't mean that she isn't romantically interested in you.

Latinas are accustomed to men taking the initiative in romance. That is why she is not likely to overtly communicate her interest in you. It is up to you to first show your interest in her. My suggestion (unless you've already corresponded, and an interest has already been expressed) is to invite her to have lunch with you, or to meet you for a walk, or to have coffee. This is a first communication that shows you are interested in her. But don't be surprised if she brings a female friend with her. It is common. Keep asking for the simple dates, until she is willing to go out to dinner with you alone, or perhaps to the movies. At some point you will get the message that she is interested, if she is. Once you have been out alone a time or two, there is nothing wrong with bringing up for discussion your interest in her. She will either tell you that she sees you only as a friend or that there may be some possibilities.

Things do move much more rapidly during a tour such as that offered by T.L.C. Worldwide. The girls are aware that time is limited and that they must move quickly if any kind of relationship is to be established. If, during one of the parties, a girl doesn't seem to want to continue a conversation for long, or appears restless, forget about her. If, on the other hand, she keeps showing up at your side, or lingers for a long time to talk, then you can be sure that you have her interest. If you like her, encourage her and stay with it. Ask her out for the next day.

Don't be a butterfly (*mariposa*). If you flit from one girl to another, you can be sure that none of them will have interest. Roving husbands and infidelity are constant problems for Latinas, and if you give behavioral signs indicating that you would make that kind of husband, you can be sure that she will back off.

Another indication of interest is when she invites you to meet her friends. The invitation is a clear indication that she approves of you as a person. She would not risk a potential embarrassment by bringing someone she wasn't interested in to meet her friends. Family is a different matter, however. You should never marry someone without meeting her family, but you must give her the lead in this. A girl is likely to strictly limit the number of men that she introduces to her family, both to protect her family and to protect her own reputation within the family. An invitation to meet her family is a good indication that she is taking you seriously. But that is not always the case. I have been invited many times to girls' homes simply because they found me interesting and thought that their families might, too. In those instances I was not being invited as a romantic interest, but simply as a friend.

The only reliable rule of thumb that I can offer is ...when in doubt, ask.

Propositions

Latin Americans are generally much less aggressive in communication than are Americans. There is one area, though, in which they differ, and that is when a man makes a sexual proposition to a woman. Surprisingly enough, it is quite acceptable to do so if you are reasonably well acquainted. In the U.S. it is considered to be in bad taste to just come right out and propose a liaison, but it normally isn't in Latin America. She might be shocked, but at the same time will probably be flattered.

It must be done with a bit of style, though. Latin women are accustomed to suggestive comments (*piropos*) in the street, but the *piropos* never are requests for sex...they merely show, hopefully in a creative manner, how much the man appreciates the woman, ("Such dangerous curves, and me without brakes!") and how much he would enjoy taking her to bed.

By the same token, when making a proposition, you don't ask her for sex. You simply make the proposition that you do it. Something to the effect of "I'm really excited by you and would really like to make love with you. How do you feel about it?" It might or might not get the results you want, but the chances are that she will be pleased by your interest and not be offended at all. The worst that is likely to happen is that she will laugh and tell you to put the ring on her finger first. In any case, she won't make you feel like the idiot you would feel like if you tried that in the United States.

Danger Signs

» 1) When, in a letter (and before any kind of commitment is made) a girl says that she has some kind of emergency and desperately needs money, throw away the letter and forget her. It is probably a lie. I get offended whenever a girl asks for money, even if there is some sort of relationship. It's not that I mind giving it, but I would like to make it as a gift of my own volition. If you are corresponding with a girl, it doesn't hurt to send a little money to help her with the correspondence. Ten dollars here and there is not likely to do much damage, and can help her pay postage and pay for the photos you would like to have of her and her family. Do not send more than that during the course of correspondence, until a commitment is well established, because you may very well be establishing a dangerous precedent, leading her to appreciate you more for your money than for you. Remember that she got along fine before you entered her life, and she can continue to get along without your money. All you owe her at this point is to cover her extra expenses in corresponding with you. Even after a commitment has been made, it is very unwise to send money to begin wedding preparations **unless you have already met the lady and her family** and are convinced that she is the right one. More than one man has been fleeced in this way.

» 2) When a girl frequently expresses how much she would like to live in the United States, take a real close look at the relationship. There's a possibility that she's interested primarily in you as her ticket to the U.S.

» 3) When a girl declares her love for you within the first few letters, beware. She's either an air-head, a hopeless romantic, or trying to cut some corners. In any of these cases it probably won't be good for you.

» 4) Once you have met, if she insists on bringing friends or family along with her on all of your out-ings, you may be in for trouble. It is normal to have someone else along for the first few dates, although that isn't always the case. If the pattern persists, she probably isn't interested in you personally, but is en-joying your generosity to entertain her and her friends. If trips to the beach or to restaurants regu-larly include her family, it's the same thing. I don't object to it if she asks in advance if she may include friends or family. It gives me the opportunity to tell her whether it is possible or isn't possible. It may sim-ply be that she wants to give me the opportunity to know her family. I don't mind that. However, on a few occasions, the group was simply waiting for me to show up. Guess who gets to pay for the excursion, and guess who doesn't always have the money.

» 5) I consider it a wise choice to dump a girl at the very first sign of deception or dishonesty. Don't per-mit lies and don't permit theft.

» 6) I have had some American men tell me that when they married their wives they also married her fam-ily. It is true that once you are married you are con-sidered to be part of the family, and family members are generally expected to help out for the welfare of all. However, some families view American men as having inexhaustible deep pockets, and where they were once looking out for themselves, they now ex-pect the American man to take over that responsibil-ity. This may be something that you would find acceptable. I absolutely do not. If you see signs of this developing, I think a deep discussion with your girl-friend or wife is in order. Once married, you should help her family to some extent if you can afford to do so, especially if any income that she was producing before went to help her family. But you are definitely not responsible for their welfare.

» 7) It is traditional in Latin America for girls, once they marry, to spend much less time with their girlfriends. If she doesn't cut back some after a commitment is made, it would be to your benefit to examine the nature of her commitment to you.

Chapter 12

Love

Falling in Love

Falling in love is more of a North American concept than Latin American. Remember the old song with the words "love and marriage go together like a horse and carriage"...romantic drivel from the 1950's? Traditionally, in Hispanic culture marriage is a social institution related more to perpetuation of family ties and the development of a new family unit. Marriage never was, and still isn't (for the most part) something perceived as being mainly for the satisfaction of the man and woman involved.

I remember reading many years ago the idea that "falling in love" is a psychosocial mechanism designed to get men and women to suspend their rational judgment just long enough to get married, at which time they can come back to their senses and live with the mistake they made. I got a big kick out of it at the time because it seemed to fit the situation I was in at the time. Whether it is true or not, every psychologist will tell you that "falling in love" is basically a narcissistic act in which we idealize the other person and make him/her into reflections of our own deeply felt needs. We don't really fall in love with another real person, but our idealized version of that person.

Latin American women fall in love too, and when they do it's essentially the same thing that Americans experience. It just doesn't happen as frequently nor as easily, and when it happens it isn't necessarily seen as a prelude to marriage. Marriage is seen as something far more serious than something to satisfy the emotional needs of the two people involved.

Growing in Love

As I write this, I am envisioning the indignation of some Hispanic lady who lives in the United States reading this and having the thought of "What the hell does he think he knows about how I feel!" Well, whoever you are, I actually don't know how you feel. I can only go by my observations and the many talks I have had with girls in our programs in Latin America. If I offend you, I apologize.

Given the above disclaimer, let me proceed. Latin women are romantics at heart but are immanently practical in their behavior. Men frequently wonder how it is that a Latin American girl can marry him with full intentions of devoting her life to him after having become acquainted mostly through correspondence and having had very little cumulative time actually together. It has to do with the way such decisions are made. He will have been assessed on the basis of his behavior as to whether he will make a dependable and caring husband. She will have decided whether he will be faithful and whether he will take care of her in the future. She will especially be interested in how he treats her when they are together and will want to be sure that he is a gentleman.

I can't say that physical attraction isn't a part of it, because it usually is to some extent. But I can say that when it comes to choosing a husband, physical attraction is far down the list of important characteristics; much farther down the list, in fact, than on your own list.

Actually, given that she has met a good man who has some interests in common with her and who will treat her well, she expects to be in love with him some day, and she probably will be. But this isn't "falling in love." This is what I call "growing in love." It is a process of developing affection through knowledge and trust, and the love coming out of the process is something that can only be developed through time. It is, in fact, the opposite of "falling in love," which I see as an abandonment of rational judgment in favor of fantasy. It is rational judgment itself that promotes "growing in love," thus allowing full development of affection. Psychologically and socially the method is far superior to the usual North American approach to marriage. It produces more stable and enduring marriages. It does, though, require that you suspend your normal expectations regarding love long enough to allow the process to work, because it is not an overnight thing.

Being Romantic

So far as I know, almost every woman in the Western world responds to a man when he is romantic. By being romantic, I mean remembering birthdays, anniversaries, and the like, but I also mean coming up with some occasional surprises; such things as bringing home flowers from time to time, going out to dinner on the spur of the moment, whispering sweet nothings in her ear, and bringing the occasional gift. Frankly, I have never been very creative about such matters myself, and I am certain that my life has been a little more drab than it would have been had I paid more attention to being romantic.

The reason I bring this up is that you have some pretty tough competition when it comes to Latin men. They are very romantic...at least until marriage, and it would be very much to your advantage to see if you can even the score. Your girl may not want to marry a Latin man, but you can be sure that she appreciates his roman- ticism. Your being romantic can hasten the growing in love process for both of you. Not only will she like it, but you may find yourself being more loving just by getting the practice.

Chapter 13

Pastimes

Pasear

I mentioned the Spanish verb *pasear* in an earlier chapter while discussing the traditional *paseo*. The verb means "to march," "to walk," "to pass." There is another meaning that doesn't have a direct translation into English. A frequent pastime enjoyment is to simply hang around, visit friends, go to one place or another, or just walk around. It is a good way to pass the time enjoyably without spending much money. This is called *"pasear,"* too, and is probably what most people enjoy doing more than anything else when they don't have some specific plan in mind. Your lady may very well mention *pasear* when she is writing to you about what she enjoys doing, and that is what she means.

Dancing

There are very few Latinas that don't enjoy dancing. Most Latin music is so eminently danceable that it even makes a poor dancer like me want to get out on the floor. Dancing and moving to the rhythm is encouraged from childhood on, so it's no surprise that Latin ladies like to dance. Don't concern yourself too much if you aren't light on your feet. I have always been very clumsy in moving legs and feet, and no matter how much time I put into trying to learn to dance, it still comes out laughable. Still, other things are likely to be more important to her, and at most you will be depriving her of just one of the things she likes to do with you. Those of you who are good dancers, though, especially if you learn to dance Latin style, are going to have a very important social skill.

People go to dance in a variety of places. Every city has *discotecas* with a night club atmosphere. Some restaurants have bands and dance floors. All cities also have *salones de baile* which are large open-floored dance halls with tables around the walls, some with live music and some with recorded music. Just about every small town will also have a *salon de baile*, usually mostly open and with a thatched or tin roof.

Until a girl has formed a steady relationship, she is likely to go to the dances with several of her other unattached friends, and they will dance with similarly unattached men. Unlike most American dance halls, the presence of unattached women doesn't mean at all that they are there to be picked up by the men. True, it is an opportunity to meet, but most are there for the dancing.

Parties

Parties are usually very different functions than those in the United States. Most are social affairs to be enjoyed by people of all ages, married and single. The occasion can be a birthday, wedding celebration, anniversary, or just about any other kind of conceivable reason. Singles parties, so common in the United States, are very rare. I can remember only one that I went to, outside of those sponsored by T.L.C. Worldwide, and a number of young married couples were also present. While at most parties beer and liquor will be served, it is considered to be in very bad taste for anyone to get drunk, and usually the women don't drink anything stronger than Coca Cola. Parties are seen as a way to have some good, clean fun, not to get drunk, raise hell, and pick up a girl.

Outdoor Activities

Except for going to the beach, outdoor activities are not as popular in Latin America as in the United States. Camping (except at the beach), boating, sailing, skin-diving and such are activities enjoyed primarily by the upper class. I suspect that the cost of the equipment needed has a lot to do with that.

But wherever there are beaches, they are popular. So are bikinis.

Chapter 14

Meeting Her Family

Why It Is Important

There are three important reasons why you need to meet her family. First is to gain more knowledge of her. It is important to see the setting in which she became an adult. It is important to gain insight into how her family functions as a unit and how she fits into it. The patterns that she learned as a child will tend to persist over her lifetime, and it is a good idea to know as much as possible about them before you marry. It is a common saying that if you want to know what kind of woman a girl will become, just take a look at her mother. I don't know how accurate the saying is, but there is usually at least a grain of truth in all folk wisdom. You also need to notice whether there is friction or tension in the family, since, to some extent, you will become part of it. You need to observe whether or not her family is respectful toward her and vice-versa. There will be reasons behind either respect or disrespect. In general, her family is part of her, and the more you can know in advance the better prepared you will be to deal with her.

The second reason is that her family wants to know you, and she also wants them to know you. She is going to want feedback from her family as to what they think of you. You may not actually need to ask for permission to marry her (unless she is young), but it is important that she has the approval of her family. It is important to her that she remain part of the family unit, even if she lives 3,000 miles away with you, and it is also important that, since you are marrying her, you will also be welcomed into the extended family. I am aware of instances where couples married in spite of family disapproval, but it complicated things. Actually, all you have to do is be a decent person with them and know enough about their culture to avoid offending anyone.

Third, it is important that you show respect to her extended family, and that requires meeting them. It might happen all at once in one large gathering, as it happened with my first Latin wife, or it might happen over a period of time, as it did with my second one. But, no matter how complicated or time consuming, it is vitally important that you meet every relative that she considers significant. To not do so would be offensive.

When the Occasion Comes

If a group occasion has been chosen to introduce you to the extended family, some courage may be required on your part, because a face-to-face meeting with twenty strangers can surely be intimidating when you are the guest of honor. I've found, though, that the objective really isn't to cast a jaundiced, critical eye upon the potential groom. It's really more a matter of paying honor to him and offering him a welcome into the family.

Actually, getting to know an extended family usually comes after meeting closer members of the family, such as parents and siblings. But whether it is a large group or just a few people, there are some things to be aware of. Unlike in North America, where a smile and a nod of the head is sufficient to acknowledge members of a group, that is not so in Latin America, and you will be viewed as stand-offish and cold if that is all you do. It is essential that you greet each and every person individually and introduce yourself. That will inevitably involve shaking hands with all of the men. The custom of shaking hands with women varies from country to country. It is customary to do so in some countries, but in some others it is appropriate only if the woman offers her hand first. Study up on the local customs as much as possible, and if you still don't know, ask your girlfriend.

It isn't necessary to say a whole lot to the people you are being introduced to. They will not expect you to speak Spanish well, and they will also be aware that it is a new situation for you. Just smile and be as open and friendly as possible. Actually, although I speak Spanish well, I frequently use the approach of appearing ignorant, but of good will, to many of the strangers I meet, especially those who are in some position of authority, such as customs inspectors and mothers. I have found that Latin Americans are particularly willing to be helpful and considerate if you don't seem to know what you are doing, but want to learn.

At Her Invitation

It is particularly important that you don't try to rush the occasion of meeting her family. When I first began my introduction service, I stressed to my customers that it was important to meet the girl's

111

family before marrying her. But there was another point that I neglected to make. One of my customers came down to Costa Rica to meet a girl that he had been corresponding with, took her out a time or two, and demanded to meet her family. The girl was highly offended, and considered the man to be a pushy, bad-mannered boor. And she was right. It is true that you need to meet her family before marrying, but it must be at her invitation.

I dated my Costa Rican wife for at several months before she invited me to her home. Prior to that we had met at appointed times and places, but I was under strict instructions to never go to her house. I knew about where it was, but I wasn't supposed to show up. I finally got invited to a Sunday dinner for the purpose of meeting her family. Why had it taken so long? I didn't know at the time, but it turned out that I was the very first boyfriend that she had ever introduced to her family, and it was an especially important event for both her and the family. She didn't want to make the mistake of inviting a man into her family circle until she was very sure that it was probably going to be a lasting relationship. Of course, I lived in the same city, had no intentions of leaving soon, and she realized that she could take all the time she wanted.

Because of time constraints, things happen a whole lot more quickly on T.L.C. Worldwide tours. The girls realize that the man is only going to be around for a few days, and if anything is going to happen, it has to happen then. It is common for a man to meet a girl on Friday evening, have dates with her Saturday morning and after-noon, and get invited to meet her family on Sunday. Of course it doesn't involve the extended family at this point, but the meeting with her parents gives them a chance to know the man that she expects to be corresponding with, and perhaps establish a permanent relationship with. It is easier for her to proceed if they know what is happening and with whom it is happening.

Chapter 15

The Role of Religion

The Catholic Church

Latin America was settled by the Spaniards and Portuguese, and they brought Catholicism with them. In fact, conversion of the native Americans to Catholicism was one of the moral justifications for subjugation. Latin America today is approximately 95% Catholic. The remainder is a smattering of Protestant churches, and, family by family, Jehovah's Witnesses, Seventh Day Adventists, and Mormon missionaries are making a few conversions. Every country also has its Asian and Middle Eastern immigrant populations, and they have brought their religions with them.

The Catholic Church is important enough in Latin America for Catholicism to exist as the formal state church in every one of the countries. The United States, of course, specifically forbade a state church in its constitution. The question of relevance to you, particularly if you are not Catholic, is just how much is her religion going to affect the relationship between you and the Latina you decide to marry.

Cultural Aspects

Interestingly enough, as pervasive as the Catholic Church is in Latin America, it does not maintain a strangle hold on the people. I say this in the sense that people do not tend to be highly dogmatic about the religion. We have all known people in the United States, of one church or another, who believe in their religion to the exclusion of any other, who are highly dogmatic, even fanatic, and if they are not trying to convert you, usually try to avoid you if you are not of the same religious persuasion. I have never observed this phenomenon in Latin America, at least not within the Catholic Church. Perhaps it comes from the Latin tradition of "live and let live," but I think that more than anything else, Catholicism is seen as the mother religion to other churches, and since it is so woven into the culture and shared by so many other people, there just simply isn't any point in being dogmatic about it.

My first Latin American wife, a Panamanian, was a devout Seventh-Day Adventist and went to church as regularly as possible. I am pretty neutral about religious matters, but I occasionally went along with her. One day I asked her about her feelings regarding the Catholic Church and received an enlightening answer: "Oh, but I will always be Catholic too." I think that most Latin Americans experience the Catholic Church, as she did, as being part of their cultural fabric rather than as a religion as such. It is fundamental to their thinking, but not something that has to be thought about.

Up until the time I left home I was a Methodist, sang in the choir, and went to church most Sundays. Although I never quite became an agnostic, I later went through many years of questioning, during which time I avoided formal religion as much as possible. I still have an aversion to formal religion, although not so strongly. However, about fifteen years ago, I went through the necessary classes and became a Catholic (believe it or not, I failed the first time around and had to start over. According to my favorite priest, I was the first convert ever to fail classes in their diocese). I didn't become a Catholic because I believed in the doctrine. That didn't matter to me then, and it still doesn't. It was actually because of two priests in Tampa, Florida who became good friends with me, who frequently shared glasses of wine with me, and who eventually invited me to participate in church activities. From that, I realized that I needed the community of a church.

I mention this because I later discovered that there is a tremendous difference between the Catholic Church in North America and in Latin America. Although the formal structure is laid down by decree from the Vatican, the actual structures in practice are distinctly different.

Anthropologists have long made an interesting observation: Religious structure tends to resemble family structure, no matter what the religion or the culture of which it is a part. Hispanic culture emphasizes the family unit as being the focal point of living, whereas we in North America emphasize the individual. Latin American Catholicism has a Holy Family structure not at all unlike that in the day-to-day family. God is seen as being somewhat remote, just like father, and needs to be approached by means of an intermediary, who is Jesus. Jesus, much like an older brother, is more accessible, but an intermediary can also help in His case. The closest intermediary is the always the gentle, caring, kind, and long-suffering Virgin Mary, who in day-to-day life is represented by the mother in the family. The various saints are perceived much like real life patrons, helping people to get out of trouble or helping them to get what they want. The Latin American family actually bases daily behavior on these role perceptions.

The Catholic Church in North America has a more individualistic emphasis and does not rely as much upon Virgin Mary as an intermediary or upon saints as patrons. And it relies upon priests not as intermediaries, but as interpreters of doctrine and as social shepherds. In this sense, they are not very different from their Protestant colleagues.

Does It Affect You?

There were a few women in my introduction program who specified that they would marry only a Catholic man, but they were very few. Quite a few, however, stated that it was important to them that their husband believed in God. I think that the particular religion is not so very important, because Catholicism in Latin America is more of a general cultural thing than a matter of specific religion, but it can be important that her husband have at least a basic religious faith.

There are a few specific rules that the Catholic Church has laid down than can affect you, but probably not to any great extent, whether you are Catholic or not.

» 1) The Catholic Church does not condone the use of artificial birth control methods (and the only effective ones are artificial). Most modern Latin women have seen the impracticality of this and are willing to use contraceptives without feeling guilty about it.

» 2) The Catholic Church is strongly opposed to abortion and most Latin American women are, too. It is generally not seen as an option. It is also illegal in every Latin American country.

» 3) There is a clear distinction between civil marriage and church marriage. Anyone can have a civil marriage, and it is accepted as legitimate by the church. A church marriage is accepted as legitimate by the state in all of the countries, and does not have to be accompanied by a civil marriage.

» 4) Only Catholics may marry in the Catholic Church. If you are not Catholic, your only option is a civil marriage. This generally isn't of any concern to the Latina.

» 5) A church marriage cannot be terminated with divorce. The marriage is legally permanent unless an annulment can be obtained from the church, followed by a state approved legal divorce.

» 6) The Catholic Church may put pressure on both of you to have your children baptized in the church and reared as Catholics.

» 7) It is unlikely that any pressure will be put upon you to convert to Catholicism by either your wife or the Church.

Discussion of these issues prior to marriage may prevent any later misunderstandings. Our experience is that Latinas are very accepting and tolerant of religious beliefs outside the traditional Catholic church.

Chapter 16

Across the Distance

Correspondence

Writing and receiving letters is a very good way of getting to know another person. People frequently write things that they would be unwilling to say face-to-face, so correspondence can actually be more intimate than talking. Communicating by letter also forces people to consider carefully what they say, which can be a real benefit to a cross-cultural relationship. Even if you meet your lady during a tour or during travel, you are likely to get to know her mostly through correspondence. The following tips can help you:

» 1) When you write, tell a lot about yourself. Describe your daily life, your work, your hobbies, your goals, your thoughts, and your feelings. Tell her about your family and your friends. Ask her about the same sorts of things. Be specific. Ask her about her family, their ages, names, what they like to do, etc. And be detailed when you tell her about your life. People throughout Latin America know Americans mostly through what they have seen on television or in movies. We know how inaccurate that is. Most Latin Americans consider North Americans to have a violent culture. That's because of the movies. She'll appreciate knowledge that you can give her about how Americans live. After all, she's considering living there.

» 2) Unless you write in Spanish, be sure that you keep your language simple. Write in "high English." Do it properly and don't use slang or colloquialisms. Even if she understands English, she probably learned it in school or from books, and will not understand anything but proper English. Don't use big words or complicated sentences. She may very well be sitting there with a dictionary trying to figure it out. Make it as easy for her as possible.

» 3) Start learning Spanish (or Portuguese if she's from Brazil). She will be flattered that you are making the attempt. Put as many words from her language in your letters as possible.

» 4) The chances are that she will have a friend who can read English and translate your letters for her. If you are having trouble with her Spanish and don't have a friend who can help you, you can probably locate a Spanish teacher from the local public school system or college to help you.

» 5) Letters to Latin America take a while to get there. Mexico requires about a week, Central and South America about 10 to 15 days, depending on whether she lives in the capitol city or out in the boondocks. Use only airmail. Surface mail can take months to arrive. Check with the post office regarding current international airmail rates. It goes up from time to time.

» 6) It varies from country to country, but the postal employees in all of them are less dependable than you are accustomed to. Mail is frequently lost, abandoned, or stolen. Theft of mail is not treated as seriously as it is in the U.S., and a postal employee caught stealing mail is likely to get only a slap on the wrist.

» 7) Don't send much money through the mail. It will probably arrive nine out of ten times, but the tenth time someone else will be spending the money. Theft of mail has become more of a problem in recent years because of the large numbers of immigrants moving to the U.S., working, and sending money home to their families. Letters from the U.S. are targets.

» 8) Registered mail is more likely to arrive than regular mail, but there's no guarantee of that either.

» 9) Postal systems vary a great deal. Some countries deliver mail directly to homes or businesses. Others have no home delivery at all. For instance, most mail in Panama goes to general delivery because P.O. boxes are scarce and there is no home delivery. Most mail delivery in Costa Rica is directly to the home, which is complicated, because Costa Rica doesn't have street addresses, and most of the streets don't have names. Somehow the letters usually get there.

» 10) I don't recommend it for the first letter (unless you have already met), but it would be a good idea to send her some International Reply Coupons (available at the post office) to help with her expenses in buying stamps. She will be able to trade the coupons directly for stamps at her post office. As an alternative you could send her some money, but most likely the money would be spent for something else.

» 11) If you don't want to wait for the long turn-around time for letters (a month or more), try using FAX. Almost all cities in Latin America have telephone offices where international phone calls can be made and where FAXs can be sent and received, and you can easily locate a commercial FAX service near you. I used this method of communication regularly with my wife in Costa Rica whenever I was out of the country. It's cheaper than phone calls and a lot faster than mail. If you choose to use FAXs, you'll need to send her some money to help out with the expense.

Sending Money

Sending money is a touchy subject for me. It's true that I'm a bit tight-fisted, but I also have reservations about leading girls to expect more money from me in the future. Getting money through the mail can be habit forming, and when it's my money I don't want the habit to be formed. It's your decision, though, but I strongly suggest that you wait until you have established some sort of relationship before sending money.

Money can be sent through the mail there is a chance that she won't receive it. Be sure that the money is not visible through the envelope. Unless you are sending the money to Panama or Puerto Rico, where U.S. dollars are the national currency, the dollars will have to be converted to local currency. She can do that easily enough, but don't send anything smaller than a $10 bill. Money changers, including banks, don't want to handle anything smaller.

For the most part, checks, even certified checks, are worthless to her. She probably won't be able to cash it, and even if she deposits it to her account, it will be at least a month before she can use the money. The same goes for money orders of any kind, including international money orders. She also cannot use travelers checks, because they have to be countersigned. If you send unsigned traveler's checks it is the same as sending cash.

Aside from sending cash, I see only two viable alternatives, and I only like one of them. If she has a bank account, you can ask your bank to wire the money directly to her account. It takes about three to five days for the process to be completed. The last time I had my U.S. bank wire money to my Panamanian bank it cost $40 for the service charge. That's kind of steep. The method that I prefer is to use Western Union. Western Union has offices in all of the major cities in Latin America, and the money is usually available within minutes. All she needs is her identification card and your name to pick up the money in either dollars or the local currency.

Sending Gifts

In a word... don't. She might be very pleased to receive a gift, but it will usually be more trouble than it is worth, and it may very well cost her more money than you paid for the gift. Any kind of gift showing up in any kind of package that doesn't look like a letter is going to end up in customs. They will open the package and place a value estimate on the contents if it is a taxable item, and most items are. She will then be notified by mail to go to the customs office, pay the duty, and pick up the package. If she doesn't live in the same city where the customs office is located it would be a problem for her. Furthermore, some of the contents may never make it to her. For instance, I went to the Costa Rican customs office to pick up a package, and while waiting, I overhead two lady employees discussing (they assumed that I didn't understand Spanish) which clothing items they would take home from the package they were examining. This is not uncommon.

Phone Calls

It is a delightful experience to hear, for the first time, the voice of someone that you have been corresponding with. It makes her all the more real to you. But please wait until you have corresponded a bit. You need to establish whether or not she can speak English (unless you can speak Spanish), and you need to plan out your conversation in advance, at least to the extent that you will have something definite to talk about. Keep in mind, too, that just because she can write in English doesn't mean that she can also speak it. When you do talk with her, speak very slowly and clearly, enunciate each word, and do not use slang. Even if she has studied English and speaks it, she will probably not be familiar with slang nor with many phrases common to us. It will be book English for her, so keep that in mind.

Be careful to whom you give your phone number. Some girls might pay for the call, but most will call you collect, and you will probably accept the call even if you aren't sure who it is. It can get very expensive very quickly. If she has a telephone (and many do not), try to arrange a date with her, and make the call yourself. Check with your long distance carrier about the best rates for calling to that particular country. Many carriers have promotions, for limited periods of time, that can save you a lot of money, and if you mention that you are considering one of their competitors, they will go to the trouble to locate a discount for you. Also, of course, certain times of the day are cheaper for international calls (it varies from country to country), and weekends are always less expensive.

Another option, if she doesn't have a phone, is to have her call you collect, ask her for the number she is using, and then call her back by direct dialing. You can dial direct to all of the Latin American countries (although in some areas, long distance calls cannot be put through to coin telephones), and it is a lot less expensive than using an operator or accepting collect calls.

Chapter 17

Ins & Outs of Marriage

Getting Married

No two countries have exactly the same laws regarding marriage and divorce, but there are enough similarities that we can discuss it in generalities. For marriage in any of the countries you will be required to have a passport, birth certificate, and if you are either widowed or divorced, a certificate of death or a final divorce decree. All of the papers will have to be taken to a consulate of the country in question, located in the United States if you are a U.S. citizen. The documents will have to be "authenticated" by the consulate and translated by an authorized translator into Spanish (or Portuguese). The translation can be done in the Latin American country if the consulate does not have an arrangement with a translator. I am not familiar with the other countries, but Panama charges $30 for each document authenticated, and likes to have 24 hours to do it in (even though it only takes about 5 minutes). I have always had my lawyer get the translations done in Panama. If you are prepared to get married, have these documents ready when you go, because you will not be able to marry without them.

In her home country she will be required to show evidence that she is not married. This is usually accomplished by her going to the National Civil Registry, which maintains records on births, deaths, marriages and divorces. They will issue her a document showing that she is not currently registered as being married. If both of you are Catholics and want to be married in the Catholic Church, it will be necessary to make arrangements directly with the church and they will take care of the necessary documentation of the marriage. In some countries, civil marriages can be performed only by lawyers, in others either judges or lawyers can be used, and in some, only judges. They take care of all the paperwork and documentation of the marriage. But in all cases, you will have to turn over to them the documents that were authenticated by the consulate in your home country, and she will have to turn over the proof that she isn't married.

It is possible for you to marry her in the United States, but first you have to get her there, and that can be a bit of a problem. Unless she already has residence in the U.S., she will have to enter on either a tourist visa or fiancee visa, either of which can be difficult to obtain. Read the section on Visas to get the details. Normally, the simplest and fastest way of doing it is to marry her in her home country, apply for a resident visa, and bring her into the country in that manner. If she qualifies, and it's a big if, a tourist visa can frequently be obtained in a matter of hours. Resident visas usually require several weeks to process, and a fiancee visa (which must originate from within the United States) can easily take six months.

Chapters 44 and 45 explain in greater detail what is needed for marrying abroad and immigration options for your fiancee.

Divorce

I am not familiar with divorce laws in most of the countries. It may very well be that there are some that require court action in which fault must be demonstrated. I am only familiar with the laws of Costa Rica and Panama, and in both cases, an uncontested divorce is a simple no-fault procedure handled by lawyers, not requiring a court appearance. It is simple, but by no means quick. Both countries have a 2-year waiting period once the divorce petition is filed, and then it takes about 6 months after that to make it final. It is my understanding that divorces can be obtained in the Dominican Republic within a matter of days. It is the Las Vegas of Latin America, and quite a few people go there for divorces. But, even if the divorce is obtained in the Dominican Republic and the marriage was made in Panama, for instance, it still takes two years for it to become final in Panama.

I know of instances in which American men married in a foreign country, but divorced their wives in the United States. That is fine for him, but grossly unfair for her unless he is willing to see his U.S. divorce through the court system of the country in which he married. Unless she has the money to process a divorce through her court system, she essentially remains married to him legally (in her country), while he has the freedom of being a single man. Please don't abandon her in this manner. At least be kind enough to have the divorce decree authenticated at a consulate of her country and send it to her.

Chapter 18

Keeping Her Happy

Culture Shock

When a person leaves his own culture to live in another culture, he inevitably suffers what anthropologists call "culture shock." Your new wife will be suseptible to culture shock if she comes to live in the U.S. with you. Cultural anthropologists are generally required to live in and study another culture for a minimum of two years in order to earn their Ph.D. degree. The term "culture shock" was coined to describe what happens to them as they immerse themselves in another culture and learn to live according to the terms of that other culture.

It doesn't happen to tourists, and usually doesn't happen to people who know that they will be returning home fairly soon. It happens when people have to actually adapt to a new culture and live in it on its own terms. It has happened to me on several occasions, and it was bad, even though I knew that it would come and was anticipating it and knew that in six months or a year I would be over it. It will happen to your Latin American wife, and it will probably be even worse than mine, because she is not going to be expecting it.

What is culture shock? It is felt as a mixture of depression, sadness, homesickness, and anger. Especially anger. It is caused when a person is forced to deal with everyday situations in ways that they are not accustomed to dealing with them. It comes from having to interact with people in new and different ways, and from the behavior of others that is not expected and is different from the behavior of people in their own culture. It is basically a stress response.

Culture shock doesn't set in right away. Usually the first few months in a new culture is exciting. It is new and different, and it is fun to learn the new ways of doing things. The culture shock begins to set in when one believes that he knows most of what needs to be known, then begins to discover that what he believed to be the case isn't true at all. It is sort of like marrying someone that you believe you know, then discovering that you didn't know the person at all. There's anger, sadness, depression, and all those other things that go along with disillusionment, and then you finally settle in and make the best of it.

That is what is going to happen to your new wife when you take her to the United States to live. If you can anticipate it in advance, you can plan for it and help her to get through the process. After the initial excitement comes culture shock, then comes acceptance, and eventually full participation in the new culture. You can help her through it by being patient.

Meeting Other Latins

It *will be* helpful if you can find other Latin Americans of her same social class with whom she can socialize. This can usually be accomplished through enrolling her in an English language class. Most larger towns now have adult education classes in English where most of the students' native language is Spanish.

This is especially true in California, Texas, and Florida and in other areas that have received large numbers of Hispanic immigrants. Having friends that speak her native language can give her a sense of being connected, and at the same time, especially if they have been in the U.S. longer than she has, they can teach her strategies of adapting and educate her about her new home.

It is especially important that she has the opportunity to get out of the house occasionally while you are at work. Boredom will be her worst enemy. Having friends that she can visit or go out with frequently will help a great deal. As soon as you can, see to it that she learns to drive and has transportation. It will not be good for either of you for her to be totally dependent on you as her entire social world.

Visiting Home

The happiest wives get to go home occasionally. Please see to it that she gets to visit her family at least a couple of times a year. Yes, it's expensive, but very important.

Chapter 19

ᒍ*idbits of Wisdom*

Jidbit #1: Living together without marriage
may be possible, if that's what you and she prefer.
It's not uncommon in Latin America. Your problem will be getting her into the U.S. and keeping her
there. Tourist visas are normally only valid for three
months, (although occasionally longer) and fiancee visas
are always only valid for three months.

Tidbit #2: Expect her to become more like American women as she spends more time in the United States.
It's inevitable. Your good fortune is that she will almost
surely retain the Latina character that you value so highly.

Tidbit #3: Latin humor is almost, but not quite, the
same as Anglo humor. Sight gags in movies get a lot of
laughs. Jokes with unexpected endings are funny. Slightly
off-color jokes are popular with both men and women. You
will occasionally see people laughing at people or animals
in trouble or in pain. Don't make fun of other people. The
butt of your humor won't like it.

Tidbit #4: You may have some legitimate complaints about some of the ways things are done in her country. Keep it to yourself. Don't compare her country to yours if hers comes out on the short end. Look for positive things to comment about.

Tidbit #5: In the United States married women are usually clearly identified by a wedding ring worn on the third finger, left hand. There is no such consistent tradition in Latin America. Wedding rings may be worn in that position, but they may as likely be on the right hand and on the middle finger. Many married women don't wear wedding rings at all. Some wear what appears to be a wedding ring, but it may have come from her mother or grandmother, and she may not be married at all. So, don't bother to look for wedding rings. Look at her behavior, or ask her if she's married. There is no other way to know for sure.

Tidbit #6: Don't even consider marrying a prostitute. Some men have the feeling that they will be able to convert the girl into a good wife. It isn't likely. She may not be promiscuous after marriage, but most girls have gotten into that line of work because they enjoy the wilder life style, and have chosen the easier way out, not just because they need the money. You can be sure that she will have become hardened toward men and sex. This may not be apparent at first. All prostitutes, have to become good actresses in order to be successful with a variety of men, and she can fool you as well as those who preceded you.

Part III

Customs in Daily Life

Chapter 20

In the Home

Family Is Sacrosanct

Guests are usually treated royally. Always remember, though, that the Latin family is usually very close, and the family always comes before any outsider. Don't take sides if a dispute arises.

If You Get Invited Home

If you accept an invitation to visit someone's home or to have dinner with the family, it's usually OK to show up anywhere from half an hour to one hour later than the hour planned, although North Americans are known to be more prompt than Latins. It might be best to ask if you should appear *"al punto"* (to the point). It is not the same in all countries however. Check in the section dealing with individual countries for variations. It is considered good manners to say *"con permiso"* (with permission) as you enter the door. Do not just pick a chair and sit down. Most people have their own private space, including "their chair." Wait for the host or hostess to point to a chair. If you have dinner with a family, plan on staying around afterwards for some social time. It is considered bad manners to eat and run. Deny any temptation you may have to help clear the table or wash dishes. This is considered to be women's work, and no matter how well-intentioned you may be, don't do it.

Relationships with Household Help

Many middle-class and most upper-class families have servants. That is something that we North Americans are not accustomed to. Accept it as normal and do not comment on it. It is best not to be especially friendly with servants, but say thank you and please. Be respectful without being chummy. It is not a good idea to make your own requests directly to servants. This could be seen as undermining the authority of the host or hostess. Simply ask your host to request that the servant do whatever it is that you need done.

Meals and Mealtimes

There is a great deal of variation between the countries with regard to what is eaten and when it is eaten. Refer to Part 7 for specifics. There is a great deal of variation in mealtimes, too. In Mexico and most South American countries, the noontime meal is the heaviest, and dinner is lighter and eaten as late as 9 or 10 PM. Central American mealtimes are similar to the United States, with lunch being the lighter meal and dinner being eaten around 6 to 7 PM. Working people usually have 1 1/2 to 2 hours for lunch and normally go home when it is possible.

Table Manners

Table manners are fairly consistent throughout Latin America. Most people eat in the European manner, with knife in the right hand and fork in the left, without changing hands when cutting or eating. But you also frequently see the American custom of changing hands. The knife is also frequently used to push food onto the fork. The napkin is generally left on the table and not placed on the lap as is normally done in the U.S. One important rule is that both hands must remain visible and above table level.

It is not considered to be good manners to put one hand in your lap when it is not in use.

Visiting

It is very common for visitors just to drop in without phoning in advance. This is perhaps related to the fact that not all that many people have phones. I still find it sort of annoying, but that's the way it is. I keep myself fairly busy even when I'm at home, and usually prefer to keep on doing whatever it was that I was doing when the guest dropped in. That's not the Latin way though. To the Latin American, friendship is more important than any activity he might have been involved in.

Use of Space

Homes in cities throughout Latin America tend to be crowded very closely together. They frequently share common walls, the front door opens directly on the sidewalk, the edge of which is on the street. Front yards are not common in the cities except in newer areas. Back yards aren't either, although many houses will have a patio either in the center of the house or within a walled area in the back. Suburban homes tend to utilize space more like North American homes, although the rooms are likely to be smaller.

Because of the way the extended family works, there are likely to be many more people living in less space than the American is accustomed to. Latins in general seem to feel comfortable very close together. They tend to sit closer together (even strangers) and stand closer together while talking. This can make an American feel uncomfortable. Whenever I sit or stand somewhere, I try to do it next to a pretty girl, and that way I can enjoy the experience of a close encounter.

Pets

Latin Americans generally do not view dogs and cats with the same affection as North Americans, although there are certainly exceptions to this. One girl refused to see me any more after I pushed her sleeping dog off the porch. Generally, though, dogs are looked upon more as protection for the house than as pets. As for cats, there simply aren't that many of them around, and I rarely see house cats. Parrots are commonly kept as pets, and frequently allowed to roam around the house. Perhaps that is why they don't want cats around.

Pet food is showing up more and more in supermarkets, so it may be that pets are becoming more popular. In the U.S. we generally try to feed our pets whatever kind of food they like best, and we assume that it has to be meat based, or at least meat flavored. Usually dogs in Latin America eat table scraps only, and there normally isn't a whole lot of meat in their diets. Dogs learn to eat rice, beans, bread, or whatever happens to be available. Just last week I observed a puppy obviously enjoying a mango.

Chapter 21

Communicating

Meeting People

To meet people all you have to do is walk around with a pleasant expression and a smile on your face. By smile, I don't mean a big silly grin. With that, they either don't want to interrupt the joke you are telling yourself or they think you may be nuts. Just have a countenance that shows you are open to friendliness. Latins are remarkably adept at reading expressions of mood, far more so than Americans, and if you are feeling negative that day people will either stay away from you or will want to help you with your problem.

Quite frequently people, especially men, will simply walk right up to you, ask you where you are from, and start a conversation. By the same token, you can walk up to someone and ask him/her how to get to such and such place, and in that manner start a conversation. The person might even walk you there, giving you even a better opportunity to get acquainted. Don't hesitate to ask a person, male or female, to join you in having a Coke or coffee. It is a good way to begin a relationship.

Greetings

People are much more inclined to make eye contact in Latin America. It doesn't really mean anything special. It's just the way they do things. I make a practice of maintaining the eye contact long enough to smile and say hello. There are several ways of doing this: *"hola"* (especially to children and women), *"buenas"* (to any adult), *"buenos dias"* (good morning), *"buenas tardes"* (good afternoon). *"Adios"* (goodbye) is sometimes used in passing between strangers. When said coyly to the opposite sex, stretching out the last syllable, it is a flirtatious communication that you would like to get acquainted with that person. *"Adios,"* incidentally, is not a word that you normally use to say goodbye, even though that is what it means. It is used when you don't expect to see the person again for a very long time, or never again at all. To say goodbye to someone you'll be seeing again soon, say *"hasta luego,"* which means "until later."

When men first meet, or are introduced, it is essential that you offer to shake hands. Not to do so is an insult. Men friends, after they have not seen one another for a day or two, also shake hands as a greeting. They also shake hands upon parting. Especially good friends who have not seen each other for a longer time may embrace and pat the other's back, or shake hands while patting the shoulder. I have read that close men friends sometimes kiss one another on the cheek. Perhaps so, but I have never observed it.

Women may or may not shake hands upon meeting or introduction. It depends both upon the circumstances and local custom, which varies from area to area. In

Colombia, for instance, the women don't shake hands, but grasp one another's forearms. Women who are friends, even if they have only recently met, may kiss one another on the cheek, both when they meet and when they part. There is some variation in this from one country to another, and in some places they will kiss on both cheeks. Actually, they are not both really kissing. One will present her right cheek and kiss into the air, and the other will either kiss the cheek or come close to it. There is a subtle status differential here. The one who is doing the presenting is either the older of the two or is of higher social status. Keeping an eye on this can give you some clues to an aspect of the relationship that even they may not be aware of.

Once a man is accepted as a woman's friend, he is also expected to kiss her cheek. She presents the cheek and he does the kissing. It is wise to wait for the woman to initiate this phase of the friendship, and she will when and if she is ready. A woman may or may not offer to shake hands with a man. It is a regional variation, as well as a personal choice. It is common in Panama, but not in Costa Rica. Your best bet is to be alert, nod, smile, and greet her (*"con mucho gusto,"* or one of the other variations), and if she offers her hand, shake it lightly.

Friendliness and Its Implications

It is quite common in the United States to greet someone with friendliness one day and ignore him the next day. It shouldn't be done that way in Latin America. Your initial friendliness might even have seemed excessive on the first occasion, but once you have set the level of friendliness, it is expected to continue at that level. You can become more friendly, but not less friendly and it will be puzzling and disappointing if your greeting isn't just as enthusiastic.

Physical Distancing

People tend to stand closer in line together, bunch up tighter in a group, and sit closer together than in the U.S.. Most noticeable to Americans is that Latins usually stand closer together while talking. I no longer notice it, and I guess I do it naturally now myself, but occasionally Anglo friends will mention it to me, and it's something I read about from time to time. Just accept it unless bad breath is bothering you. If you back off, you will either offend the person or he won't notice and will just follow you. I don't mind the close packing in lines or squeezing together in groups. I have enough good sense to try to stand in a bunch of ladies. My only concern is that crowding makes it easier for pickpockets.

Eye Contact

Extended eye contact is the norm in Latin America, either between strangers or friends. Staring is common, and they don't see anything wrong with it. That will be especially true since you are a foreigner, dressed differently, and probably physically different, and thus an object of curiosity. Usually I just smile back, which usually gets me a smile, or if it goes on too long and is annoying me, I wink. That gets a response every time, because winking is not common in Latin America.

You will find that women you are talking with will make a great deal more eye contact than you are accustomed to. This may lead you to believe that she is attracted to you, which may be the case, but it is still just the normal way of doing it. People are supposed to maintain eye contact during conversation, and to not do so is considered rude, although looking down is done as a sign of submission.

Conversations

Conversations can get loud and boisterous, with lots of gestures, especially between men. It doesn't mean they are angry, but just enjoying the give and take. Interruption doesn't mean they aren't paying attention, either. Interrupting regularly means that they are involved in the discussion, and to not interrupt occasionally would indicate that attention is wandering.

Gestures

Latin Americans use body expressions a lot more than Americans. However, different gestures can mean different things in the different countries, and some that might be safe in one country might be insulting in another. So you need to take some care until you are sure. Eventually, if you spend enough time in Latin America, certain gestures will become second nature to you.

Here are some of the gestures that I find useful, and they are safe for use in any country:

» I don't know: Shrug with your arms held down and your palms facing forward.

» Come here: Pretty much the opposite of come here in the U.S. Hold the arm out, palm down, move your fingers back toward you and out again. Keep repeating.

» Good-bye: There are some variations on this, but is pretty much like in the U.S.

» More or less: Palm facing downward, fingers spread, tip hand from side to side.

» To say "no": Wag your forefinger from side to side.

» Keep your eyes open (caution): Put tip of the index finger under one eye and pull down.

» To indicate a tightwad: Bend forearm upward, and with cupped palm of the other hand, tap the elbow. Caution: If the fist is closed, and the elbow is hit with force, you've issued a potent insult.

» To indicate money: With palm facing upward and index and middle fingers together, rub the thumb quickly over the tips of the two fingers.

» To indicate excellence: Put the tips of all five fingers together, kiss them, then move the hand straight ahead and spread the fingers. Commonly used to compliment the quality of food or the beauty of a woman.

» To indicate a small amount, or "just a moment": Same gesture as in the U.S., except much more commonly used. Curl the last three fingers toward the palm, extend the index finger and thumb parallel to each other, with about an inch of space between them.

» Caution: The commonly used "OK" sign is not so commonly used in Latin America, and in some countries resembles an obscene gesture. I would suggest avoiding its use.

Gifts

Gift giving in person is always appropriate. When you visit from the United States take a small gift along for her and her children, if she has any. Perhaps several small, relatively inexpensive gifts will be best. It is better that they not be especially personal until you know her well. Printed T-shirts (they like large sizes) are always well received, and so are things that she can decorate her room with, such as prints for the wall. Take along a number of small, inexpensive gifts for children so that you will also be able to give some to her nieces and nephews. Don't spend much money on the initial round of gifts. To do so can not only raise expectations, but can also arouse envy from family members who cannot afford to give nice gifts.

Chapter 22

In Public

Public Displays of Affection

You are going to have to use your best judgment on this matter. Look around and see what others are doing. Holding hands and kissing in public is acceptable in some settings, in some areas, in some countries. In others, it is not. For instance, it is common to see couples holding hands, kissing, and hugging on the street in Costa Rica. One normally conservative lady in Costa Rica that I was interested in thoroughly embarrassed me in a Pizza Hut restaurant one evening by hanging all over me. This was before I got to know the country, and was accustomed to Mexico, so I asked her to please cool it. She was so offended that she wouldn't kiss me for days afterwards. However, what she was doing was perfectly normal in that setting in that city.

No matter what the country, people in rural areas and small towns are much more conservative in public than in the city, and its best not to do more than hold hands in public.

When it comes to public displays of affection, Panama is much more conservative than Costa Rica. You rarely see kissing in public, and not that often do you see lovers holding hands. Colombia is more conservative than Costa Rica, but less so than Panama. All of the countries are different. So just look around you. You can also follow the lead of your girlfriend. If you want to walk through the park holding hands, give it a try, and if she doesn't think it is appropriate, she will let you know.

Dress Codes

Latin American women tend to be much more concerned with appearance than their counterparts in the United States. A higher percentage of their budget is spent on clothing, and they put a lot of effort into seeing that their hair and make-up looks good. Men seemed to be less concerned about it. Usually it is only among the businessmen and professionals that they especially try to dress well.

The most common clothing for men in the street are jeans with a T-shirt and athletic shoes. Women are likely to be attractively and sexily dressed, perhaps also in jeans, but frequently with high-heeled shoes, and often wearing tight, short skirts. But, sexy clothing in Latin America doesn't necessarily mean available for sex. It is a matter of looking interesting for the males and showing off her best attributes. It is also a matter of style, and it has been this way for many years. It is characteristic for both men and women that clothing is clean and well-pressed, even if it is just jeans and T-shirt.

Unless it is for your own wedding, it is unlikely that you will need to take a suit with you. Coats and ties are usually worn only for special occasions or for business. Dress nicely, though. Shirt and slacks are needed for when jeans aren't appropriate, and leather dress shoes will be more appropriate than athletic shoes for some occasions. Since you will probably be doing a lot more walking than you normally do, bring comfortable footwear. If you wear anything larger than a size 10, you will have a hard time finding it in Latin America.

A jacket will be needed at higher elevations (anything over about 3500 feet). Shorts are never appropriate in most areas, especially in cities, but are fully acceptable in coastal resort areas. Shorts are not acceptable where I live in David, Panama, but I wear them anyway because it is so very hot. People have gotten used to my wearing shorts and it doesn't bother them. If you want to break tradition, go ahead, but it will most definitely mark you as a foreigner. No matter where you are, though, do not wear shorts into offices. I have seen signs in front of government offices absolutely prohibiting smoking, drinking, and shorts...in that order.

Noise

Latin Americans don't seem to mind noise. The crowded cities are as noisy as you are likely to find anywhere on earth, with buses, trucks and cars sporting mufflers designed to enhance the sound. Music is usually played loudly in homes, and the dance halls can be deafening. Expect it, and don't get a hotel room near where people will be dancing on weekends. It's not all that common, but occasionally young men will walk around with their ghetto blasters at full volume, certain that they are doing everyone a favor by providing the music. Loud music and the sound of traffic drives me nuts, and I usually have to look long and hard to find housing where it is fairly quiet. The trade-off often has me waking up to roosters crowing in the morning.

Chapter 23

Dining Out

Kinds of Restaurants

In all of the Latin American cities you can find first-class restaurants rivaling what you can find in the United States. You can also locate restaurants in great numbers that wouldn't be allowed to operate in the U.S. In most cities you can also locate fast-food restaurants that originated in the U.S., such as Kentucky Fried Chicken, McDonald's, Burger King, Pizza Hut, etc., and their food is almost the same as you are accustomed to.

Most of the locals eat their restaurant meals in small simple restaurants serving local foods. They are usually inexpensive and offer ample servings. Most offer a set-price complete meal called *"comida del día"* (meal of the day), *"comida corriente"* (common meal), or *"almuerzo ejecutivo"* (executive lunch). Several other names are used in the various countries. Simply look for a chalkboard or hand-lettered sign on the wall. They usually consist of meat, chicken, or fish and rice, beans, perhaps a green vegetable, and *platano* (large cousin of the banana). It's a good way to get a filling, fairly well-balanced meal at a reasonable price.

Restaurants serving international foods and ethnic foods can be found in all cities. You can find Texas-style barbecue, Peruvian seafood, French haute cuisine, Chinese, Korean, and Japanese food, Middle-Eastern food. Name it and you can probably find it. Except for the ubiquitous Chinese restaurant, these are mostly up-scale restaurants with at least a touch of elegance, and are considerably more pricey than restaurants offering local menus.

Reservations are rarely required. Jeans and athletic shoes are rarely appropriate, coats and ties rarely required. Most restaurants do not have a maitre d' and you are expected to select your own table and sit down. I suggest looking around first to see if someone is available to seat you, and if not, select what you want.

Waiters and Waitresses

Generally, as in the United States, the more up-scale restaurants will have waiters (*meseros* or *saloneros*); the more ordinary restaurants will have waitresses (*meseras* or *saloneras*), because they will work for less money. Ordinarily the better the restaurant, the better the service. Waitresses in the more ordinary restaurants often seem to have no training at all and provide service that would be more appropriate to feeding her family at home.

Quality of service also seems to be directly related to whether the government requires a service charge to be added to the bill. In Costa Rica, for instance, it is required that the restaurant add 10% to all checks, which is to serve as the tip. Since tips are automatic, there simply isn't much motivation to provide fast, pleasant service. As a consequence, except in the better restaurants, service is frequently slow, surly, and inattentive. In Colombia no service charge is normally added, with the result that the service people have to stay alert if they are to earn good tips.

You have become accustomed in the United States to the waiter or waitress occasionally checking by the table to see if there is anything you need. If they can't check by frequently, they will usually at least glance at the table from time-to-time to catch a signal from you. In Latin America, except at the better restaurants, you are usually pretty much on your own once you have received your meal (I have always been impressed with service in Mexico, however), and sometimes it is hard to get the waitress' attention. Usually the way to do it is to call out *"señorita"* or *"señor"* loudly enough to be heard. You may or may not get a response. I occasionally simply get up and walk over to them and tell them that I need some attention. Costa Rica has a practice that I consider to be eminently practical, but that is considered to be bad manners in the rest of Latin America. They hiss loudly, and because it is a different kind of sound than a voice, it is easily heard, and never fails to get attention.

A frustrating (to me) practice in Latin America is that whatever dish is available first is what is served, and it doesn't always conform to what ought to be logically served first. And frequently there doesn't seem to be much of an attempt to get everyone's food on the table at approximately the same time. It is generally expected that a person will begin eating as soon as his food is placed in front of him, without waiting for the other people. This makes some sense, because they may be served at various times, and if you wait, your food may be cold. The better restaurants do make an attempt to serve people all at the same time and with the appropriate dish, and their service will be as good as you are accustomed to.

Ordering

Whether on a date with your girlfriend, or in a large group of people, it is customary that each person order individually. It is best that the person who is going to pay speak up with enough authority to get the waiter to his side first, because it is expected that he be the first to order. Unlike in the U.S., where a gentleman often allows his date to order first, you order, and then she orders. It is not customary for the man to order for her. All orders from the same table will be put on the same check unless you specifically request differently.

Most restaurants have menus (*"menú"* in Spanish), but in Mexico the menu is often called *"la lista"* (the list). As a young man just beginning work in Mexico, I once sat down in a little roadside restaurant on my way to some obscure town out in the desert, and asked the waitress to bring me *"el menú."* She took a very long time getting back to me, and instead of bringing me a piece of paper, she walked to the table with a steaming bowl of soup. What I had accidentally ordered was *"menudo,"* a soup made of beef stomach. That was the day I learned to call it *"la lista."*

It's always a good idea to ask if there is something especially good that day. Frequently a restaurant will be able to make a special purchase of something that isn't on the menu and it's likely to be fresh, and frequently different. In that manner I have been able to eat fresh-water shrimp delicately broiled with garlic and butter, and on another occasion, steamed crabs in an area where crab normally wasn't available.

Paying the Bill

he most important piece of advice here is that separate checks are rarely requested in Latin America, and if you can reasonably avoid it, don't. If you need to split up the check it's best to do it after you leave the restaurant. No matter how large the group, one person is expected to be treating the others and it is a matter of his pride that he pays for everything, including the tip.

Since it's going to be fairly obvious that you are a foreigner, it's quite all right to pull out a pocket calculator and make a conversion of local currency into dollars for your better understanding. While you are at it, it might not be a bad idea to examine the check to see if the addition is correct and that the prices correspond to what you saw on the menu. Waiters can make mistakes, and some pad the bill.

A common error that Americans make is in request-ing *"el cheque."* A *cheque* is something that people write against bank accounts. The proper word is *"la cuenta,"* which means "the count" or "the account." Simply say *"la cuenta, por favor."*

Tipping

he proper tip in Latin America in restaurants is approximately 10% of the cost of the meal, including beverages. This is normally left on the table for the waiter or added to the credit card. Don't leave tips on tables that are outside on the street, in high traffic areas in the restaurant, or when beggars are nearby. The chances are that the waiter will not get the tip.

Take a look at the check and see whether a service charge has been added. If it has, you are under no obligation to leave a tip, since this is the tip. In Costa Rica, at least, a service charge is obligatory in all restaurants (required by law). Only when the service is especially good (which isn't very often) do I leave a tip in addition to that.

In the United States you have probably become accustomed to leaving bills rather than coins on the supposition that the waiter will be offended if you leave anything smaller than a dollar. Waiters and waitresses don't look at it that way in Latin America. Leaving 10% in coins for just a cup of coffee is just fine.

Children

Don't be surprised to see children of all ages along with their parents in the finest of restaurants. Children usually go along with parents when they go out in the evening. Usually they are well-behaved, but they are rarely disciplined even if they start running around the restaurant and pestering other patrons.

Frequently children of the restaurant owner will also be in the restaurant. Lots of times when I see this I think of W.C. Field's response when he was asked how he liked children (he said "boiled," if I remember correctly).

Chapter 24

Pace of Life

Mañana

The word "mañana" means tomorrow. Except that the word doesn't necessarily mean tomorrow. It may mean "eventually," and it frequently does. Getting things done, especially with government offices, frequently seems to take forever. To us, the people simply don't seem to ever get in much of a hurry to accomplish things. However, this is also a frequent complaint about many European and Asian countries, as well. It may be that we, ourselves, are in too big of a hurry.

To wait for things that seem unnecessary is frustrating to anyone who has a specific goal to accomplish. It annoys me too, but not nearly as much as it did before I found a few ways to adjust to the system. First, I plan as far ahead as possible, calculating what items can be accomplished simultaneously. If it involves getting three government permits, for instance, I will hire three different lawyers, one to work on each permit. I already know that the lawyers are going to drag their feet and I know that the bureaucracy is going to be slow. Three working at once will be faster than one working three times.

Second, I try to get to know, well in advance, people that will be valuable to me in the future. This is normal practice in Latin America, where one cultivates a number of well-placed *patrones* to help get things done. These may be community leaders, bankers, policemen, or government bureaucrats, and they are usually flattered that you need and are asking for their help. They can make things move faster when you need it.

Third, I use bribes when it will help. Bribes, incidentally, are viewed more as tips in Latin America when they are used to get something done more quickly (they are not viewed in this casual manner when it is a matter of getting out of a jam). It can put your documents at the top of the pile instead of at the bottom, where they would be if you didn't offer the tip. This may seem unfair to you, but it's the only way I can compete with the other people offering bribes. Unless you know, or can meet, the person that can help arrange the *mordida* ("bite" or bribe), you will probably need to use a go-between, such as a lawyer who knows that person.

Fourth, when my presence is required (and some waiting is almost always involved), I always take along a good paperback book or some writing materials. As long as I can find a place to sit down, I can make the time productive. Count on it, though. You will spend a lot of time waiting for things to get done in Latin America. When everything fails, as it sometimes does, I buy a good bottle of imported Cuban rum, go home, and try again the next day.

Punctuality

In Costa Rica the people refer to themselves as *"Ticos."* If you ask a Costa Rican to meet you at 6 PM, they will frequently ask: "Tico time or Gringo time?"

If it's Gringo time it should be as close as possible to 6 PM. Tico time could be anywhere from 6:30 to 7:30 PM. That's typical throughout Latin America. You've got three options. If it is a girlfriend that you feel needs to get accustomed to gringo time, you can just leave at 6:15, and tell her the next time that you never wait more than 15 minutes. Eventually she'll get the message. The second option is to adopt the local time and show up late yourself. The third option is to show up on time and take along something to amuse yourself while you're waiting.

Actually, when you are invited to someone's house for dinner or for a party, you are showing better manners when you show up about 30 minutes late, and usually an hour isn't pushing things. An appointment with a doctor, lawyer, businessman, or government official should be met punctually. You may have to wait a while, or you may not, but if you are not there when scheduled, he may very well leave and do something else. In fact, he may leave anyway.

Waiting in Line

How frustrating it can be! Not so much for the wait, but what happens while you are waiting. People, sometimes groups of people,

167

will spot a friend somewhere near the front of the line, go straight to the friend and move right into the line with him. That puts you back however many places there were that were butted into.

Friends come before customers, too. You can be next in line in the bank, waiting for the teller, when up walks a friend of the teller, who is then taken in front of you. So many times I have waited in a lawyer's office, ready for my appointment, and next in line, when in walks a friend who proceeds to take an hour of his time. So common and so frustrating.

Frequently, lines don't form at all where lines would be more efficient. You may have to use your elbows like everyone else to get on the bus or into the movie theater. Don't hesitate to push or shove when it seems the only way to get things done. You may be the only one left standing outside if you don't. In some countries things are handled a little more orderly than others. Costa Ricans are great for lining up, whether in banks or at bus stops. They will wait patiently for their turn (unless there is a friend further up the line). Panama is a little less orderly, especially at bus stops, but one inviolable rule is that women go first and the old go before the young. Supermarkets and banks will sometimes have check-out counters and cashiers strictly for retirees so that the elderly don't have to stand too long. Mexico is one of those countries where anything goes. Lines don't form. People just bunch up around the focal point and get in as best as they can.

The Virtue of Patience

Patience is a virtue in Latin America.

Chapter 25

Public Services

The information in this chapter is general. For more specific information on individual countries please see Part 7.

Mail Systems

At the moment most mail systems in Latin America are nationally owned and operated as monopolies (usually inefficient), although several of the countries have been discussing privatization of theirs, and several others have already done so. There are a few international couriers operating in certain countries in Latin America which offer their subscribers post office boxes in Miami with rapid air delivery of mail to their Latin American offices.

None of the Latin American mail systems are as efficient and reliable as the U.S. Postal Service, although most are a little less expensive. Some countries are better than others in this respect, but mail is frequently lost, stolen or misplaced (perhaps one out of ten letters mailed from the United States will not make it to its destination). The main factor affecting this is the fact that so many of their citizens are working in foreign countries (especially in the

U.S.) and sending money to their families in Latin America. Dishonest postal employees look for mail likely to have cash or checks (which can be easily cashed) enclosed and steal those envelopes for opening later. Punishment is so minimal for this offense that the risk is justified. For this reason, your mail to any Latin American country should not appear to contain money or checks.

Mail can be received at just about any post office through general delivery if addressed to you, *Correo General, Entrega General,* or *Lista de Correos,* City, Province, Country. You will need positive identification, such as a passport (or copy), to retrieve your mail.

All countries offer post office boxes (but in some areas they are so scarce as to require years of waiting) and general delivery. Some countries, but not many, have home delivery. More citizens probably use general delivery than any other method of receiving mail. Because of mail theft, delivery problems, and the fact that only a minority of people use bank checking accounts, bills are almost always paid in person, and usually with cash. Mail systems are also rarely used for advertising. Most countries do not have mail deposit boxes on street corners, and in those countries where there are a few, mail is not picked up regularly. The only reasonable option is to mail letters in the post office.

As a point of passing interest, few Latins ever lick postage stamps. In fact, in Costa Rica it is illegal. All post offices have moistening devices available.

Telephone Systems

Some telephone systems are modern and efficient, some are antiquated, poorly maintained, and don't always work. All countries have coin or token operated telephones, and frequently these are the only telephones that people have access to. Home telephones are scarce in many countries, and waiting periods of up to several years are common in order to get a phone. In some areas there is a black market for phone lines, in which numbers are offered for sale at high prices. Argentina, which recently privatized its telephone system, used to have waiting lists 20 years long. Now it is possible to get a line within a week. Several other countries are also privatizing their telephone systems, and improvements can be expected as a result of international capitalization.

All countries have, in major cities, government international telephone offices where phone calls to anywhere in the world can be made and paid for at the office. Ordinarily they also incorporate FAX services, and FAXs can be both sent and received. They may offer telegraph and telex services as well.

Transportation

The vast majority of people in Latin America do not own cars. For this reason almost any place can be reached by bus, and cheaply. The biggest problem is in finding the right bus to take you to where you want to go. I have found that taxi drivers can usually take you to the right bus stop (*parada de buses* or *terminal de buses*).

Intracity buses are usually retired school buses from the United States, often gaily painted and with fanciful names. In some countries you pay when you get on, in others you pay when you get off. Be very careful in crowded buses when you must stand. They are favorite haunts for pickpockets. In most of the countries, except in rural areas, there are designated bus stops at which you must wait for the bus. To get the driver to stop, when you want to get off either yell *"¡parada!"* or whistle. I personally prefer whistling, but I haven't been able to do it any more since the day that I got hit in the mouth by an irate Nicaraguan.

Intercity buses are usually much nicer and with more comfortable seats. Some are retired Greyhounds, others are made in Brazil by Mercedes Benz. Mexico and Costa Rica also produce buses. Generally you buy your ticket in advance and have a reserved seat for through buses. In the case of buses that stop in all the smaller towns you pay the driver directly. If you can, take your luggage inside with you. I've never lost anything by having it put in the luggage compartment, but I know people who have.

Taxis are inexpensive in Latin America despite the generally high cost of gasoline. They are an effective means of getting from one point to another. In some areas meters are used and in others the drivers simply operate on the basis of zones. If your taxi has a meter, check to see that it is starting out with no previous charges on it. It is best to ask in advance how much it will cost you to get to where you are going. I've never had any problems in most cities, but those of San José, Costa Rica are notorious cheats. It is also not a good idea to leave luggage in the taxi while you are doing something else. Sometimes they just drive off with everything and leave you behind.

Taxis can usually be rented for the day. Unless you just want the freedom of driving a rental car it is normally much more of a bargain to hire a taxi. Taxi drivers know what areas will probably be of interest to you, and it will be a lot safer than if you drive. There is absolutely no country in Latin America where people drive safely, and until you get experienced in demolition derby driving you are taking your life in your hands.

Restrooms

Planning in advance where to locate a restroom can be an important matter, especially since diarrhea can be a traveler's companion and often strikes at the most inconvenient moment. I have found that the best sources of emergency restrooms in a city are chain fast-food restaurants, such as McDonald's. They are usually fairly clean and don't object to your using the restroom since they have no way of knowing whether you will be making an order afterwards. Other possibilities are hotels and regular restaurants. You may need to explain that you have an emergency.

Toilet paper is not usually provided in restrooms in Latin America, and it is a good idea to take along your own. The little packets of Kleenex serve quite well and are easy to transport.

You will frequently see wastebaskets placed alongside toilets. This is for the disposal of toilet paper. Many of the sewer systems in Latin America don't work particularly well with toilet paper being flushed down the toilet, and if you see a wastebasket placed for that purpose, please use it. You may save some poor fellow the work of having to use a plunger.

Chapter 26

Authority

Military

All of the Latin American countries except Costa Rica and Panama have military organizations, and most also perform police functions. As you are traveling through Latin America, you will be occasionally stopped at roadblocks or checkpoints. This is usually of no significance to the tourist, and is generally nothing to be concerned about. Simply be courteous, show your identification and whatever else they ask for. Unless they suspect you of smuggling arms or drugs, or unless they want to collect a bribe (not particularly common), you will be waved on your way. Otherwise you may undergo an inspection. If this happens, be polite and respectful and do whatever they ask you to do. Do not, under any circumstances, offer a bribe. If that is what they are after, it will be requested. Then you may negotiate it.

Police

Most of the countries have, just as we do in the U.S., distinctions between traffic cops, criminal police, investigators, city police, national police, rural police, and so forth. It varies from country to country.

Every country in Latin America has more police corruption than is found in the United States. It is mainly because bribery is more tolerated, and accepting a bribe doesn't constitute the crime that it does in the United States. Some countries have less of this than others, and it seems to be directly related to whether the police are paid livable salaries or not. In Panama, for instance, corruption exists, and bribes occasionally get paid, but it is not common. Policemen are usually polite and considerate. You get your ticket and go on your way. In Mexico, on the other hand, corruption at all levels is a way of life, and bribery is accepted as part of the policeman's normal income. For that reason, the tourist is frequently accused of crimes or violations that have never occurred. The object is to extort a bribe.

Do not ever offer a bribe. Again, you will be asked for it if that is the intention. This will usually come in the form of a suggestion that you can pay your fine on the spot and not have to go to court, thus saving you time and inconvenience. The court, of course, never gets the money. You are then put in the position of asking how much the fine is. My suggestion is to offer one-fourth or less than what he wants, explaining that you simply don't have much money. Negotiating will follow, and hopefully you will settle on something you can live with. If it gets out of hand, simply ask him to take you to the police station to talk with whoever is in command, or tell him that you would rather go to court. That will usually reduce the demand or eliminate it altogether.

Admittedly, it is infuriating to have a sleazy policeman demanding money from you in a country where you have neither the time nor inclination to receive justice. Basically, he has you by the you-know-what, and you have no other choice than to cooperate. My suggestion is to maintain your composure, don't smile or be friendly, and negotiate. Losing your temper will usually just cause you problems. Don't be afraid, though, and if you are, try not to show it. The reality is that he can only push the issue so far, and he knows how far it is.

Several years ago, while I was driving a loaded pickup truck through Mexico, on my way to Central America, I was stopped for extortion three times within forty miles. The first policeman, in town, caught my glance and waved me over. He opened the pickup door and got in (an illegal act in itself). He proceeded to insist that I unload everything in the truck so that he could inspect for arms. I told him that it was an impossibility and to please show me the way to the police station. We went a few blocks and he motioned me over again, to inform me that we could avoid my inconvenience by paying him $200. I started up the truck and began driving again. Again he stopped me, and we finally settled for $20. He pointed out, quite accurately, that he could arrange an overnight stay in jail for me, and that by morning there likely would not be anything left in the truck. Boy, was I pissed.

Half-an-hour later I was stopped by two cops at a document inspection roadblock. They pointed out pretty much the same thing, and I settled for $5 apiece. In another half-hour I came to a construction detour, and the traffic cop directing traffic pulled me over and asked me why I didn't have commercial numbers painted on the door. I told him that with a foreign vehicle I didn't need them, and that if he didn't get out of the way I was going to run him down (I was super pissed by this time). He suggested that it wouldn't be a very good idea, and would I at least give him enough money for a cup of coffee. I did.

The Napoleonic Code

The most fundamental principle underlying the American system of criminal justice is that a suspect is considered innocent until proven guilty, and if demanded, he has the right to be tried by a jury made up of citizens. You will not be offered this opportunity in any country in Latin America. Under the Napoleonic Code (established by the Emperor Napoleon in France), it is up to the defendant to prove his innocence rather than the other way around. Trials are often conducted by tribunals, and innocence or guilt is determined by judges. This can be problematical. I will have to say, though, that in Costa Rica, the only country in which I have closely observed the process at work, it does seem to result in justice being done, and usually fairly quickly.

Lawyers

Don't leave home without one. At least if you live in Latin America. Although lawyers serve pretty much the same functions as they do in the U.S., they also do quite a bit more. They are essential for the filing of the most apparently insignificant documents, which in the U.S. would be left to paralegal or handled by the individual involved. They are also essential for the most minor legal infractions. I always take a lawyer with me to traffic court, for instance, because I am fully convinced that he can argue my case better than I can. Do not, under any circumstances, try to argue your own case with a criminal charge.

Your legal rights are not the same as they are in the United States, and you can wind up in a mess of problems if you don't have a lawyer to help you. Fortunately, since there are so many lawyers around, their fees are usually considerably lower than in the United States.

Chapter 27

Fiestas, Ferias and Feriados

Fiestas

The word "fiesta" means party. It can refer to the small get-togethers that we refer to as parties in the U.S., but generally is applied more to festive events and celebrations.

Most children have *fiestas de cumpleaños* (birthday parties), which are frequently elaborate, to which both children and adults are invited. Almost invariably there is a *piñata*, originally a clay pot filled with small gifts and candy, hung above the floor, which the blindfolded children try to break with a stick. Nowadays they are usually made of papier maché or cardboard and decorated with crepe paper. There are probably fewer injuries than with clay pots. Now all they have to worry about is the blindfolded kid whacking another one with the stick.

There are also *fiestas de quinceaños* (fifteenth birthday party), in which a girl's coming of age (at 15) is celebrated. These are frequently large, elaborate, and expensive affairs. Fiestas are also held to celebrate wedding anniversaries and weddings themselves. Mariachi bands or trios (even in countries other than Mexico) are frequently hired to serenade the wife.

Many holidays are referred to as *"fiestas"* because of the merry-making and celebrations accompanying them.

Ferias

The word feria literally means "fair." There are all kinds of *ferias*. In Costa Rica, for instance, most communities will close one of the streets for one day every week so that farmers can set up tables and sell their produce directly to the consumers. These happenings are called *ferias*. David, Panama has an annual *"Feria Internacional de San José"* lasting for five days or so, in which artisans from all over the country (and from other countries, as well), come and set up booths to sell their wares. Boquete, Panama, a lovely small town in the mountains, has an annual *"Feria de Café y Flores"* (Festival of Coffee and Flowers) that lasts a couple of weeks, in which artisans sell their products, food vendors sell food, and carnival rides excite the children. Traveling circuses and carnivals are also popular and are also called *"ferias."*

Feriadas

Feriadas are holidays. Every country has its own particular set of holidays, and usually they are numerous. Refer to Part 7 to find out about the individual holidays for each country. You should be aware of holidays before you visit, because it will affect what you will be able to do while you are there.

Certain religious holidays are common to all Latin American countries because they are associated with religious events within the Catholic Church. These are:

» *Epifanía* or *Día de los Reyes Magos*—January 6, Epiphany, or Day of the Wise Men
» *Miércoles de Ceniza*—Ash Wednesday
» *Domingo de Ramos*—Palm Sunday
» *Jueves Santo*—Holy Thursday
» *Viernes Santo*—Good Friday
» *Día de Pascua*—Easter Sunday
» *Día de los Muertos*—Day of the Dead, November 2
» *Nochebuena*—Christmas Eve, December 24
» *Día de Navidad*—Christmas Day, December 25

In addition, each country, region, city, and town usually has its own patron saint, with a holiday set aside in the saint's honor.

Christmas Eve and Christmas Day are celebrated throughout Latin America. A special dinner is usually eaten on Christmas Eve, with gifts being given, as part of a large family gathering, after dinner. Santa Claus is not part of the picture, but decorated Christmas trees are common, as are nativity scenes. Frequently people attend a midnight mass after the celebration at home. Christmas Day is usually occupied with large family gatherings.

The most significant religious holidays of all occur during Easter Week. Ordinarily, almost all businesses are shut down from Thursday afternoon until Monday morning, although some will be open for part of Saturday. Most buses don't even run during those days, and taxis are scarce. Unless you have friends that you can spend part of the weekend with, you are likely to be lonely, because the streets are deserted. It depends on the country to some extent, but Easter is usually somber and for family. The fun-loving Costa Ricans flock to the beaches, however, and if you think that you may be in the mood for going to the beach, you'd do well to make your reservations well in advance.

New Year's Eve is celebrated much as it is in the United States, and New Year's Day is frequently reserved for nursing hangovers. The traditional hangover cure, incidentally, is *sopa de mariscos*, seafood soup.

Almost everywhere in Latin America, *Carnaval*, the equivalent of our Mardi Gras in New Orleans, is celebrated. It specifically refers to the three days preceding Ash Wednesday, but the dates actually vary widely throughout Latin America. At best, you can say that *Carnaval* will occur sometime in March or April. Rio de Janeiro has the most famous *Carnaval* in the world. It is a time when caution and restraint are thrown to the wind, and when some of the wildest parties known to mankind are thrown. Panama also has a widely-known *Carnaval*, but it is somewhat more subdued than that of Rio de Janeiro.

Chapter 28

Forms of Address

Names

Hispanic full names (*nombre completo*) consists of the given name (*nombre de pila*, usually just referred to as *nombre*), second name (*segundo nombre*), followed by two surnames (*apellidos*), those of both the father and the mother. The father's surname (*apellido paterno*) comes after the given names and is followed by the mother's surname (*apellido materno*). Thus a person might be formally named María Felicia Romero Gonzalez. Romero is the father's surname and Gonzalez is the mother's surname. This would normally be written as María Felicia Romero G., using the initial of her mother's surname.

There are several reasons for using two surnames, not the least of which is that a woman does not assume her husband's surname upon marriage. His name is considered the more important of the two when naming offspring, thus his surname comes first, but it is traditional, that the mother's surname be part of the full legal name.

In daily use people will frequently use only there first surname, but there are many instances, including legal, where both must be used to avoid the stigma of illegitimate

185

birth, although in the case of actual illegitimacy, it could be embarrassing. Had María Felicia Romero Gonzalez been born illegitimate she would have the legal name, María Felicia Gonzalez Gonzalez, having had only her mother to give her surnames. Under those circumstances she would probably use her full legal name only on legal documents.

It is also especially helpful to have a second surname in a list of names such as in a telephone directory. Due to the frequent use of the same given name in a family it can get confusing. For instance, a grandfather, father, and son frequently have the same first name and same second name; the only distinguishing feature would be the second last name, which is the first family name of each of their mothers.

Because of the nature of extended families in Latin America, it is fairly important to be able to keep track of who is related to whom, and in what manner. The use of the mother's surname helps a great deal in this. Both parents of my Costa Rican wife came from the same rural area and both were born in the same village. Because I knew my wife's second apellido I was able to quickly spot relatives on her mother's side that I would never have recognized otherwise.

Last Names of Married Women

If María Romero Gonzalez marries Gerardo Paredes Rios, her name does not become Mrs. María Paredes. Her legal name will continue to be María Romero Gonzalez. However, she may be referred to as María Romero de Paredes (which means that

María Romero is the wife of Paredes). She may also simply drop the common usage of Romero and call herself María de Paredes (except on legal documents).

Note that a woman never uses her husband's first name as part of her name. She is never, for instance, Mrs. Gerardo Paredes. A man introducing his wife never uses his own last name as part of hers. Mr. Paredes would introduce his wife to you as María Romero.

Nicknames

The most common kind of nickname is the *"apodo."* It is a descriptive nickname, usually describing a physical condition or circumstance of the person's life. One of my favorite bus drivers on the Costa Rica-Panama run is called *"Chino."* I'm not sure that anyone knows his real name. *Chino* means Chinese. *Chino* is not Chinese, however, but his eyes do have a slight slant to them, and his skin has a faintly yellowish cast to it. There may have been some Chinese ancestry somewhere, but he looks just vaguely enough Chinese to be called *"Chino."* A very slender girl might be called *"Flaca"* (skinny). One of the darker skinned children in the family might be called *"Negro"* (black), even though there is no African ancestry whatsoever. A person who is overweight, or who once was, may be called *"Gordo"* (fat). Someone originally from Nicaragua, but now living in Colombia might be called *"Nica"* (Nicaraguan). A person who acts somewhat wild might be called *"Loco"* (crazy). These terms are used in face-to-face address as well as to refer to that person. They are not meant in a negative way nor are they experienced negatively. If anything, they are sort of like terms of endearment. I would suggest, though, that you know someone fairly well before you call him *"Gordo"* or *"Loco."* Especially if you haven't heard anyone else call him that.

Another kind of nickname is the *"nombre hipocoristico."* It is an alteration of, or a substitute for a given name. It can be a shortening (Feli for Felicia; Lupe for Guadalupe; Mari for María); a diminutive (Felicita for Felicia; Lupita for Guadalupe); or a standard alteration of a name (Manolo for Manuel; Lola for Dolores; Pépe for José).

Common Titles of Address

Señor (for a man), *señora* (for a married woman), and *señorita* (for a single woman) are titles of courtesy. Divorced women may use either *señora* or *señorita*, widowed women usually prefer *señora*. If you don't know what the marital status is, it is best to address younger women as *señorita* and middle-aged or older as *señora*. The titles may be used alone, in combination with the person's given name or surname, or in combination with the person's profession. They are abbreviated as *Sr.*, *Sra.*, and *Srta.*

Until you think you would feel comfortable calling someone by his/her first name, it is best to call him *"Sr. Gonzalez"*, *"Sra. Morales"*, *"Srta. Garcia"*, or whatever.

The titles, when used with a first name, are usually to show respect for age or social position while at the same time a degree of friendship is being expressed. Younger people, for instance, frequently call me "Sr. Jim". I might prefer to just be called Jim, but I'm stuck in the Latin American system of respect for old folks.

The three titles can also be used with the name of his/her profession (but not followed by that person's name). Examples are:

"*Sra. abogada*" (female lawyer, married), "*Sr. profesor*" (male professor), "*Srta. maestra*" (female teacher, single), "*Sra. doctora*" (female doctor, married), "*Sr. ingeniero*" (male engineer).

Titles of Respect

he words "*don*" (used in addressing a man) and "*doña*" (used in addressing a woman) are titles of respect. They are not directly translatable into modern English, but are similar to the old English usage of "master" and "mistress". In the past the terms were used to address the masters and mistresses of large estates and were used for members of the nobility. At present, the terms are commonly used as titles of high respect, and are usually reserved for older, highly respected members of the community.

I always get a kick when someone refers to me as "Don Jim". It's a term of address I don't deserve, but always enjoy receiving. *Don* and *Doña* normally are used with the first name only, but it is not incorrect to use them with the surname, and the surname is frequently added to the first name when addressing a letter, or when referring the person to someone else.

Professional Titles

Using professional titles as terms of address is fairly important in Latin America, and it's to your advantage to use them when appropriate. Such titles are *"Licenciado"* (actually means anyone who has a bachelor's degree, but is normally used to address a lawyer), *"Doctor"* (anyone with a doctor's degree—M.D., Ph.D., D.D.S., etc., and some lawyers also use it), *"Maestro"* (teacher), *"Profesor"* (professor), *"Arquitecto"* (architect), *"Ingeniero"*, etc. Simply replace the "o" with an "a" (or add an "a" if there isn't an "o") when addressing a female.

Chapter 29

Correspondence & Telephone Manners

Letters

Salutations in letters are usually more formal than Americans are accustomed to. Ordinarily, when you receive a first letter from a lady in Latin America it will begin with *"Estimado Jim:"*, *"Estimado Sr. Jim:"*, or *"Estimado Sr. McLeod:"*. *Estimado* means "esteemed." Notice that the salutation is followed by a colon. Commas are not used for this purpose in Latin America. Later, as you become better acquainted, she will probably switch to using *"Querido Jim:"*. *Querido* means "dear," and is used only between members of the opposite sex or between very close friends. Remember to substitute an "a" for the "o" when writing to a female.

Salutations are virtually the same in business letters, with the person's professional title often being substituted for the *"Sr.,"* as in *"Estimado Ingeniero Gonzalez:"*.

Letter closings are varied, depending upon the amount of intimacy between the correspondents. An initial letter will probably close with *"Atentamente"* (attentively), *"Respetuosamente"* (respectfully), or *"Sinceramente"* (sincerely). Later letters may close with *"Con cariño"* (with caring, tenderness) or *"Con mucho amor"* (with much love), etc.

Addresses

When you write to a person in Latin America, always use the complete address exactly as that person has written it. Don't try to modify it into something that seems to make more sense to you, because if you do, it will probably be wrong. For instance, in smaller cities in Panama, the person may very well give you only her name, the name of the city and province, followed by Rep. de Panama. If she gives her address as Dolores Ramirez, David, Chiriquí, República de Panamá, it doesn't mean that she is so well known in David that the post office instantly knows who she is and will deliver it directly to her home. Instead, her mail will go to general delivery, where it is placed in an alphabetized cubicle where she can ask for it by her name. Panama doesn't have home delivery, and the choice is between a P.O. Box (hard to get) or general delivery. If a P.O. Box (*A.P.* or *Apartado Postal*) isn't shown in the address, it automatically goes to general delivery.

While all of the countries have general delivery (expressed as *Lista de Correos, Correo General,* or *Entrega General*), many do not have enough post office boxes available to provide them to the general public, and they reserve them for businesses. Some countries have effective home delivery (such as Colombia), and all that is needed is to provide a proper street address on the envelope. Other countries that have home delivery actually don't have street addresses, such as Costa Rica, and addresses are usually expressed as so many meters north, south, east, or west of some commonly known landmark. Since the postal system is used primarily for personal correspondence, rather than for business and advertising (resulting in a lower volume), deliveries are not made with regular routes. Instead, the mail will be delivered as needed by motorcycle.

As you can see from the above, it is essential that addresses be written exactly as provided to you, whether it makes any sense to you or not.

Answering the Telephone

This varies a great deal by local custom. Businesses and government offices will usually answer with the name of the company (or agency) just as is done in the United States. Answering home phones is a different matter. There is no standard "hello" as there is in the United States. There is a great deal of variation between countries. In some countries, such as Panama, the usual expression is *"¡Diga!"* (tell) or *"¡Digame!"* (tell me); *"¡Bueno!"* (good, referring to "good morning") or *"¡Buenas!"* (good afternoon, evening, or night) in Mexico; *"¿Qué hay?"* (what is there?) and *"¡Oiga!"* (listen) in Cuba; *"¡A ver!"* (to see) in Colombia; *"¡Hola!"* (hello) in Argentina and Uruguay; *"¡Sí!"* (yes) in Venezuela; *"¡Aló!"* (hello) in Peru, Ecuador, and most other places. *"¡Aló!"* is understood and fully acceptable in all of the countries, even if it is not the most commonly used in that particular country. To me, *"¡Aló!"* has a pleasing sound, and I use that manner of answering the telephone no matter where I am.

193

Chapter 30

Shopping

Bargaining

Just how acceptable bargaining is depends on which country it is, what kind of store you are in, and what is being sold. While bargaining, negotiating a price, is acceptable in all countries in Latin America (just as it is in the United States), it is only in Mexico that it has been developed into an art form. Otherwise, it is very much like in the U.S.

In Mexico, sidewalk vendors, vendors in open markets, handicraft sellers, etc., all expect to do some bargaining. In fact, although they want to get the best price that they can, they will be a bit disappointed in you if you don't offer less than they are asking. It is an enjoyable game for them. And you need to keep it enjoyable for yourself too. Just don't take it too seriously. It isn't a life or death matter. Please do not try to negotiate a lower price if you aren't seriously interested in making the purchase. It is unfair and unappreciated. You can make your first offer just about anywhere you want to, just as long as it isn't so low as to insult the seller. Perhaps one-fourth the asking price is a reasonable guideline. One thing that you must never do is to say that the product isn't worth the price. A better way of approaching it is to say that you hadn't intended to spend that much, or perhaps that you simply can't afford that much money. Once you have reached a point in the bargaining where you feel that you don't want to pay more, simply say thank you and begin to walk away...but not too fast. Chances are that you will be called back, and your last offer accepted.

Throughout Latin America, including Mexico, in stores in which price tags or labels are attached, or where a fixed price is shown, negotiating is not expected. That does not mean that it isn't possible. If the store owner or manager is around (or at least someone in a decision-making capacity) it is entirely possible to negotiate a reduction in price. Approach it by saying that you very much like the item in question, and will buy it if a discount can be worked out, perhaps a reduction in price of 10% to 20%. Such stores are not places to haggle over price, but with a gentlemanly approach you can frequently arrange some kind of discount if they would rather reduce the price than lose a sale.

As in the United States, you are expected to make lower offers for real estate and automobiles. In the U.S. you can occasionally get lower prices when you finance such a purchase, because a car dealer, for instance, frequently has a banking arrangement where he will receive some points back for referring the customer. That is not the case in Latin America where even such large purchases may be with cash, and where credit is something that the buyer has to laboriously work out with the financing institution. Discounts come with a cash deal quickly executed.

Stall Markets and Street Vendors

Every town in Latin America has its "stall markets," where individual entrepreneurs rent space (as in flea markets in the U.S.), sometime indoors, sometimes outdoors, where they sell their products. You can find butcher shops, vegetable stalls, handicrafts, pots and pans, shoemakers, and dozens of other kinds of shops. In some areas, Costa Rica comes to mind, certain days are set aside on a regular basis, perhaps Friday, Saturday, or Sunday, and a street is closed off to traffic. Vendors bring in their farm-fresh vegetables, put them on tables, and sell to the public. Most middle and lower-class families do the bulk of their shopping at stall markets and street markets because prices are lower. Owners of restaurants frequently do their purchasing there, too, because the produce is fresher than can be obtained elsewhere.

In some Latin American countries (Mexico and Peru, for example), street vendors make up a vast alternative economy, selling as much as 50% of all retail goods. They have no permanently fixed location (although they may have a particular street corner staked out) and they pay no taxes. Almost any small item can be purchased, ranging from watches to ladies underwear. Prepared food and drinks (not recommended for sanitary reasons), fruits and vegetables in season, and lottery tickets are available. Prices are usually reasonable, and can be negotiated if that's what you like to do.

Shopping Malls

Shopping malls, just like those in the U.S., are popping up all over Latin America in the more modern cities. The inevitable anchor stores, restaurants, and specialty shops are virtually indistinguishable from those in the United States. They are popular with the middle and upper classes, but because of the somewhat higher prices and the fact that most of what is sold would be considered luxury items by the poor, they are not frequented by the lower class.

Supermarkets

Supermarkets, some rivaling the best of the U.S., are also becoming common. Some even have housewares, hardware, and clothing departments. Most of what is found in American supermarkets is produced in the United States, but much of what is available in Latin American supermarkets is imported and somewhat more expensive than that available in the U.S. The freezing of foods for supermarket sale is not common in Latin America, and because of the high expense of transporting frozen foods for import, most supermarkets do not have much of a frozen foods section. The one exception is in frozen seafood. Seafood is frozen for export (in those countries that have a coastline) to the U.S. and other countries as a matter of course, and it is a simple matter to get it to the national market packaged and frozen. Produce departments are usually inferior to what we would expect in an American supermarket, for the simple reason that people can buy produce more cheaply and fresher from stall markets, and the supermarkets generally provide produce just as a matter of convenience for their customers. Unfortunately, supermarket managers have not learned the value of misting produce, and it's usually somewhat wilted.

If you are carrying a shopping bag, large purse, or any kind of merchandise, expect to leave it at a booth near the entrance of the store. It will be put in a bin and you will be given a numbered tag to retrieve it later. Don't let it annoy you. It is done to discourage shoplifting. The practice can even be handy if you are shopping by foot. I've frequently deposited stuff in supermarkets just because I didn't want to lug it around all day.

Convenience Stores

onvenience stores, such as those so common in the U.S., offering both gasoline and basic food supplies, are becoming popular and are fairly common in the more developed Latin American countries, but it is a recent phenomenon. So far I haven't seen any 7-11 stores, but Texaco has moved into Central America, and in keeping with the trend in the U.S., is including convenience stores as part of the package. The advantage to the consumer is that they are open much later, frequently all night, and on Sundays as well. Some even have fast-food bars.

The Corner Grocery Store

Only a very small minority of people own cars in Latin America. Most either walk, ride bicycles or motorcycles, or take the bus to wherever they are going. Because of the transportation limitations, probably more basic food items are sold in small local stores than in all other outlets combined. Every neighborhood has a small store, frequently just a house with one room and a refrigerator set aside for grocery goods, usually one within a 15 minute walk in any direction, in which the basics are available. The larger ones will offer snack foods, sodas, rice, beans, meat, chicken, canned foods, basic fresh vegetables, milk, bread, candles, kerosene, aluminum cooking pots, bottled propane, rope...just about any item that is basic to daily life. Usually a housewife won't have to go to the central market or a supermarket more than once a week, and then mainly to buy fresh produce and meat.

Prices are usually a little higher than can be obtained at a stall market or supermarket, but there are compensations. Not only are they more convenient to home, but almost all of them give credit to their regular customers, keeping a small book with their customers' names and their purchases. Debts are usually paid every two weeks, which is the usual pay period in Latin America.

Chapter 31

Education

Learning

Educational systems in Latin America differ a great deal from those in the United States. In the U.S., school systems are controlled by state boards of education and administered by local school districts. In most Latin American countries, the entire educational system, including private schools, is controlled by a national *Ministerio de Educación* which usually has ultimate control over curricula and content.

Classroom activity is much more structured and there is generally less student participation than there is in our system. Curricula tend toward the three R's, most of which is learned through rote memorization. There are few extracurricular activities, and individual creativity is not encouraged. People generally learn to read, but the habit of reading as an enjoyable and educational activity is not developed in students. Because of the limited scope of most public educational systems in Latin America (there are some exceptional private institutions), the populations as a whole are not as broadly nor as deeply educated as they are in Europe and North America.

This is not to say that there are not some very well educated people throughout Latin America. There are many. In most cases, though, they have had to educate themselves, attend private schools, or be educated abroad. Latin America has produced some noted writers and artists, but comparatively few scientists. One of NASA's astronauts, however, is Costa Rican. All of the Latin American countries have universities, and most produce doctors, dentists, and lawyers. I do not know, though, of any Latin American university that is comparable in scope or in quality to any of the better American universities. Some of the major limiting factors are that university teachers are frequently part-time and are not actively involved in their areas of specialty, a high percentage do not have the most advanced degrees available in their fields (such as Ph.D., M.D., etc.), and the libraries are usually sadly limited in their offerings.

As I write this, trying to justify such a negative view of Latin American educational systems, I am very aware that education in Latin America has been deprived mainly because of the formerly prevalent political systems of dictatorships, but as third world countries go, theirs are much better than most. Dictatorships do not fare well when they attempt to govern a well-educated population, and it is not in their best interests to produce a well-educated population. In searching my memory, I cannot come up with a single instance of a well-educated dictator, either. Come to think of it, however, neither can I remember a particularly well-educated American president, although a few have been presidential candidates. Without an appreciation of education at the highest political levels, or at least an economic motivation for a well-educated populace, strong educational systems do not get created.

Levels of Education

Formal education usually begins at about the same age as it does in the United States. Private kindergartens and pre-kindergartens are available for those that can afford it. Public school education begins at the age of six in the *escuela primaria* and continues for six years. In some countries school attendance is mandatory through the sixth grade. After *escuela primaria* the student enters *escuela segundaria* (usually called *"colegio,"* and not to be confused with the English word, college) and continues for another six years. Thus, just as in the U.S., the student is in school between the ages of six and eighteen. Upon graduation from high school, the students receive the degree of *bachiller* (not to be confused with the bachelor's degree offered by American colleges and universities).

Most students who continue with an education beyond high school normally do so in order to educate themselves for a specific occupation. This is usually done through courses taken at private trade schools. Such private schools are much more common in Latin America than in the United States, and they are comparatively expensive. Students may learn accounting, secretarial skills, foreign languages, and probably most commonly, computer skills. To give you an idea of the perceived value of post-graduate skills, David, Panama, with a population of about 120,000 people, has at least 20 such schools, churning out computer operators and programmers, beauty technicians, mechanics, accountants, ship's officers, secretaries, and other occupations, as well as people who are bilingual in English or French (skills learned to broaden job opportunities).

University Level

U*niversities* offer highly structured programs to prepare students for a degree (*título*) in fields such as medicine, law, humanities, and science. Most classes are large, and courses are taught primarily by lecture. Few, if any, electives are offered. Students must decide upon a career fairly early. Actually, the university studies themselves are referred to as a "career." Fairly frequently the girls applying to introduction programs will mention that they want to finish their *carrera* (meaning their university studies) before they get married. Also, when one asks what another is going to study in the university, it is put as "What career are you going to study." Latin American universities are not designed to provide a Liberal Arts education, but exist primarily to prepare people for professional careers.

People who graduate in different fields receive different kinds of degrees. The *licenciado* is the degree in the fields of arts and sciences; *ingeniero* is the degree in engineering; *arquitecto* is the architecture degree. The degree equivalent to the master's degree is the *maestria*; the equivalent to an M.D. or Ph.D. degree is the *doctorado*.

To give you an idea of educational deficits at the higher political levels, I provide the following story. It is true, and I read it as news in the Barranquilla, Colombia newspaper in 1995.

The Minister of Education of Colombia fired a university president because he had hired a person with a Ph.D. degree (in genetics) to teach genetics. Of course, you can't teach genetics in a major American university without a Ph.D. degree or its equivalent. However, the "Ph.D."

actually stands for "Doctor of Philosophy," which can only be obtained in specific fields (such as genetics), and is always the highest degree available in that field (except in medicine). The Minister of Education claimed that a person with a doctorate of philosophy had no business teaching genetics since he would only be qualified in philosophy and couldn't possibly be qualified in the field of genetics. How's that? Come again?

Actually, most universities in Latin America are fairly autonomous, with no external governing board, and little direct government involvement. They usually decide their own policies and teaching staff. Only those universities existing as national universities have to put up with much government interference.

Governments and universities frequently don't get along well together, as you may remember from the 1960's and early 1970's in the United States. The strain is even greater in Latin America, because universities tend to be hotbeds of political activity, most often aimed against the existing government. There are often politically motivated student strikes, with violent demonstrations, and government troops or police may be called in to put them down. Sometimes a government closes a university because of anti-government activity. I was in Bogota, Colombia in 1972, giving a series of guest lectures at a university, when student strikes and riots erupted. The government closed the university, surrounded it with troops and tanks, and closed all streets leading to the university by spreading tire puncturing devices on them. I had a hell of a time getting back to my hotel.

Chapter 32

Living as a Foreigner in Latin America

Advantages

People occasionally ask me why I choose to live in Latin America rather than in the United States, or even in some other part of the world. Theoretically, since I am retired, unmarried, and have a small, but dependable pension, I could live just about anywhere that isn't prohibitively expensive. My answer is that I live here because I like it, and that is the same response you will get from almost any other North American who lives in Latin America. I would like to tell you what it is that I like about living here, as well as some of the major and minor annoyances that accompany the pleasures.

First of all, I like the people. Having lived my childhood and youth in Texas, I was predisposed to open friendliness (although when I return for visits now, it doesn't seem as friendly as it used to be). Of all of the people I have met anywhere in the world, or *from* any other place else in the world, Latin Americans seem to me to be the most friendly and openly accessible. To me it is an unending pleasure to arise in the morning, drink my coffee, and go to town to do whatever it is that I have planned for that day. Strangers speak to me and smile, acquaintances come up to shake hands and ask how things are going, and old friends ask me to meet them for lunch. And when I say *old*, some of them are quite old. Others of them are very young. One of the beautiful things about friendships in Latin America is that age is never a consideration. That so-called generation gap doesn't exist.

Not only are the locals friendly and accessible, but being in a foreign country tends to bring other foreigners together, especially those from your own home country. I have, for instance, met far more Europeans in Latin America than I ever met in the United States, and I find that it is much easier to meet and get acquainted with my fellow Americans in Panama than it is back home.

I have found this to be true in every Latin American country in which I have spent time.

From the foregoing, it might appear that I am an especially social person who needs the company of other people. Actually, that's not the case, and for the most part, I don't like people very much. While not quite a misanthrope, I come close, and I generally prefer to be reading books, writing books, or fishing. What I enjoy about people in Latin America is the adventure and excitement of meeting and interacting with them. I never know which day I am going to meet and talk with a ship captain from Russia, meet and take to dinner a beautiful *Latina*, seduce a lady from France, have an argument with a Swedish engineer, discuss Rastafarian drug use with a Jamaican, talk about foreign policy with a lovely Israeli girl from a kibbutz, or have a philosophical discussion with a Panamanian university student. All of these things, and many others, have happened. For that reason, living and interacting with the people I meet in Latin American is a never-ending adventure.

I am, except for doing what I like to do, retired. At my present age of 58 I could easily be spending my time dancing with old ladies at Parents Without Partners parties, playing poker on Wednesday night with some similarly bored old men, or getting tan while hitting around a little white ball on some golf course. I recently noticed, in fact, that I am now qualified to join the American Association of Retired Persons. Let's just say that I prefer to be doing what I am presently doing.

Disadvantages

As I sit here, at this very moment, in front of the word processor, I am ticked off at one of my lawyers for being two weeks late in getting some papers ready, a matter which we discussed about an hour ago. Will they be ready tomorrow? Nobody knows. I am also steaming about a formerly prospective Panamanian business partner, who pulled out at the last minute this morning, leaving the other two of us holding the bag. Could this have happened in the United States? Of course it could have, and things like this happen all the time there. However, being in a culture that at times tends to be unpredictable in business matters, it is simpler to blame it on the location rather than on human weakness. And I do think that to some extent, it is a product of the culture.

The way people drive in Latin America is also a very annoying thing to me. I feel that I am taking my life in my hands every time I get in my car, and Panamanians are better drivers than most. I'm a good driver, but I'm really tired of having dents removed from fenders.

As a matter of lesser consequence (most of the time), there are five things that I miss about the United States: Blue cheese salad dressing, fried catfish, rare prime rib, morning newspapers, and interstate highways. I really can't think of anything else. Do the positive outweigh the negatives? They do by a country mile!

Costs

I have read several books and have seen a couple of videotapes that promote Mexico and Costa Rica as being retirement paradises where the living is easy...and cheap. I am not inclined to agree with all of the ecstatic conclusions. Most of it has to do with one's perception. Had I recently retired from New York City, Chicago, San Francisco, or Los Angeles, I'm sure that I would see it the same way. However, when I do go to the United States these days it is normally for a relatively short visit in the vicinity of Houston. Prices are still comparatively low in that part of the United States, and while it is not exactly a paradise, it is still fairly nice.

As best I can tell at this point, to live the lifestyle that you are presently living in the United States, it is likely to cost you just about the same amount of money to live in a comparable area in Latin America. The main difference is that you can live just as comfortably as you are living now, but with a simpler lifestyle. That statement is going to require some elaboration. Let's say that you are now living in a comfortable suburban house and have the basic amenities, including air conditioning, at least one car, belong to a country club, like to dine out occasionally, dance, and go to the movies, and so forth.

If you choose to live in the same kind of house in San Jose, Costa Rica, you will still pay $100,000 to $200,000 for it, or will pay $1,000 to $2,000 per month in rent. Your electricity will cost a lot less, though, and you won't need air conditioning or heat. Your furnishings will cost a great deal more, because it's all heavily taxed (although some very nice furniture is made in Costa Rica at very reasonable prices). Your car, either new or used, will cost at least double that in the U.S., again because of import taxes. Your country club dues will be from $5,000 to $10,000 per year, assuming that you can get in, because it's a bit difficult for foreigners. Dining out will cost about half as much as in the U.S. and movies will be about $2.00 per person. It all kind of balances out, doesn't it.

However, if you choose a simpler lifestyle, you can still be quite comfortable, and perhaps importantly to you, you won't be looked down upon if you do choose to live more simply. It is quite possible to buy a nice 3-bedroom suburban house for $35,000, or you can rent the same for $300 per month. The neighbors will be closer than you want, and your lawn will be smaller than you are accustomed to. You really don't need a car because buses go almost everywhere, and taxis are extremely cheap to hire. You can, in fact, live comfortably for about $1000 to $1200 per month per person, and if you want to do most of your own cooking and housekeeping, it can be quite a bit less.

The difference in Latin America is that it *is not necessary* to live with all of amenities that you enjoyed in the United States. I could not conceive of living without a car in the U.S., but felt no sacrifice when I did it for a number of years in Latin America. I would not want to live without a nice house with a big yard and a lot of trees in the United States. It didn't bother me here, though, because I was living like almost everyone else. That is the big difference. If you are willing to adopt a similar lifestyle to the people who already live here, your costs will not be high, but if you insist on living as you do in the United States, you will pay just about as much.

Allow me to illustrate a couple of things. I presently live in an attractive 2-bedroom house, sort of in the country (lots of roosters to listen to), large creek nearby, with a large fully-fenced yard, a number of fruit and coconut trees, garage, barbecue, good security, and no air conditioning (which at times I need). My rent is $75 per month (this is Panama, not Costa Rica) and all utilities cost about $25 per month. How do you like that? All housing costs for $100 per month. However, I am in the process of purchasing a piece of property in the mountains a few miles from here. It is only a 3/4 acre plot, presently planted in coffee trees and citrus. It has a paved road, all utilities and a large spring. The cost: $20,000. To build the house I want, which will be much better than I now occupy (and which is presently for sale for $15,000), I will need to spend about $35,000. Depending on where you now live, you may consider those figures to be quite inexpensive. This is a matter of perspective. To me they are high, because I could build (doing my own contracting, as I plan to do here) an equivalent house for about the same cost on my property in East Texas, and my two acres in Texas were recently appraised for only $10,000. Frankly, I consider those two acres to be at least as nice as the 3/4 acre that I am buying here for $20,000. I might add, though, that just a short distance away from my mountain site in Panama, a particularly nice house just sold for $250,000 to an English couple. Maybe it's the illustrious company that accounts for the price.

My reason for getting into these specifics is to show you that you just can't depend on it when somebody says that living in Latin America is "really cheap." It depends on how you want to live and where you want to do it (which country, whether rural or urban, beach front, mountains, or nondescript). Most of all, it depends on one's perspective of what is "really cheap."

Regulations

Regulations affecting foreigners living in Latin America vary significantly from country to country. To find out what they are, I recommend that you call a consulate representing the country in the United States. The chances are that they will not be able to tell you very much, but they might at least get you started. They probably have a yellow page directory for the capitol city, where they can look up a few names for lawyers that you can call. If you use a lawyer for information, try to locate one who has had experience in working with resident foreigners, because laws affecting them are actually sort of a specialty.

Now that I've given you what might be considered an acceptable approach, let me tell you what you really should do. First of all, I wouldn't consider living in any foreign country without spending some time there first. Ignore what anyone else tells you about the country, including me, because only you will know how you feel when you are actually there. One of my good friends was not at all satisfied with living where I live in Panama, and he couldn't stand Costa Rica either (nor could I, although many North Americans love it). He took a trip to Medellín, Colombia and fell in love with the place. After spending a number of months there, he decided to stay and he bought property. Personally, I don't particularly like the idea of living in Medellín or in any other city in Colombia, but he loves it. My point is that it is a personal matter, and you won't know how it feels until you are there.

Once you have decided where you want to be, you can start finding out about the regulations. Look for a good lawyer (recommended by other foreigners) with some experience in residence requirements and regulations affecting foreigners.

Legal Residence

All of the countries that I have investigated so far have some kind of permanent legal residential status available to foreigners. None of them, as far as I am aware, are as restrictive as residence requirements for living in the United States. Several possibilities exist:

» 1. Work permit: This does not give actual permanent resident status, but if you have a work permit you do not have to leave the country on a regular basis to renew your entry permit. They normally have to be renewed on a regular basis, usually every six or twelve months. Work permits are normally issued only for those occupations in which the foreigner will not be competing for work with citizens.

» 2. Business or property ownership: Some countries offer a permanent residential status to persons who make substantial investments in businesses or properties that are considered to be of importance to the economy. For instance, Costa Rica offers a special resident status to individuals who invest $50,000 or more in any business in the country, and it confers the right to work in the business in which the investment has been made. Home or property purchases do not count. Some other countries do not offer this status.

» 3. Marriage with a citizen: This confers permanent resident status, but does not provide you with full rights of citizenship. You still may have to have a work permit in order to legally work within the country, and you will not be able to vote. Every country, though, ultimately considers the welfare of their citizens, and being married to one allows you to cut through a great deal of red tape and can offer advantages which are not legally on the books.

» 4. *Pensionado* status: This is a permanent resident status available to people who can demonstrate a permanent lifetime income, independent of any employment (this generally does not affect any income earned through business ownership or investments within the country). The status is normally accorded to retired people with pensions, although at present none of the countries that I know of has put any particular age requirement on it (Costa Rica has been considering an age limit). Income requirements range from about $300 per month to $1000 per month, and is based on a level which will permit the person to live without having to work (some countries have specific requirements based on the city or area in which you intend to live). You do not have the right to vote or work, but generally will have all other rights accorded to citizens. Some countries offer substantial benefits to *pensionados*. Panama, for instance, legally requires that businesses offer significant discounts to *pensionados* in hotels, restaurants, transportation, supermarkets, health care, public utilities, etc., and vehicles and household goods can be imported without any import taxes. Many other countries offer no benefits other than the right to remain in the country.

Some Thoughts on Being an Expatriate

During the years that I worked in Latin America I always thought of myself as being a normal American who just happened to be working outside of the United States. There was never really an issue of *living* outside of the U.S., although I was spending most of my time doing exactly that. During that period of time I met many people who were, in fact, expatriates; Americans who, for one reason or another chose to make their permanent residence in Latin America. Most were retirees who went south looking for warmer climates or less expensive lifestyles. Some were draft evaders, some hiding from the law, and there were many who had personal problems back in the United States and who were trying to start a new life.

I never thought of myself as being one of these people, because I felt that I had a *reason* to be there. I now find myself being one of those people, an expatriate. Yet I still feel that I have a reason for being here, and I don't like to call myself an expatriate because I still feel very much like a patriot, but I have made a personally selfish choice to live in a place where I feel very comfortable.

Most of my American and European friends are people who, like me, retired early, and felt the freedom to live in a place where their adventurous spirit could fly free. I want it to be understood that I live in Latin America because I enjoy the *culture*, and it is a matter of my own selfish pleasure. It is certainly not because I feel more respect for political systems here (although Panama's is very close to that in the United States), nor because I have any kind of fundamental dissatisfaction with the United States. It's just that I like it here, and I never had much use for television anyway.

I never forget, though, that the only reason that we are able to do this is because we are citizens of democratic countries that assure their people of the right to live pretty much as they please. Most citizens of most countries don't enjoy that degree of personal freedom. The United States has not abandoned me just because I now live somewhere else. I am still welcome back anytime I want to return (at least officially). For the degree of freedom that I am guaranteed under our Constitution, I sincerely feel gratitude to the United States of America. I also feel a real appreciation for the *República de Panamá* and its citizens for accepting me as a resident. Neither country had any particular obligation to allow this indulgence of mine.

Welcome to "THE *Romance* ZONE"!

housands of Latinas await American men seeking relationships & marriage. Most
re less than a 4 hour plane ride. One hemisphere with unlimited opportunities !

Correspondence Methods for Establishing Relationships

Photomagazines featuring Latinas from 12 different countries is the most popular form of correspondence. Ladies are published in color with their photos and personal information. Addresses can be purchased, and gentlemen write directly to those ladies that interest him. After the initial letter exchange, couples often talk on the telephone before meeting. This method of introduction has resulted in hundreds (if not thousands) of happily married couples.

At least 550 new Latinas in every edition !

Since 1992, TLC Worldwide, Inc. has published more than 22 quarterly issues

Personal Advertisements (Mens' Listing) allow the gentlemen to be published in a brochure which is distributed to the latin ladies free. Interested latinas contact the men directly by letter. Each "Mens' Listing" is printed in Spanish and distributed to over 1,800 ladies applying for membership. These listings are shown to friends and family members which results in thousands of ladies seeing you. This product works great for first-time clients and those too busy to initiate the letter writing process. TLC Worldwide, Inc.'s Mens' Listings are prepared bi-monthly to expedite responses. They are also published in full color. Deadlines for the Mens' Listing is the last day of every even numbered month.

＊This Personal Advertisement was intentionally blurred for reasons of confidentiality.

Mens' Listings are seen by thousands of latinas.

Live-Action Videos are shot on location at one of our Singles Vacation destinations. Each video tape features 60 - 70+ ladies who give a brief interview about themselves and a modeling session. You can hear her voice, see her mannerisms, and watch her body language.

Each of these products may be purchased individually. But for greater success, consider a combination package for additional networking.

Live Videos - "The next best experience to actually being there !"

TLC Worldwide, Inc. has produced more than 30 live-action videos to-date.

See <u>Chapter 42 "Correspondence"</u> for additional product information Call T.L.C. Worldwide, Inc. at (713) 896-9224 to receive a free brochure ladies' photos & data, or visit their website at **www.tlcworldwide.com**

Singles Vacation Tours provide the opportunity to meet hundreds of Latinas in a short period of time and the security of traveling with an experienced tour company.

*See Chapter 43

Hundreds of Latinas in attendance provide unlimited introduction possibilities

6 - 8 ladies for every 1 man.

Pool, bbqs., or beach parties.

Available latinas are happy, polite and unpretentious.

Feel free to join in the fun.

All reputable singles tour operators to Latin America offer a video describing their programs. TLC Worldwide, Inc. updates it's promotional video annually, and it costs only $8.00.

Travel to Latin America is fun, safe, and inexpensive. Whethe
traveling by yourself or in an organized group, you will find Lati
Americans friendly, helpful and catering to American tourists.

Short 3 - 4 hour flights.

Excellent food,
refreshments &
purchasing power.

Beautiful sandy beaches.

Anxious ladies wanting to meet you.

Great social mixers.

Sightseeing & recreation.

Five star facilities & events.

Sunny days of pleasant relaxation.

Memorable sunsets.

Part IV

Travel Tips & General Safety

Chapter 33

Travel Documents

Passports

With a few exceptions, a passport is required for all U.S. citizens to depart and enter the United States. Passports are required to enter most countries in Latin America, but not all. A valid U.S. passport is the best documentation of U.S. citizenship available. It is foolish to travel without one because it is essential as a form of identification. Hotels usually require it, policemen insist upon it (or a photocopy), and you cannot cash traveler's checks without it. If you do not have a passport and are thinking about traveling to Latin America, you might as well apply now. If you already have a passport, be sure that it will be valid for a minimum of six months (one year is better, because some countries require it) from the time you begin your trip. Many countries will not permit entry unless your passport meets that minimum.

Application for a passport may be made at a passport agency, to a clerk of any Federal court or State court, or a judge or clerk of any probate court accepting applications, or at a post office selected to accept passport applications.

First time applicants must apply in person, and must present evidence of citizenship (such as a certified copy of birth certificate), personal identification with a photo (such as a valid driver's license), two identical black and white or color photographs taken within six months (2 by 2 inches), plus a completed passport application (DSP-11). If you were born abroad, you may also use as proof of citizenship: a Certificate of Naturalization, a Certificate of Citizenship, a Report of Birth Abroad of a Citizen of the United States of America or a Certification of Birth.

You may apply for a passport by mail if you have had a passport issued within 12 years prior to the date of a new application, are able to submit your most recent U.S. passport with your new application, and your previous passport was not issued before your 18th birthday. If you are eligible to apply by mail, include your previous passport, a completed DSP-82 "Application for Passport by Mail," new photographs, and the required fees. Fees change occasionally, and it would be a good idea to check with the passport office or post office to get the current costs.

If you must have your passport within 10 days, you will need to pay an additional fee to expedite it and provide proof of the need for this service. A passport agency can normally process an expedited passport within 24 hours. The National Passport Center (which is set up for mail applications) can usually process mail-in applications within 14 days. Their address is: National Passport Center; P.O. Box 371971; Pittsburgh, PA 14250—7971.

U.S. Passport Agencies are located in Boston, Chicago, Honolulu, Houston, Los Angeles, Miami, New Orleans, New York, Philadelphia, San Francisco, Seattle, Stamford, Connecticut and Washington, D.C.

Loss, theft, of destruction of a passport should be reported to Passport Services, 1111 19th Street, N.W., Washington, D.C. 20522-1705 immediately, or to the nearest passport agency. If you are in a foreign country, report the loss to the nearest U.S. Embassy or Consulate, and to the local police. The police probably won't help with recovery, but your copy of the report will help to get another passport issued, and will be legal proof of your right to be in the country. Your passport is a valuable citizenship- and identity document and should be carefully safeguarded. Its loss could cause you unnecessary travel complications as well as significant expense. When you are in a foreign country it is advisable to photocopy the data page (in the front) along with the page showing your entry stamp. Take the copies with you and leave the passport in your hotel safe.

Visas

Most of the countries in Latin America do not require visas of U.S. citizens, and permit them to enter with a tourist card (but you still need a passport). Some do, however, and it is wise to call the Embassy or a Consulate of that country while you are making your plans. There is also a good deal of variation with regard to the amount of time a tourist is permitted to remain in the country without obtaining a renewal. Generally the entry permit allows a stay of from 30 to 90 days, after which time one must either leave the country and re-enter, or apply for an extension. Ordinarily there is no serious problem involved in over-staying your entry permit. You will, however, be required to pay a fine (generally small), and obtain an exit permit from the immigration office. One friend of mine over-stayed his entry into Costa Rica by 22 years. When they finally caught him, he was financially incapable of paying the fine which had accrued over the 22 years, no longer had a valid United States passport, and didn't want to leave anyway, so they made him a citizen.

Those of you who wish to go to Cuba may do so, and a visa is not required, nor is your passport stamped as having entered Cuba. It will be necessary, however, for you to enter from some country other than the United States. Regular flights (as well as group tours) to Havana are available from Mexico City; San Jose, Costa Rica; Panama City, Panama; Barranquila, Colombia; and Caracas, Venezuela. Flights from other countries, such as the Bahamas and Canada, are also available. Don't be afraid of going. Cuba is not as bad as the publicity would suggest. It is a favorite vacation spot for Europeans and Canadians, and Americans are also treated well.

To find out exactly what is required and the amount of time you will be allowed to remain on your entry permit, it is best to call the Embassy of the country in question. Most of the countries also have Consulates in major U.S. cities, and they can issue a visa if it is required. The Embassy can provide you with the phone number and address of the Consulate nearest to you, and you can also call directory assistance if you are in a larger city to find out if they have a consulate nearby. The Foreign Embassy addresses and phone numbers are as follows:

» Embassy of the Argentine Republic
1600 New Hampshire Ave., N.W.
Washington, D.C. 20009
Phone: (202) 238-6400

» Embassy of Bolivia
3014 Massachusetts Ave., N.W.
Washington D.C. 20008
Phone: (202) 483-4410

» Embassy of Brazil
3009 Whitehaven St. N.W.
Washington, D.C., 20008
Phone: (202) 238-2700, 745-2820 or 745-2831

» Embassy of Chile
1732 Massachusetts Ave., N.W.
Washington, D.C., 20036
Phone: (202) 785-1746

» Embassy of Colombia
2118 Leroy Place., N.W.
Washington, D.C., 20008
Phone: (202) 387-8338

» Embassy of Costa Rica
2114 S St., N.W.
Washington, D.C. 20008
Phone: (202) 234-2945

» Cuban Interests Section of Switzerland
2630 and 2639 16th St., N.W.
Washington, D.C. 20009
Phone: (202) 797-0748
Cuban Embassy (202) 797-8518

» Embassy of the Dominican Republic
1715 22nd St., N.W.
Washington, D.C. 20008
Phone: (202) 332-6280

» Embassy of Ecuador
2535 15th St., N.W.
Washington, D.C. 20009
Phone: (202) 234-7200

» Embassy of El Salvador
2308 California St., N.W.
Washington, D.C. 20008
Phone: (202) 265-9671

» Embassy of Guatemala
2220 R St., N.W.
Washington, D.C. 20008
Phone: (202) 745-4952

» Embassy of Honduras
3007 Tilden St., N.W.
Washington, D.C. 20008
Phone: (202) 966-7702

» Embassy of Mexico
2829 16th Street N.E. 20018
Washington, D.C. 20006
Phone: (202) 728-1628 or 736-1000.

» Embassy of Nicaragua
1627 New Hampshire Ave., N.W.
Washington, D.C. 20009
Phone: (202) 939-6570

» Embassy of the Republic of Panama
2862 McGill N.W. Terrace
Washington, D.C. 20008
Phone: (202) 483-1407

» Embassy of Paraguay
2400 Massachusetts Ave., N.W.
Washington, D.C. 20008
Phone: (202) 483-6960

» Embassy of Peru
1700 Massachusetts Ave., N.W.
Washington D.C. 20036
Phone: (202) 833-9860

» Embassy of Uruguay
1918 F St., N.W.
Washington, D.C. 20006
Phone: (202) 331-1313

» Embassy of the Republic of Venezuela
1099 30th St., N.W.
Washington, D.C. 20007
Phone: (202) 342-2214

Sometimes addresses and telephone numbers to the various embassies change. Washington D.C.'s information telephone number is (202) 555-1212 for assistance in contacting an embassy. Additional satellite consulate offices may exist in larger cities that are more convenient. Check with local information or a telephone directory to see if there is a foreign embassy close to you.

Chapter 34

Travel Guidebooks

I sometimes get teased because I always travel with at least one guidebook appropriate to the country I am in. Even now, although I am a resident of Panama and have been here long enough to know much of what needs to be known, I still travel with a guidebook, and still try to convince Panamanians that they need one too. I regret that during my earlier years of traveling in the United States there were not guidebooks available for most of the areas I went. Why do I consider them important? Simply because I don't want to miss anything that might be interesting, prefer to eat in restaurants that meet my needs, and don't like to waste time looking for a hotel.

There is a wide range of guidebooks that cover every country in Latin America. Some focus on tourists with more money than time to spend and others exist to meet the needs of those who have several months for exploration, but limited funds. As far as I know, I have all of them, and am always waiting for new ones to be published. I want to see the countries not only through my eyes, but also through the eyes of others who go. I suggest that you try to do this too, because doing so will broaden your horizons and make your trip more interesting.

There is only one set of guidebooks that I consider to be absolutely indispensable: The *Lonely Planet* series of guidebooks. The *Lonely Planet* head office is in Australia (and given the adventurous spirit of the Aussies, this is probably to be expected), with other offices in France, England and the United States. For me, the books have been difficult to find in retail outlets, but residents of the United States can easily order them from: Lonely Planet Guidebooks, 150 Linden Street, Oakland, CA 94607. Ordering by telephone is easy by calling 800-275-8555; their website is www.lonelyplanet.com.

Lonely Planet is not aware that I highly recommend their books, and I have never even discussed the matter with them. They get my endorsement because, above all other guidebooks, they take local cultures seriously and go to great lengths to make local settings understandable. Although they are oriented toward budget travelers, and you may have lots of money, you still need their book. Buy an additional guide to help you find a luxury hotel. *Lonely Planet* offers guidebooks (for Latin America) as follows:

» Baja California
» Central America on a Shoestring*
» Costa Rica
» Cuba
» Guatemala, Belize, and Yucatán: *La Ruta Maya*
» Mexico*
» Argentina, Uruguay & Paraguay
» Bolivia
» Brazil
» Brazilian Phrasebook
» Chile & Easter Island
» Colombia
» Ecuador & the Galápagos Islands
» Latin American Spanish Phrasebook*

» Peru
» Quechua Phrasebook
» South America on a Shoestring*
» Trekking in the Patagonian Andes
» Venezuela

    *Denotes especially useful guidebooks.

These cover all of the countries of Latin America except for the Western Caribbean. *Fielding's Western Caribbean* provides useful information for Puerto Rico, Dominican Republic, and Cuba. Another good series of Travel guides are published by Passport Books and include *Mexico & Central America Handbook* (ISBN 0-8442-4784-7, cost $27.95) and South American Handbook (ISBN 0-8442-4783-9, cost $39.95). Either can be found in bookstores or by calling (847) 679-5500. These books are very detailed and small enough to accompany you on your travels.

To get a handle on some useful Spanish phrases, get a copy of *Spanish Lingo for the Savvy Gringo* by Elizabeth Reid, $14.95 (ISBN 1-881791-08-4). It's very entertaining and readable, not a boring textbook. In addition to Spanish, it also includes a lot of cultural information and an appendix on Spanish slang. It can be ordered by calling 800-356-9315.

Don't wait until you are almost ready to leave and can't find the appropriate guidebook in a local bookstore. Write them now for prices and order far enough in advance to get the book and have enough time to study it.

Your local library can also be a great source of travel information. The one handicap here is that you can't take it with you. You can, however, photocopy the pages you will need.

Chapter 35

Money

Carrying Cash

It is generally recommended by most travel writers that money never be transported in the form of cash. I have always done so and I have no plans to stop doing it. However, I generally do not carry more than several hundred dollars in that manner. The most practical reason for carrying U.S. dollars in the form of cash is that you can usually get a better rate of exchange for cash than you can with either travelers checks or cash advances from credit cards. There are a few exceptions to this, for instance, in Colombia the best rate is with travelers checks. In countries where there is a thriving black market for dollars (Honduras, for example) you can only use cash for black market exchange, and occasionally you can come out 50% or more ahead by using the black market.

If you are going to carry much cash, never put it in a wallet (in fact, it's best not to carry a wallet at all) and never carry more with you than you need at the time, and certainly no more than you can afford to lose. Putting it in a front pocket doesn't help because all pickpockets know to look there. I have frequently carried it in my socks because its rather difficult to pick a sock, but in the event of a physical assault that really wouldn't help much. I have also used baby safety pins to pin a cloth sack with the cash to the inside of my underwear, hoping the assailant wouldn't be homosexual. If you are going to be carrying cash, however, the best method is to use a money belt underneath your clothing.

One thing that we rarely think about in the U.S. is the condition of the paper money that we have. If more than half of the bill still exists, it can still be redeemed at banks if you are in the United States. Be very careful, though, when you go to Latin America, that your bills are in good condition. They should not be written upon, torn, or have any pieces missing. Unless they are in good condition, you probably will not be able to use them.

Traveler's Checks

Usually the easiest, and sometimes the only place to cash a traveler's check is in a bank. Some banks won't exchange traveler's checks at all and some will accept only certain brands of checks. Citibank, for instance, will only accept Citibank traveler's checks. Some banks will exchange traveler's checks during certain, very limited, hours. Fortunately, more and more hotels are now accepting traveler's checks, but usually offer the exchange at a rate far less favorable than in a bank. It appears that American Express traveler's checks are the most widely accepted in Latin America, and most major cities have an office where they can be purchased and where claims for lost checks can be filed.

Be sure to take your passport to the bank with you when you want to exchange a traveler's check. It is a necessity throughout the region.

Credit Cards

Don't leave home without one. Actually, I got by quite nicely for some 20 years in Latin America without a single credit card. I did occasionally have to call my bank in the U.S. and ask them to wire me some money, but it would have been much simpler to have had a credit card for a cash advance.

It is only fairly recently that credit cards have been especially useful in Latin America, and for some things it is now a necessity. A credit card is usually required to rent a car, for instance, and a sufficient remaining credit line to cover the deposit must be there. Some hotels require a credit card, and many require either a credit card or the room rent plus a deposit paid in advance. Most of the budget hotels do not accept credit cards. Credit cards can be used in the better restaurants throughout Latin America, and most up-scale stores also accept them.

Visa and Mastercard are the most commonly accepted cards, but quite a few establishments also take American Express cards in addition to regional Latin American cards.

Western Union

All of the larger cities in Latin America have Western Union offices, and money can be wired to you in a matter of minutes, as long as you have someone at home who can send it to you. The cost is rather high, and is based on how much money is being sent. But it's fast and dependable and serves well in an emergency. It is also one of the few reliable ways to send money to your lady in Latin America. Their toll free number is (800) 325-6000.

Bank Wire Transfers

Some banks will accept wire transfers which have been sent to you from your bank in the United States, and most banks will accept a wire transfer to your account if you have one in that bank. The process requires about three days, and can cost you up to $40 for a single transfer. Western Union is much faster, and if a relatively small sum is being sent, less expensive.

Currency Exchange

In every Latin American country except Panama and Puerto Rico (which use U.S. dollars as their basic currency), you will find it necessary to change your dollars into their currency. Here are some things to consider in exchanging money:

» 1) Exchange rates may change daily.

» 2) Exchange money in cities or major tourist areas. The farther into the hinterland you go, the lower the rate tends to be. In rural areas it will be difficult, even impossible, to make a currency exchange.

» 3) Change as much as you think you will need. Exchange rates are better for larger amounts of money.

» 4) However, if the local currency is inflating rapidly, change less, because your dollar will be worth more later.

» 5) You usually get a better rate of exchange for cash as opposed to traveler's checks.

» 6) Never exchange currency in the United States. The exchange rates are very low, and any international airport you will be entering in Latin America will have places where you can exchange your dollars for enough local currency to get by until you can go to a bank.

» 7) Generally, the best rate of exchange is at a bank. Ask, however, whether a commission is charged on exchanging traveler's checks.

» 8) Usually you will find more or less the same rates at money changers (*casas de cambio,* or *cajas de cambio*) as you will at banks, without the lines and waiting in a bank. Know the rate of exchange first, however.

» 9) The black market usually matches or exceeds bank rates, and sometimes, after hours or on weekends, it may be your only choice. Be very careful, and don't hand over your money until you have personally counted the money handed over to you. It is illegal, but rarely taken seriously.

» 10) You almost always get a very poor rate of exchange in hotels. That is why I suggest that you not use a credit card to pay hotel bills. Get a cash advance on your card from a bank and use that to pay your hotel bills. You can come out way ahead. Inasmuch as this is not always the case, check with both bank and hotel to see what credit card rates of exchange prevail that day.

» 11) Check your newspaper before you leave to find out the official rate of exchange in the country you are visiting. The New York Times, available in most cities, always provides this information. This will allow you to calculate which option is likely to be most advantageous for you.

Chapter 36

Getting There

Driving

Except for Mexico, the only sensible way to travel to Latin America is by air, unless your reason for going is for the travel experience itself. I have driven to Central America several times, and have met land travelers in Central and South America who have gotten there from the United States by bus, train, hitch-hiking, bicycle, motorcycle, automobile, van, trucks with campers, and trucks pulling house trailers. So, it is possible. But, in my opinion this should be considered as adventure travel. You can, in fact, except for the Darrein Gap in Panama, drive almost all the way to the southern tip of South America by highway (or at least by "road").

Once you get to Latin America, of course, there are a variety of ways to get around. You can use airplanes, trains, buses, automobiles, bicycles, motorcycles, horses, mules, burros, and feet.

If your reason for considering driving to Latin America is for the purpose of living there and having your car with you, there are several important things to consider. First, it usually costs very little more to ship your vehicle to your chosen country than to drive it (frequently it is cheaper), and it is a whole lot safer and easier. You will need to do some shopping around to get the best shipping rates. When I was considering shipping a car to Panama, I found rates ranging from $675 to $1250 (in 1995 from the Gulf Coast), which is quite a spread. I decided to drive, mostly for the adventure, and my total costs of driving from Texas (not including the week of debauchery in Costa Rica) came to about $1200. Not only do you pay for gasoline, food, lodging, and bribes to policemen and customs officials, but every country charges you for the privilege of crossing their borders.

Second, you'd best check into the expense of import duties in your particular country (some, in fact, do not even permit the importation of used automobiles). The cost can be as high as 300% of the value of the car. The formula is complex, but Panama charges about 15% of the car's value (based on depreciation from new cost), and Costa Rica charges about 150% (higher if it is a luxury car). Colombia doesn't even permit the importation of used vehicles. Before making your decision, I highly recommend talking with the Embassy or a consulate of the country in question.

I have a friend, and know several other people, who regularly buy and drive vehicles to Central America, where they sell them for a profit. This can be done if you buy a 4-wheel drive Nissan or Toyota vehicle, preferably diesel. They pay the import duty, go through the process of paperwork, then sell the vehicles when they are through using them (six months to a year), and make a profit of $1000 to $2000 dollars each time. But they do buy cheap and sell high. I haven't done it yet, and haven't yet seriously considered it, but if you feel adventurous, it exists as a possibility.

If you decide to drive, take along plenty of spare parts, leave with good tires, double the amount of money you think you will need, and be prepared for delays and expense at all of the border crossings. And allow more time than you think will be necessary. Never drive at night. Potholes, vehicles without headlights, and cattle on the highway are just three of the problems. In some countries bandits are the more serious problem. Be aware also that border crossings are not open at night, and after hours or weekend service can cost you more.

I have always driven alone, but I do not recommend it. If you have a breakdown, you will need someone to remain with the vehicle while you go for help. Otherwise wheels, tires, and other parts, along with the contents, will probably not be there when you get back. I have been lucky, and a tool kit and spare parts have also helped. Perhaps it is because I am getting older and feel less confident than even last year (when I drove the last time), but I definitely plan to ship my next vehicle.

Air Travel

This topic could easily be expanded to several chapters because there are so many factors that could be considered. If you are especially interested in going for bottom dollar, without concern for schedules, I suggest that you buy one of the many travel books that are available. Some of them have some excellent suggestions for saving money. Usually when I originate my travel in the United States, I am concerned about getting the least expensive ticket available that also has a guaranteed schedule. I am not interested in stand-by, tours, clubs, clearinghouses, consolidators, or bucket shops. You can save some money by looking into them carefully, but at the same time you may sacrifice scheduling reliability.

If your interests are similar to mine, try the yellow pages or pick up the weekly travel section of your nearest big-city newspaper. You will probably find an advertisement from a travel agency specializing in Latin American travel. Most of them buy block tickets which are highly discounted, and which they can sell at a discount to you. Unless you have a fairly competent local travel agent who is willing to spend some time with the computer searching out the lowest available prices, try a specialty travel agent. And, unless you just like to spend unnecessary money, there is no point in going directly to the airline and paying for a full-price ticket. Travel agents cost no more to use, and they can usually save you money.

Normally, since I live in Panama as a resident *pensionado* (and receive a 25% discount), I originate my flights from Panama. Even with the discount, I pay approximately the same price for round trip Panama/United States tickets as someone in the U.S. who buys his ticket in the United States, would pay. No matter where you are going in Latin America, it is cheaper to buy your tickets in the U.S. for all international flights if your initial flight originates in the United States. Buy tickets for all of your international flights before you leave. Once you get to your destination, and want to travel around within that country, buy your tickets locally for local flights.

Keep in mind that Latin American destinations have high seasons and low seasons, roughly corresponding to rainy and dry seasons, with the dry season having the higher fares since that is when tourism is higher. Also, in tourism oriented countries, hotel rates are higher than in off-season.

By just looking at a map it is hard to appreciate just how large some of the Latin American countries are. It is also hard to realize that the cities in any given country may be separated by high mountain ranges or virtually impenetrable jungles. Add to that the fact that most of the Latin American highways are narrow and poorly maintained, and cities that are separated by only 200 miles might require a long day of bus travel to go from one to the other. For these reasons, air travel is widely utilized within Latin America. Much more so than in the United States. Unless your interest is in sightseeing, which I highly recommend, plan on doing quite a bit of local flying. Passenger airlines connect every major city that I know of, and it is surprisingly inexpensive and safe.

Important telephone numbers for the two main domestic air carriers to Latin America are American Airlines (800) 433-7300 and Continental Airlines (800) 231-0856. You can also call local travel agents found in the yellow pages or Sunday travel section for comparison shopping.

241

Chapter 37

Getting Around

Travel by Air

Plane travel in Latin America can often be the only practical way to get from point A to point B, and sometimes is the only way to get to some places, including remote ruins, jungle lodges, and isolated towns. It also offers the advantages of covering long distances quickly and arriving less tired than if you go by car or bus. There are a few disadvantages. It is more expensive than buses, both for the flight and for taxi rides between the airports and downtown (but still is likely to be less expensive than renting a car). You can also get locked in by bad weather (although buses are sometimes locked in by landslides), and flights are sometimes canceled if there are not enough passengers to make the trip profitable.

Intercity Buses

It depends on the country and the bus, but bus travel can be a delightful experience or a nightmare. Intercity buses can be comfortable and air conditioned, especially if they travel between major cities, and some routes offer reserved seating with nobody standing in the isles. Rural buses, on the other hand, may very well be ancient, retired school buses from the United States, packed as tightly as they can be jammed.

Intercity bus travel comfort is closely related to highway conditions. Highland Peru has some of the worst roads in Latin America, and bad stretches can also be found in Guatemala, Costa Rica, Colombia, Bolivia, and the Brazilian Amazon. Much of it depends on the season, and roads get perceptibly worse during the rainy season when it is difficult to fill potholes. Highways and roads in Panama, Chile, Argentina, Uruguay, Brazil, and most of Venezuela are usually pretty good.

In the more remote areas, buses may be stripped to their bare essentials, worn out, and held together by baling wire. When all the seats are filled, the aisle is then packed to the limit and beyond, and the roof is loaded with cargo, including chickens and the occasional goat. At the other extreme, you will find very comfortable buses in Costa Rica, Panama, Venezuela, Argentina, Colombia, Brazil, Chile, and Uruguay. Some even have sleeping compartments and a restroom. The bus lines with the better buses always offer reserved seating with tickets purchased in advance, and there is usually no standing in the aisles.

Most major cities and towns have a *terminal de autobuses* (central bus terminal) in which the various bus companies have information boards showing routes, departure times, fares and whether the bus is direct or otherwise. The biggest and best terminals also have restaurants and various other services (be prepared, incidentally, to pay for the privilege of using restrooms).

There are a number of advantages to bus travel. You can get to just about anywhere by bus, even to the most remote village, and you can do it very cheaply. Local residents rely on buses to get to wherever they are going because so few people own cars and for this reason buses have to be inexpensive. I have had some very delightful experiences riding on all sorts of buses, mostly because of the people I have met. If you speak even the most basic Spanish, it is easy to get into conversations with your seat mate or with other people at bus stops. People are almost always pleased to meet and talk with foreigners. I meet the occasional girlfriend in this manner, and I have met a number of fellow American or European travelers this way. Although I have a car in Panama, I frequently take the bus simply for the adventure of social interaction.

There are some disadvantages, too. Many of the bus stations are badly crowded and infested with pickpockets. The toilets are sometimes so nasty that you try not to use them. Buses themselves are often very crowded, and if this bothers you, you will be bothered quite a bit. Bus stops on intercity routes are far apart, with several hours frequently between them. Since very few buses have restrooms, this can get uncomfortable, especially if you happen to be suffering with diarrhea at the time. Quite often, though, buses will stop to let someone use the bushes. Take your own toilet paper! Although in some countries, such as Costa Rica, bus schedules are exact and carefully adhered to, in many other countries they are loose and you will have difficulty predicting when you leave and when you will arrive. Finally, in the litany of disadvantages, some bus companies have horrible safety records, with poorly trained drivers and badly maintained buses.

Intracity Buses

Traveling around a city by bus, depending on the city, can be a good way to get around. They are very inexpensive, and you are likely to meet some interesting people in the process. Again, there are some disadvantages. The biggest problem I've encountered is in finding the right bus stop, and then knowing which bus to get on. Asking questions is the only way that I've found to do it. And it pays to ask not one, but several people. Frequently in Latin America people will give you an answer even though they actually don't know, and it makes sense to find at least two people that tell you the same thing.

The other problem is crowding during rush hour. A frequently heard comment is "at least sardines are dead when they are packed."

The crowding I can put up with as long as I can find a couple of women to stand between, but because of the crowding, buses are popular hangouts for pickpockets, especially in Guatemala City, Mexico City, Bogotá, Colombia; Managua, Nicaragua; and several other capitol cities (in Mexico City, crowding has gotten so bad that women now ride buses separately from men in order to reduce the problem of unwanted intimate touching). If you do ride a crowded bus, put your folding money in your socks or some other safe place.

Taxis

Taxis can be the best way to get around within a city, and they are inexpensive in Latin America.

They are usually easy to hail on the street (except during rain or rush hour), and regular taxi stands can normally be found in the centers of all cities. You do need to know well enough where you are going to be able to give the driver information to get you there. Unless you are reasonably conversant in Spanish, it is a good idea to have the address or directions already written out for him. If you can do so, ask what the cost will be for the trip. I've generally found taxi drivers to be reasonably honest about the fare, but have also had some loud arguments about it. Occasionally I have also been cheated.

Car Rental

There are advantages and disadvantages to renting a car. Some of the advantages are:

» 1) Cars can take you just about anywhere, including places where buses don't run (which aren't many).
» 2) You are not locked into someone else's schedule as you are with public transportation, which gives you a sense of freedom.
» 3) You don't have to bother with reservations, tickets, and waiting in lines.
» 4) You can change your schedule when you want to.
» 5) You can stop whenever you want to or need to, whether to admire a view, to take in a tourist site, or to take a leak.

Some of the disadvantages are:

» 1) They are usually outrageously expensive (only in Panama are rates similar to the U.S.), and except for in Venezuela and Mexico, gasoline is very expensive.

» 2) It can be dangerous. Local drivers, especially taxi and bus drivers, are terrible. Costa Rica, for instance, has the highest fatality rate per mile driven of all countries in the world. Passing on hills and curves are common, as is turning without giving signals.

» 3) In many areas the roads are in very bad condition, making them more dangerous.

» 4) It is both expensive and difficult to find parking in larger cities.

» 5) Cars are frequently vandalized unless parked in guarded lots or in garages.

In my opinion, the benefits of car rental don't really justify the risks and expense unless you particularly want to travel in areas outside the cities. They are much more trouble than they are worth in cities. Should you decide to rent a car, you need to know the following:

» 1) You must have a passport, a valid driver's license, and a credit card (or a lot of cash).

» 2) During peak travel periods such as Christmas, New Year's, *Carnaval*, or Easter, make a reservation as far in advance as possible.

» 3) Major companies do not have cars available in every city and town, but smaller companies usually do.

» 4) Get by with the smallest car possible. They cost less to rent, less for fuel, and are easier to park.

» 5) Make sure that the car you get is the newest one available, with the lowest mileage.

» 6) Most cars in Latin America have stick shifts.

» 7) Try to arrange an unlimited mileage agreement.

» 8) Examine insurance charges and deductibles carefully. This is fertile territory for rip-offs.

» 9) Expect to be lied to by the rental agent and read everything carefully.

» 10) Get everything in writing and make the assumption that verbal assurances mean nothing.

» 11) Examine very carefully the condition of the car before driving off, and be sure that every scratch and ding is noted in writing.

Chapter 38

Entering Countries

Immigration

Upon entering a country, the first step is to go through immigration *(migración)*, whether by land, sea, or air. If arriving by air, simply follow the crowd. If there isn't one, follow the signs to *Migración*. You will be asked to show your passport and/or any other entry documents that you may have. It is normally just a routine matter of rubber stamping your passport to show the date you entered the country.

Customs

The next step after leaving *Migración* is to proceed to the baggage pick-up area and get your luggage. Then get in line and move up to the customs inspection area *(Aduana)*. You may or may not be asked to open your luggage. Partly it depends on local policy, partly on how crowded it is, and partly on how you look. I normally just put the bags on the table and start to open them. This is taken as a sign that I have nothing to hide, and I am frequently told not to bother, and to just pass on through.

Some items that you are bringing in may be taxable. Normally, however, tourists are not examined carefully for taxable items. Also, belongings that are obviously used are ignored. If, however, you are entering with new items in their original packages, you may be required to pay tax on them, especially if there is more than one of the same item. They want to collect tax on items that are for resale, but if you explain that they are gifts for friends, you are likely to have no problem.

There are two things that you should never attempt to bring in to a foreign country: firearms and illegal drugs. Either can land you in jail. Agricultural products, such as cuttings and seeds, won't get you into trouble, but they will probably be confiscated if found.

Once you have made it through customs the next step is to get transportation to where you are going. Be very careful with your luggage at this point. Usually someone will ask to carry it for you. This is fine. I normally use the service. But, be sure that they are in uniform or have an identification tag showing that they are supposed to be picking up your luggage. Once your luggage is outside, watch it with an eagle's eyes. Many airports are safe, and have police standing around for security, but others aren't.

Changing Money

You can change your dollars into local currency at most international airports. This may be in the form of booths or counters, but in many cases individuals will be walking around calling out *"¡dólares!"* or *"¡cambio!"* Usually they are okay, but have in your hand only the exact amount that you want to change. The rate of exchange usually isn't as good as you can get in town, and it is a good idea to change only enough to see you through until the time that you can get to a bank or *casa de cambio*.

Getting to Your Hotel

If someone is not meeting you, and if your hotel has not arranged to pick you up, you will have to use some form of public transportation, and since airports are generally some distance from city centers, it can be an expensive proposition. Until you know your way around that particular city, I do not recommend buses. You can easily get lost or robbed. Usually the only two reasonable options are taxis and collectives. Quite a few airports have collective (*colectivo*) services, in which microbuses or taxis will take a number of passengers for a set price, and drop each off where he wants to go. The cost is usually quite a bit less than going as an individual in a taxi. I also frequently look for a single individual waiting for a taxi and ask if they would like to share the cost of a taxi into town. Most are happy to do so.

Chapter 39

Accommodations

Motels

You will occasionally see a sign announcing a *motel*. The word doesn't mean the same as it does in the United States. Invariably it will be a single floor building with parking adjacent to each room, and it will be surrounded by a high solid fence blocking off the view from the outside. *Moteles* in Latin America are built to accommodate lovers, not to provide shelter for travelers. They may rent by the hour or by the night, and if you can't find any other place, you can probably arrange to stay as if you were in a hotel.

Pensiones

Pensiones are very common in Latin America and can be excellent and inexpensive places to stay. They are normally small and offer few amenities, and may be converted residences. They are, in essence, like the boarding houses that existed in the United States except that most do not offer meals. Prices can frequently be negotiated, especially if you will be there for a week or more.

Hotels

Hotels in Latin America range from the seediest possible, accommodating cheap prostitutes, to the finest 5-stars you can find. My suggestion is to make use of one of the many travel guidebooks available to help you find the sort of hotel you are looking for. If you happen to get stuck without a guidebook, taxi drivers can frequently be of help. Most of them have arrangements with several hotels, and earn a finder's fee for bringing customers, but in any case they will have knowledge of a variety of hotels. Tip them for helping you out. Here are a few pointers regarding hotels in Latin America:

» 1) Only the better hotels will accept credit cards.

» 2) Almost all will require payment in advance or a credit card number to serve as a deposit.

» 3) Almost all will require your passport for identification.

» 4) The better hotels frequently have mini-bars with soft drinks, liquors, and snacks. They are always outrageously priced, and unless you don't mind the expense of the mini- bar, have a taxi driver take you to a supermarket and liquor store for your supplies. Some, however, don't allow guests to bring their own consumables. I have found several good ways to smuggle them in.

» 5) Nobody cares about the marital status of a couple that checks in. But, unlike in the United States, when you get a room in a hotel, you haven't rented the room. You have rented a place to sleep. If you bring in a lady later (sometimes even a male friend for a short visit), you are going to have to pay for two, and she will have to produce identification. If the woman appears to be a prostitute, most hotels will not permit her to enter without a little bribery to

the desk clerk, and frequently even that won't work.
Prostitutes normally have their own arrangements
with particular hotels.

» 6) In the elevator, the symbol "PB" means *Planta
Baja*, which is the lobby floor.

» 7) In the shower, "C" doesn't mean "cold." It means
"caliente" (hot). "F" means *"frío"* (cold). Usually the
symbol is accompanied by a color code, with red as
hot and blue as cold. But always check before jump-
ing in, because sometimes the plumbing is reversed.

» 8) Many of the less expensive hotels and *pensiones*
do not have central hot water, but instead use what
are commonly called "suicide showers." In this case
there is a shower head with an electrically operated
heating coil. Some are automatic and others have to
be manually turned on. In either case, it is better not
to touch the units with wet hands or while standing
in the shower. I've never heard of anyone being elec-
trocuted, but I have occasionally made the mistake
of accidentally touching the units while showering
and have received mild shocks.

» 9) Many hotels in tropical areas do not have hot
water at all, although the better ones almost always
do.

» 10) Air conditioning may or may not be available,
and fans may or may not be available. The better hotels are always air conditioned.

Chapter 40

Staying Safe

Crime in Latin America

Generally speaking, you are physically much safer in most cities of Latin America than you are in North American cities. Your wallet and camera, however, are much more likely to disappear. Every city is different, though, and those in which there is very little law enforcement are riskier than others. Most crime against foreigners in Latin American cities is a matter of taking property, and it rarely involves physical violence. Here are some safety suggestions:

» 1) Stay out of unsafe areas. How do you know what areas are unsafe? Look around you. It is no harder to spot unsavory characters in Latin America than it is in the United States. If you see them around, especially in groups, you are in the wrong place. Cross the street, run if necessary, and catch the first bus or cab and go somewhere else. But mainly, stay out of the slums. I will admit that I had some fun times in the slums. But it was when I was younger, tougher, and could run much faster. I don't even consider it now.

» 2) Prostitutes can be problems. Frequently they will distract a man while a companion picks the pocket. It is also fairly common for them to give a "Mickey

Finn" (a knock-out drug) and rob men while asleep. Never take them to your own place, and be very careful where they take you.

» 3) Don't wear jewelry. It is a magnet. I never wear rings or gold necklaces, and my watch originally cost $8. Dress as nicely as you want, but leave off the trimmings.

» 4) Assume that if you are carrying a camera, some-one will try to pull it out of your hand or off your shoulder. Assume also that someone will have a knife or razor to slit the strap. I have replaced the original straps of my cameras with lightweight chains. You might consider doing the same.

» 5) In hotels it pays to examine the windows. If a win-dow is accessible from the outside, don't put your valuables on a table near the window where a hand with a stick can reach in and take them.

» 6) Stay sober on the streets. Intoxication is an invita-tion.

» 7) Don't carry a wallet. I do now, because I live in a town just as safe as any midwestern U.S. town, but I never do when I am in a city. Take with you only what you need. Put your folding money in your socks. If you are wearing jeans with a watch pocket, that pocket serves well, too. Front pockets aren't any better than back pockets, regardless of what some guidebooks tell you. I once had a tri-fold wallet, care-fully placed in the left front pocket of tight jeans, lightened by some $200. Oddly enough, only the money was taken. The wallet and credit cards were left, as were all of the other contents except for a Zippo lighter that was also in the pocket. That, sir, was talent, and pickpockets have lots of talent in Latin American cities.

» 8) It is hard for an American tourist not to look like an American tourist. Try, though, not to look vulner-able. Act as if you know what you are doing and where you are going. Be friendly, but if you can, con-vey the impression that you will twist the head off of anyone who tries to bother you.

Chapter 41

Learning Spanish

If you are seriously looking for a Latin American wife, there is absolutely no excuse not to learn Spanish (or Portuguese, if you are considering Brazil). It is not a difficult language. The pronunciation is easily learned because it is regular, and most of the verbs are regular.

I learned with only a grammar book, dictionary, and immersion. I think, though, that a basic course would have made things a lot easier. Unless you live in the wilds of Montana (or some such place), you will be able to find a course in Spanish. Check into your local community college. Most have evening courses. Adult education programs frequently offer Spanish courses. At the very least, buy a grammar book, a dictionary, and a series of audio tapes that teach Spanish. You owe it to your future wife.

A good book to help you get a handle on some useful Spanish phrases is *Spanish Lingo for the Savvy Gringo* by Elizabeth Reid, $14.95 (ISBN 1-881791-08-4). It's readable and entertaining, not a textbook. In addition to Spanish, it also includes a lot of cultural information and an appendix on Spanish slang. It can be ordered by calling 800-356-9315.

Some gentlemen take advantage of modern technology and get some assistance from computer software programs. Letters can be prepared in English or Spanish and then converted into the other language. Only consider bi-directional programs (from one language translated into another, and then back to the original typed language). This will help with idea and sentence structure. Be aware that every country has it's individual idioms and ways of constructing sentences, and your letters will appear somewhat stilted to her, but still the communication will be accurate. Contact a local software store for their recommendations for programs.

If you are in a hurry and don't have time to study Spanish, take with you a Spanish-English dictionary and an electronic pocket translator. I don't especially like the electronic translators because they do not give alternative meanings as a dictionary does, but they are much more enjoyable to use with your lady. Both of you will get a kick out of punching in the words and seeing how they come out.

If you are unwilling or unable to do any of the above, don't worry too much about it. Somehow, communication always seems to take place when two people want it to. So does mis-communication, especially when you don't want it to.

Part V

How to Meet That Special Lady

Chapter 42

Correspondence

===

You may have already been provided with a lot of information regarding the correspondence process. Here I want to discuss the relative merits of the three methods offered by T.L.C. Worldwide, Inc.

Catalogs

TLC Worldwide regularly publishes photo catalogs of selected Latin American women every three months. The women are new in each catalog, and there are usually more than 500 photographs, along with some personal data about each lady. Promotional brochures are free (they know how to wet your appetite), but you have to buy the addresses. You will need to see current T.L.C. literature to get the current prices. Free promotional photo brochures can be obtained by calling (713) 896-9224. Speak slowly and clearly when you leave a message to avoid any delays in your request.

Personal Listings

Men's personal listing advertisements work a lot like the lady's catalogs do, but in reverse. T.L.C. advertises widely in many countries in Latin America. Each girl who writes in for information receives a free copy of the men's listings, which include photographs, biographical data, and addresses. While there is no actual information available about how many women get to see the listings, it is very clear that they get passed around to friends, and every man pictured gets a very wide exposure, possibly to several thousands Latinas. Your only problem in this situation is that you are likely to get dozens to hundreds of letters, and you will have to select those to which you will respond. Some men have used form letters, but I do not recommend it. A short, hand-written note along with a photo is the best way to get things rolling. Personal listings work best for gentlemen too busy to initiate the letter writing process, or those just beginning the international romance experience. We strongly encourage all gentlemen to participate in a personal listing advertisement.

Videotapes

During each of the T.L.C. Tours, they arrange a separate room for photography near the ballroom where the receptions are being held. Here, each girl who wishes to join the program is photographed for publication in the next photo catalog. A videotape is also made, in which she is able to tell you some things about herself (sometimes in English, sometimes in Spanish, but more often a mixture of the two).

The advantage of viewing a videotape is that you get to hear her voice, see her expressions, and watch her body language and movements. It is the next best experience to being with her in person. T.L.C. normally photographs more than 200 women during each tour, but far fewer wind up in the final edited videotapes. Bruce and James are very selective about who gets in, and you are sure to have the cream of the crop in the videos. However, only a small number of the ladies in those countries in which there are tours are actually able attend, based on their location. While the videotapes are certainly the best way to be able to see the ladies, only a small percentage of the T.L.C. participants are presented, and the catalogs offer a much wider selection.

Whichever method you choose (and you might well use all three at once), it is still a matter of correspondence, and you will eventually need to make a trip to visit that special lady. Correspondence is an excellent way to get to know another person with whom you may share the rest of your life.

Chapter 43

Tours

T.L.C. Worldwide conducts about six tours per year to Mexico, Colombia (Cali and Barranquilla), Panama, Venezuela, and Honduras. If the number of marriages that have come out of the tours are any indication, it is an excellent way to meet your life-mate. Over 1/2 of the tour participants are engaged or married as a direct result of these tours. The tour concept will be much easier to understand if I describe for you how a typical tour is organized. Normally the very best hotel in the city is used (assuming that certain important criteria can be met). A large ballroom is reserved for the two weekend receptions (at each of which are normally a minimum of 200 women, different each night), catering is arranged for refreshments and appetizers, a disc jockey is contracted, door guards are usually hired, and a number of T.L.C. girls who speak good English are hired to work as interpreters and assist clients with introductions. T.L.C. is convinced that an elegant setting enhances the reputation of their activities, and everything is in good taste, carefully planned and dignified.

The men usually arrive on Thursday afternoon or evening, and ordinarily (except for stragglers) someone will meet them at the airport and arrange transportation to the hotel. Fridays are pretty much free days. Normally small groups of men will go out for sightseeing. T.L.C. always has suggestions as to what might be interesting. On Friday evening the first of the two main social receptions gets underway around 8 PM. I say around 8 PM, because the first of the girls usually start showing up by seven, hoping to get first shot at the guys. About midway through the evening the music stops, all of the tour participants are seated at long tables, and one of the interpreters goes from man to man with a microphone, interpreting if necessary, allowing each to say something about himself, so that all of the girls will have a chance to know a little about each guest. Then the music resumes, refreshments are served, and the party continues, usually ending around 1 AM, although many people go to discotheques afterwards.

Saturday is a repeat of Friday, except that some new ladies attend. By Saturday many of the men will have met ladies from the Friday reception and have dates during the day.

On Sunday afternoon there is usually a pool party with refreshments and barbecue, either at the hotel or some other choice location. Each man is given one special invitation on Friday, which he may use to invite the girl of his choice (from either Friday or Saturday night) to the pool party. T.L.C. also invites a number of especially attractive girls to make up for any who received invitations, but didn't show up.

Mondays are free days. Most men will have met one or two special girls by this time, can choose whom they are most serious about, and will have dates or be meeting her family. Staff is available to help with interpreting. On Tuesday morning the tour is officially over, and most men head for home, although frequently some will have begun something they are not ready to leave behind, and will stay over a few more days.

There are some steps that you can take that will make a tour more productive. Clothing is important to Latin Americans. For these events the girls dress in their finest clothing. You will be doing yourself a favor, and make a good impression, if you wear a coat and tie to the receptions. A 3-piece suit isn't necessary. A sport coat will do fine, but dress as nicely as you would for a reception in the United States, especially since you will be a guest of honor.

You will be astonished at the number of women at the receptions. You will not be able to remember all whom you meet. Be sure to carry a notepad for jotting down phone numbers and addresses.

There will certainly be women who will want to meet you, but who can't because of the others surrounding you, and there will be those whom you would like to meet, but find that you don't have the time to talk with them. I suggest that before you leave home have some calling cards made up with your photo and address. The photo is needed so that they will remember who you are. Unless you want to receive collect calls, it would be a good idea to leave off your phone number. You can then pass out the cards to whomever you wish for corresponding in the future. It will be easy enough to write in your number if you want a collect call from a specific lady.

Another suggestion is to purchase International Telephone Calling Cards before you leave. You can give these to your girlfriend (if you have made your selection by then) to assist her in calling you later. I suggest that you designate specific times and pre-plan when you will communicate.

A Letter

T.L.C. sent a letter to previous tour participants, encouraging them to make open-ended
comments on their experiences and especially on
their impressions of Latin American women. One particularly articulate letter we are printing in its entirety
(excluding last name and address). The letter is authen-
tic, complete, unaltered, on file, and is reproduced by
permission of its author.

(from) Fred B.
Louisiana

T.L.C. Worldwide, Inc.
Attention: James McLeod
P.O. Box 924994
Houston TX 77292-4994

Dear Dr. McLeod:
Per your request, I am submitting answers to
your questions concerning my experiences on
my trips to South America. I have only been on
two trips, and am planning my third trip for
sometime this summer, but I have had some ex-
periences that I would not mind sharing with
you that you might find relevant for your book.

1) Positive and negative aspects of Latin
women: On the negative side, I would say that
one of the most common complaints made by
many of the men who visit Latin America, is
that the women there tend to be rather emo-
tional, having a low threshold for anger, frus-
tration, etc. Another common complaint is that

the women do not have a respect for the time of others, though this does not apply just for the women. A time could be set for a woman to come by a man's house, and if she cannot make it on time, no matter what the reason causing her to be late, she will not call, or make any attempt to let the guy know that she will be late. This was a very irritating bad habit of the women there, and in spite of talking with guilty individuals, the problem occurred over and over again.

On the positive side, the women are very happy, and seem to have a real enthusiasm for life. They tend to not be materialistic and instead, look towards the more obvious characteristics of a personality that are important in a relationship, such as honesty, reliability, sincerity, etc. Latin women also are known to be truly committed to a man, once she feels secure and safe in this man's presence. They appear to be very family oriented, with the family usually being more important than occupation or other interests.

2) Possible positive results: The most positive factor to consider in a relationship is the commitment offered by both parties. No man could ask any more concerning commitment than what is offered by these women in Latin America. Once a woman feels good about a relationship, she is committed for the long term and will see a relationship through the worst of times. This is in direct contrast to the women of the U.S. who may walk out of a relationship at the first sign of difficulty or rough times.

3) *Men traveling to South America in search of a romantic partner will experience some obstacles in their search, which can turn into problems without proper attention:*

☐ a) *Language barriers can be an obvious obstacle, so it makes sense for anyone thinking about traveling to South America, to freshen up on their Spanish somewhat, with a tutor or even a home study course, before going. Although interpreters are available most of the time, a man will find himself seriously handicapped when he finds himself alone with the woman of his dreams, only to find that he can't communicate effectively with her. The women of South America are definitely impressed with a man when she knows he can communicate some basic ideas in Spanish. And if a man is going to all the trouble of making a trip to South America, spending a serious amount of money, and spending lots of time to find a woman, it is logical to assume that, should a man discover the woman of his dreams, he will have to learn the language, so why not get a head start by studying a little before going on the trip.*

☐ b) *Another possible obstacle that might be a problem is making the determination if your woman is sincere in caring for you as a person, or is she just looking for a trip to the U.S.? This is not too hard to figure out, but to the unsuspecting man, who is eager to find the woman of his dreams, he may be lured into thinking that a woman cares for him, when in reality, she just wants a ticket to the U.S. If a woman expresses her wish to come to the U.S. shortly after an introduction, it is an obvious warning that her intentions may not be sincere. Any man needs to utilize extreme caution in talking about bringing a woman back to the States shortly after an introduction, because there has been no time for the two persons to get to know each other, or to discover what each wants out of a relationship.*

☐ *c) A third obstacle that does occur relates to trying to determine if your lady friend is interested in you or your pocket book. While it is true that all women attempt to marry up the "social-economic" ladder, it is a different situation when a woman asks a man for money for personal things early in a relationship. It is common courtesy for a man to pay for taxi fares, collect phone calls, etc., but when a woman begins asking for money to have her nails done, to pay her bills, etc., the red flag should go up immediately. This happened to me, after I had already formed the conclusion that this woman was after money and a trip to the U.S., and not truly interested in me. The first clue came when she took me to one of the most expensive restaurants in the city, and then repeatedly expressed her interest in coming to the U.S. to get married, after only having three outings! I said no to her concern about getting married, and the relationship went no further. So, a word to the wise should be sufficient.*

4) Positives and negatives with tours:

☐ *a) Many men will be awestruck at the number of attractive women, and will act like a kid in a candy store, trying to sample a little of all available, instead of forming a few good relationships, and proceeding from there. While it is important that a man should speak with and make friends with as many women as possible, it is also important to find the two or three women that are attractive, and then work at de-*

275

veloping relationships with these, then if nothing develops, go on to some of the others that are on the list.

☐ b) Due to time constraints placed on most tours, men will have to act decisively in meeting women at the socials. There is not much time to stand idly by, wishing for some beautiful dish to walk up and make conversation; this is the time for all men to come out of their shells, and have conversation with as many women as possible, striking up friendships with the ones he is most interested in. Because of the time constraints on tours, a man may only be able to barely get acquainted with a woman, when he finds it is time to leave, but then the relationship can be carried on via correspondence, and arrange made for another trip sometime in the near future.

☐ c) The most obvious benefit of taking a tour is that a man can meet as many women as he desires in a short span of time, and then make a decision which ones he is interested in, then proceed from there. He can see visually how a woman carries herself, how she dresses, and how she functions in a social atmosphere, all of which may be difficult or impossible to determine from correspondence. Another benefit of the tours is meeting other men from all over the U.S. who are taking a trip for the same purpose, and a camaraderie develops that makes the trips so much more fun and entertaining. I presently am in frequent correspondence with two men that I met on tours, and we are planning other trips to South America in the future.

5) Positives and negatives with correspondence:

☐ a) If a man is not financially capable, or his schedule does not allow a tour as part of his agenda, then correspondence is in order. Many women prefer to get to know a man by correspondence, because they are mainly interested in the character, morality, etc., and these traits will become obvious after correspondence has taken place. Writing letters for a few months prior to a trip not only lets people become more acquainted, but is ideal from a financial standpoint, while it allows some time for a man who truly wants to meet any of the women he may be writing, to save some funds to take that tour sometime in the near future.

☐ b) The most obvious negative concerning correspondence is that if a person is not completely honest and sincere when writing, the other might be in for quite a surprise should a meeting ever take place. But my opinion is that this does not occur that often, since most people, both from the U.S. and South America, are honest and sincere, and attempt to portray a legitimate picture of themselves when writing.

☐ c) Another potential negative of correspondence is the time it takes for mail to deliver letters to and from each country. Regular first class mail can take 17 or 18 days, and there is not even a guarantee that mail will be delivered in this period of time, due to the unreliability of the mail systems in South America. For those who choose to not wait for five or six weeks to hear back from their women, the next option is express mail for $18.00, which should be delivered in 3 to 5 days, but again, there is no guarantee as to actual time this can take either. And more importantly, if a man spends too much of his money on sending express mail, he is using up the money that could be used on an upcoming tour.

6) Things that men should know before beginning a search:

☐ *a) Men that cannot speak one word of Spanish will have a handicap.*

☐ *b) Each man should know what qualities he feels are important in a woman, or else much time will be wasted in chasing after the wrong woman.*

☐ *c) Most of the women are very traditional, with church and family being the basis of most of their lives.*

☐ *d) The majority of women in South American countries do not leave home until marriage; therefore, if a woman has never married, she may still live at home and must therefore abide by the rules of the house, including what time she must return from social outings.*

☐ *e) All South American countries live in a different world as far as time is concerned; punctuality is non-existent, and it is not uncommon for a woman to show up 30 or 45 minutes late for a social outing. There is not much that a man can do about this, other than accept it, and realize that this will be difficult, if not impossible to change.*

☐ *f) Have realistic expectations: If a 55 year old man is 5'2" tall, it is unrealistic for him to be searching for a beauty queen 18 years old that is 5'9" tall. The same rules for courting women in the U.S. apply in South American countries, with the exception that women in all Latin American countries prefer to marry men much older than themselves, and it is not uncommon for a woman to marry a man twice her age.*

☐ *g) Women of Latin American countries are not as materialistic as American women; most could not care less what kind of car a man drives, or*

278

how much money he has in the bank. What
most women care about is stability in a relationship and the ability of a man to care for her
and the family.

☐ h) American men are considered a "desirable
catch" to South American women. This naturally is comforting to American men, but it
should not dictate a man's behavior to these
women. Some men in a similar situation might
try to take advantage by scoring with as many
women as possible, like sampling all the pieces
in the candy store, but before long, word will
spread about this type of behavior, and men
might find it difficult to get women to go out
once this occurs. So it is best that a man treat
all women with a great deal of respect, not expecting a sexual encounter on the first date, and
generally not taking advantage of the great esteem they hold for the American male.

☐ i) No man should take a tour with the intent of
bringing back a wife. To do so would put pressure on each and every social encounter, and
could force a man to make some hasty decisions. Instead, a man should go on a tour with
the idea in mind of having lots of fun, while
meeting lots of pretty women who truly want a
serious relationship. A first tour should be made
with the idea in mind of meeting as many
women as possible, then getting to know two or
three by correspondence, and then scheduling
another tour in the near future. I know of no
situations here in the U.S. where a man goes to
a party with the intention of finding a wife. Instead, he goes for the potential of social interaction, meeting some interesting people, and
making friends. So social gatherings on tours
should be treated the same, with men attending
in order to meet some quality women and to become well acquainted over time. Setting a goal

279

of finding a woman on one tour, not only takes the fun out of meeting lots of different people, but could lead a man down a path of ruin if he should be too hasty in choosing someone in the span of a few days to spend the rest of his life with. It will be a lot less expensive to take another trip to meet more women than to have to deal with the financial and emotional turmoil that would occur should a man make a hasty decision concerning the woman he marries.

Dr. McLeod:
I hope these thoughts are helpful. Not much organization or planning went into these ideas. I just put them down as they came to me. Good luck on your project.
—Fred

Part VI

Legal Aspects of Marriage & Immigration

Chapter 44

Immigration Options

General Overview

After a relationship has been established abroad the task of getting your fiancee into the United States legally is at hand. Normally you will have to have your fiancee or wife processed through the Immigration and Naturalization Service (I.N.S.). Depending on numerous factors this process could be as little as 2-3 months or as long as 8-12 months. Knowing your options up front will help you make the best decision for both of you regarding your future immigration.

If you can prepare your own tax return, then you can file the appropriate forms with I.N.S. yourself. Some I.N.S. forms are provided free to the public by visiting a local office or by calling. You could also hire a lawyer (Board Certified in Immigration Law), but they are normally quite expensive. T.L.C. Worldwide Inc. sells an *Immigration Guide* for only $99.00 which contains official I.N.S. forms arranged in a logical, organized, chronological order. This kit can keep you one step ahead in the preparation aspect since you already have the actual documents that will be sent to your fiancee from the American Embassy. Periodically T.L.C. has this kit reviewed by a Board Certified Immigration Attorney and we feel it's worth many times the price.

There are essentially three methods used to bring your foreign fiancee or wife back to the United States to live with you: Fiancee (K-1) Visa, Petition for Alien Family Member (your spouse), or Tourist Visa.

Fiancee Visa

This visa will permit your fiancee to enter the United States with the intention of the two of you marrying within 90 days of her arrival. If after that period of time no marriage occurs, then she must return to her country of origin.

This visa normally is the quickest (3-5 months) in getting your fiancee to the U.S.

a. Requirements

» 1. Both of you must be unmarried (no pending divorce), and thus legal to marry.

» 2. You must have met your fiancee in person within the last two years. Typically this meeting will occur in her native country.

» 3. You are a U.S. citizen.

» 4. There exists an "intent" of marriage between the two parties to become married within the 90 day period of her arrival. For this reason it is a good idea to keep all telephone bills, letters between the two of you, and any announcements regarding the future wedding.

» 5. Fee of $75.00 sent to the regional I.N.S. office along with the related paperwork. This petition will be reviewed, and if approved will be sent to the American Embassy in her country. The American embassy will then forward the appropriate papers to your fiancee to schedule an interview & to complete her application. Only after this interview (with her visa approved) will your spouse be permitted to enter the United States. Only then should you arrange airline tickets for her.

b. Forms and Documentation Needed

The Petition, forms filed with the Immigration & Naturalization Service (I.N.S.)

» Forms I-129F (Pink Form)
» (2) Form G-325A (one for each of you.)
» Fee of $ 75.00
» 1 Photograph each of your fiancee and you. (Specifications apply)
» 2 certified copies of each of your birth certificates
» Copies of all divorce and death certificates if either party was previously married
» Other documents proving the couple has personally met within the last 2 years and have the intention of marriage (Do not file these documents unless requested.)
» The Application (Interview at the U.S. Embassy after I.N.S. approval)
» Form OF-230, Parts 1 and 2.
» Affidavit of Support (Evidence), Form I-864
» Fiancee Visa Petition approval from I.N.S. in the U.S.A.
» All other documents originally filed with the petition including correspondence, telephone calls, and wedding announcements
» Long-form certified birth certificates for the applicant and any accompanying child
» Passports valid for at least six months beyond the interview date for the applicant and any accompanying child

» (3) photographs each of the applicant and any accompanying child
» Completed Medical examination of the applicant
» Appropriate Fee

In this interview your fiancee will be asked questions regarding how the two of you met and how well she knows you. Most of these questions will be asked from the information you provided I.N.S. in the form I-129F. Your fiancee should be calm, relaxed and confident in this interview. As long as the two of you entered this engagement in good faith you have nothing to worry about.

Petition for Alien Family Member (Your Spouse)

This visa will permit your wife (after marrying abroad) to legally enter the United States. The specifics of "Marrying Abroad" will be covered in the next chapter. After you have successfully married outside of the U.S.A., you will need to apply for a Petition for Alien Family Member, Form I-130 form with the Immigration and Naturalization Service (I.N.S.).

For unknown reasons this visa can take longer to process than the Fiancee K-1 Visa. Normal processing takes anywhere from 4-12 months. If any document is submitted incomplete or wrong, the delay could be even longer. After returning from your honeymoon you will submit the appropriate paperwork to the regional I.N.S. office nearest you.

Completely read the instructions for each form. Forms and documentation needed after the marriage ceremony:

A. Petition to I.N.S (forms filed with the Immigration and Naturalization Service)

» Form I-130

» 2 Forms G-325A (One for you and one for your spouse) with photos

» 1 photograph each, of you and your spouse (2 photographs total) one of each G-325A

» Your Long-Form (Certified Copy) Birth Certificate, the "Long Form" is the one containing the names of your parents.

» Your spouse's Long-Form (Certified Copy) Birth certificate.

If Either you or your spouse were previously married, certified copies of:

» All marriage certificates (for both)

» Divorce and/ or Death certificates showing termination of all previous marriages (for both)

» Marriage Certificate (foreign marriages)

» Certificate of Translation (notarized)

» $80 Fee

B. Acknowledgement Notices from the I.N.S. Regarding Your Petition:

1. I.N.S. Receipt notice (normally sent to you within 30 days from your petition date.

2. This I.N.S. Petition Approval is sent to the National Visa Center in Portsmouth NH 03801-2909 (normally within 3 months)

3. Approval from National Visa Center, sent to the U.S. Embassy in your wife's country of residence

C. Final Processing at the U.S.A. Embassy (your fiancee's interview)

*Originals and certified copies **only!**

» Passport
» 4 Photos (signed), per I.N.S. specifications
» 1 Front Side
» 1 Back Side
» 1 Without Signature
» 1 Extra
» Form 230 part I
» Form 230 part II
» Birth Certificate
» Marriage Certificate
» Divorce Decree, if applicable
» Financial Evidence, Form I-864
» Medical Examination
» Birth Certificate of children under 21
» $200.00 Fee, no large bills

After everything is approved, she will be permitted to join you. After she is approved, you can then purchase her airline ticket.

Tourist Visas

Tourist Visas are issued by the American Embassies abroad. They are not issued routinely in third world countries unless an applicant (your girlfriend) has assets, property, and political or social status. This policy is to ensure that unskilled, poorly educated people will not enter the United States and burden our economic system and welfare or social programs. If the applicant can demonstrate their willingness and the probability to return to their homeland a visa could be granted. Thus, for most single ladies without substantial property, a tourist visa is really not an option for visitation or immigration.

If the lady you are interested in has a tourist visa already, then you're lucky. She can visit you without you leaving the country. If she does visit you and you marry her, you will simply file form I-485 with a local office I.N.S. to apply for her resident card and adjust her Visa status.

Cautionary Note: Do not become involved with any persons who claim to be able to purchase tourist visas in foreign countries. Typically these are illegal scams which could jeopardize your fiancee's ability to apply for a Fiancee Visa or a Relative (Spousal) Visa at a later date legitimately. Never list inaccurate or incorrect information in any of these filings.

Chapter 45

Marrying Abroad

General Information

After several months of letter writing and telephone calls your desire to meet the lady of your dreams will be at its peak. You will need travel plans, supporting documentation, and a list of items "not to forget." These items include duplicate copies of important documents such as your passport, travelers checks, airline tickets, etc. You will need a valid U.S. passport for almost every country that you wish to visit. (See Chapter 33).

Your fiancee should meet you at the airport upon your arrival. She can help you with hotel accommodations, general sight seeing, and of course restaurants and the local nightlife. A very important piece of advice here is to meet her family. Good people are raised in nurturing family environments. Be somewhat suspicious if her family has no real interest in you, or they do not welcome you with open arms. Remember, you traveled to meet her and her family, but you are not obligated to marry her. Hopefully all goes well, the love between you is established, and the two of you contemplate marriage.

If you were relatively sure of your intentions before departing, you will need the appropriate paperwork to accomplish your goals for marriage in her country. If you plan to marry abroad, you must telephone or write to the embassy in which your fiancee is a resident (See Chapter 33). Often these countries also have satellite consulate offices in larger cities. Call directory assistance in the city nearest you to determine if a local foreign embassy exists. They can provide you with a detailed checklist of requirements needed to marry in their country. Visiting, calling or writing your local INS office may also benefit you. It's better to have too much documentation than not enough. Below are items you will generally need, but specific information from the country you will visit should be confirmed beforehand. Your fiancee can also help gather information to minimize any future setbacks.

Required Documents to Marry in a Foreign Country

A. Requirements, never-married U.S. Citizens:
» U.S. Passport And Photocopy
» Certified Birth Certificate (with seal of authenticity) and photocopy
» Sworn Statement from Consular Section stating that you are single (Fee approximately $10.00 or equivalent in the local currency)
» Resident Card and Photocopy (only if you are a resident and not a U.S. citizen).

B. Requirements, Previously Married Persons: Single by Divorce
Present Birth Certificate and Court-Certified Copy of the

Divorce Decree (may need to be translated into Spanish and accompanied by a Certificate of Accurate Translation).

Single by Widowhood
Present the Death Certificate

C. Requirements for Your Foreign National Fiancee
(your fiancee and the attorney's responsibility):
Engaged over 21 years old
» Photocopies of identity cards of the engaged
» Photocopies of identity cards of the two witnesses
» Photocopies of the Birth Certificate of the engaged (the name has to be the same as the identity card)

Engaged under 21 Years Old
She can only marry if the parents shown on the birth certificate give the authorization at the time of the wedding, or if one of the parents is deceased, the death certificate is necessary of the deceased parent. If both parents are deceased, then the grandparents have to give the authorization.

Possible Additional Requirements:
» Public announcement of the future wedding
» Medical Certificate
» Baptismal Record (in Colombia)

In summary, perform the following to minimize any problems regarding marrying abroad before departing.
» 1. Telephone the U.S. Embassy Abroad and/or her foreign embassy (in the U.S.A.) for the necessary documents needed. Telephone numbers to foreign embassies are located in Chapter 33 and in the government publication "Tips For Travelers To Central And South America" booklet or visit their internet site at http://travel.state.gov/.

293

» 2. Your fiancee can help you locate an attorney and gather additional (country-specific) information.

» 3. Consider purchasing *T.L.C. Worldwide's Immigration Guide* containing official forms (See ordering information at the back of this book.)

The Economics of a Courtship Abroad

Getting married is expensive. But then again, so is the price of a new pickup truck loaded with options. A recent article in *Bride* magazine placed the average cost of a domestic marriage at over $25,000 not including the engagement ring or honeymoon. Initially you might think that an international courtship would be even more expensive, but the fact is that forming a relationship abroad can be accomplished at a mere fraction of the cost of marrying in the United States.

Latin American ladies have not been conditioned by Hallmark, the jewelry industry, or her friends and family that the amount of expenditures incurred by the man on dating expenses (and the subsequent marriage) are directly tied to his level of love and devotion.

Everyone recognizes that overspending for special occasions (holidays and weddings) does not enhance any future happiness or guarantee a lifelong marriage. Almost all of our clients prefer small civil ceremonies which consist of the immediate family members and close friends, rather than the ambiance of a "Lifestyles of the Rich & Famous" wedding.

Of course individual expenditures will vary. The following should give you some idea of the expenses associated with establishing a relationship and marrying your new latin bride.

Estimated Courtship Expenses

	Low	High
Purchasing ladies' addresses or a personal listing ad	$150.00	$1000.00
Postage, Photos	50.00	200.00
Telephone calls	150.00	600.00
Passport & Photos	75.00	75.00
T.L.C. Immigration Kit	100.00	0
Immigration Attorney	0	1500.00
Airfare	400.00	800.00
Hotel (5 nights)	200.00	625.00
Dating	200.00	700.00
Wedding	200.00	1000.00
I.N.S. Fees (approximate)	400.00	400.00
Lady's one way airfare	300.00	600.00
Miscellaneous	500.00	?
Estimated Totals	$2,725.00	$7,500.00*

*There really are no boundaries on the high limit. We feel this high limit falls within a "reasonable test" based on feedback and discussions with numerous married couples.

These figures are by no means a guide-line or a budget. Rather, they are rough estimates for you to begin your own calculations to determine the feasibility of a marriage abroad. Numerous factors could increase these totals which we feel are realistic based on numerous years of feedback from our clients. Most men are pleasantly surprised at the low cost of their marriage plans and expenditures in a foreign country.

Larger weddings, repeat visits, lawyers fees, or meeting several ladies on different excursions could add to your cash outlay. But remember, you shouldn't be marrying abroad to save money, but rather to find a more compatible life-mate. You can't put a price-tag on this, or the positive life experiences you will reap daily from meeting the lady of your dreams.

Part VII

Guide to Latin American Countries

Chapter 46

Argentina

Republic of Argentina *(República Argentina)*
Area: 1,072,067 square miles
    Second largest country in South America.
Population: 34,600,000 (mid-1995)
    Average annual rate of increase, 1.3%
    Density per square mile, 32.2
Labor force: 12% agricultural, 31% industrial, 57%
    services.
Capital: Buenos Aires
Largest cities: (est. 1991) Buenos Aires
    (2,961,000); Córdoba, (1,180,000); La
    Matanza (1,121,000); General Sarmiento
    (647,000); Rosario (950,000, 1983); Morón
    (642,000, 1983).
Religion: Roman Catholic 90%.
Literacy rate: 95%
Languages: Spanish, English, Italian, German,
    French.
Immigrant ethnic subgroups: Descendants of Ital-
    ian and German immigrants. Also Welsh.

Geography

With an area slightly less than one third of the United States and second in South America only to its eastern neighbor, Brazil, in size and population, Argentina is a plain, rising from the Atlantic to the Chilean border and the high Andes peaks. Aconcagua (23,034 ft.) is the highest peak in the world outside of Asia. It is bordered by Bolivia and Paraguay on the north, and by Uruguay on the east.

The northern area is the swampy and partly wooded Gran Chaco, bordering on Bolivia and Paraguay. South of that are the rolling, fertile pampas, rich for agriculture and grazing, and supporting most of the population. Next southward is Patagonia, a region of cool, arid steppes with some wooded and fertile sections.

Tourist Information

Visa: Not needed by U.S. citizens. A free, renewable 90-day tourist card is issued upon entering the country. Passport required.

U.S. Embassy: Buenos Aires, Columbia 4300
Phone: 774-2282

Customs: Usually routine for foreign visitors, although they may be interested in any electronic equipment you are bringing. If you arrive from on of the Andean countries there may be a drug search.

Money: The monetary unit is the *peso,* divided into 100 *centavos.* The new *peso* was introduced in 1992 at a par with the U.S. dollar and is currently holding its value against the dollar. Cash dollars can be exchanged at banks and *"casas de cambio."* Traveler's checks are difficult to change, and have sizeable commissions. Dollars are widely accepted in lieu of pesos.

Postal System: ENCOTEL, the postal service, is also responsible for telegraph, fax, and telex services. The system was riddled with corruption, and many items never arrived and were often opened if they appear to contain something valuable. The system is now being privatized, and is likely to be highly improved. All mail to Argentina should be sent by registered mail.

Telephone System: Collect telephone calls are possible from most (but not all) long-distance offices. Offices in major cities have direct lines to overseas operators. Most public telephones use tokens (*"fichas"*), available from kiosks and telephone offices. The telephone system, once one of the worst in Latin America, was recently privatized and is now reported to be modern and efficient.

Health: There are very few health hazards. No vaccinations are required. Many common prescriptions are available over the counter. Urban water supplies are usually potable.

Risks: Argentina is much safer than most other Latin American countries. You can travel safely in most areas of Buenos Aires at any hour, but watch out for petty theft. Police frequently stop motorists for minor violations that carry high fines with the expectation that a bribe will be paid.

Cultural Specifics

Greetings: When introduced, men shake hands with other men. If men and women are introduced by a woman friend, they sometimes kiss, but usually shake hands. Women usually kiss other women when they're introduced. Close male friends hug one another in greeting. Women who are friends shake hands with both hands and kiss one another on both cheeks. Men and women friends usually kiss. Use titles when appropriate. They are important in Argentina. Use titles with the last name. At large parties, introduce yourself. Shake hands and say goodbye to each person when you leave.

Dress: Remember that Argentina is in the Southern Hemisphere, and while North America is having summer, it is winter there, and the further south you go, the colder it will be. Warm clothing will be needed from June to August. Central heating is not common. Casual wear for men is a sweater, shirt, and pants, or just shirt and pants. For women, casual wear is a top with very chic pants or a skirt. Argentines dress more formally than in other parts of Latin America. Don't wear shorts on the street, although they are fine at the beach or swimming pool. Bathing suits are conservative in comparison to many other Latin American countries. As in many other parts of Latin America, Argentines are very conscious of what other people wear, and evaluate them on that basis.

Meals: Breakfast is usually eaten between 7:00 and 8:00, and is light. Lunch is usually eaten about 1:00 PM. and is a complete meal, usually including beef (very popular and inexpensive in Argentina), and concluding with espresso style coffee. 4:00 PM to 6:00 is tea time, in which cakes or cookies are served with coffee or tea. Dinner is usually served around 10:00 PM and is a complete meal similar to lunch, normally including steak and salad.

Table Manners: If you are the guest of honor, expect to sit at the head of the table. Some families serve family style, others have a maid to serve each person individually. Argentines cut meat by holding it with a fork and cutting through the tines of the fork.

Dining Out: Argentines eat a lot of beef because it is so widely produced. In fact, some of the beef we eat is imported from Argentina. Much of the cuisine, though, is Italian and Spanish. Buenos Aires (frequently called the Paris of Latin America), however, has a large immigrant population and there are many German and French restaurants and Jewish delicatessens along with the usual Chinese restaurants and American fast-food restaurants.

Tipping: Give hotel porters $1.00 for all your bags. Taxi drivers don't need to be given tips. Airport porters should receive 25 cents per bag. Unless a tip is included in your restaurant bill, leave 10%.

Holidays: New Year's Day (Jan. 1); *Carnaval* (Saturday before Ash Wednesday through Tuesday); Maundy Thursday (Thursday before Easter—only some offices are closed); Good Friday; Labor Day (May 1); Anniversary of the 1810 Revolution (May 25); Malvinas Day (June 10); Flag Day (June 20); Independence Day (July 9); Anniversary of the Death of José

de San Martín (August 17); Columbus Day
(October 12); Immaculate Conception (December 8); Christmas (December 25).

Chapter 47

Bolivia

Republic of Bolivia *(República de Bolivia)*
Area: 424,162 square miles
Population: (est. 1995) 7,400,000
    Average annual rate of increase: 2.03%
    Density per square mile: 17.5
    58% urban
Capitals: Sucre (judicial) and
    La Paz (administrative)
Largest Cities: (1992) La Paz (711,000); Santa
    Cruz (694,000); El Alto (404,000);
    Cochabamba (404,000)
Religion: 85% Roman Catholic
Literacy Rate: 78%
Languages: Spanish, Quechua, Aymara (all official)

Cultural Information

High percentage indigenous population, most descended from Incas and previously existing groups. Quechua 30%, Aymara 25%, Mestizo 25-30%. With two major Indian groups and several lesser ones, Bolivia is the most Indian country in Latin America. Over 50% of the population are of pure American Indian descent and maintain traditional cultural values and belief systems.

305

Geography

Bolivia is totally landlocked as a result of a war with Chile. It is roughly the size of Texas and California combined. The country is a low alluvial plain throughout 60% of its area to the east, drained by the Amazon and Plata river systems. The western part, enclosed by two chains of the Andes Mountains which has three of the highest peaks in South America, is a high plateau with an average altitude of 12,000 feet. More than 80% of the population lives on the plateau which also contains La Paz. At an altitude of 11,910 feet, it is the highest administrative capitol city in the world. Lake Titicaca, shared with Peru, is the highest navigable lake in the world at 12,506 feet. Islands in the lake have ruins of the ancient Incas.

Climate

Because of its topography, Bolivia has a wide range of altitude related climates. In its Amazon basin area to the east it is always hot and humid. In the high plateau area of the Andes Mountains, freezing temperatures are common, and snow is not unknown in La Paz between March and August (the southern hemisphere winter).

Tourist Information

Visa: Not required for U.S. citizens. Maximum stay 30 days, extendable. Passport must be valid for at least one year beyond the date of entry. Onward ticket is required, as is sufficient funds for the stay, although these require-

306

ments don't appear to be taken seriously. Your passport (or copy) must be carried at all times.

U.S. Embassy: Banco Popular del Peru building, at the corner of Mercado and Colón.

Money: The official Bolivian currency is the *boliviano*, divided into 100 centavos. There is no black market for currency. Do not change more money than you are likely to spend, because the *boliviano* is virtually worthless outside of Bolivia. Money is normally changed in *casas de cambio* rather than in banks. Cash brings the best rates. Outside of La Paz, travelers checks bring 3% to 5% less, and in the smaller towns it may be impossible to change them. American Express is the most commonly used travelers check. Visa and Mastercard are in common use.

Telephone System: ENTEL, the telephone system, offers FAX, telegram, and telex services. Pay phones are common and use tokens, which are available at candy stores and from newspaper vendors.

Health: Bolivia is not a particularly unhealthy country, but sanitation is generally poor and you need to pay attention to what you eat and drink. You should not drink tap water. Because of the high elevation of the *altiplano* you will need to give yourself several days to acclimate and should not plan on strenuous activity at first. Malaria and yellow fever precautions should be taken before going to the Amazon basin section of Bolivia.

Cultural Specifics

Greetings: When first introduced, people shake
hands, with members of both sexes. Women
who are good friends kiss on both cheeks, and
close male friends give each other a hug and
shake hands. Even if good friends meet several times during the day, they will greet one
another each time. Use titles (such as for a
teacher, lawyer, etc.) As in other Latin American countries, they are important to Bolivians.

Public Behavior: Women frequently walk arm-in-
arm and teenage girls often walk along holding hands. It is considered bad manners to eat
on the street. If someone pats you on the
shoulder, it is a sign of friendship. Mestizo Bolivians identify with their Spanish heritage
rather than with the Indian, and it is an insult
to call someone an Indian. Indians are not referred to as *indios*, but rather as *campesinos*
(peasants).
Do not attempt to photograph Indian women.
They believe that a camera can capture their
souls. Indian men don't usually mind, but
may ask for payment.

Dress: Be prepared for the different climates of Bolivia. La Paz is cold all year, whereas some
other areas are hot all year. For casual wear,
both men and women wear jeans, but neither
wear shorts. Don't wear Indian clothing, because they will think that you are ridiculing
them, and non-Indians consider it strange. Indian women wear bowler hats. Men should
not wear them.

Meals: Breakfasts are light, usually made up of
bread, butter, and jam, accompanied by hot
milk with a little coffee added. Lunch is usu-

ally served between noon and 2 PM. It is the main meal of the day, and will usually consist of soup followed by a main course. Steak is popular, as are rice and potatoes. Afternoon "tea" is frequently served around 4 PM and may involve tea, coffee, and pastries. Dinner may be eaten as early as 7:30 or as late as 9:30, and is usually a complete meal.

Table Manners: When invited to dinner at someone's house, always arrive 15 to 30 minutes late. It's rude to be prompt, because your hosts may not be ready. A special guest may be served first, but it's usually the father who gets that honor. Children may eat earlier or separately in the kitchen. Food is usually put on the individual plates in the kitchen and then brought to the table. Keep your hands above the table, and never eat with your hands (not even chicken). Stay about 30 minutes after the meal, then leave.

Dining Out: Although many restaurants are open all day, many other restaurants serve only two meals. Lunch is served from 11:30 to 2:00 and dinner from 6:00 to 9:00. Fixed price meals are usually available for both lunch and dinner. Many of the dishes are spicy and hot.

Tipping: It is not necessary to tip in restaurants, because it is included in the bill. Don't tip taxi drivers. Airport porters should be given the equivalent of 50 cents per bag.
Gas station attendants should be tipped 25 cents if they wash the windshield and check the oil.

Holidays: New Year's Day (Jan. 1), Monday before Ash Wednesday, Shrove Tuesday, Ash Wednesday, Good Friday, Holy Saturday, Corpus Christi (the Thursday after the eighth Sunday

after Easter, Independence Day (Aug. 6), Columbus Day (Oct. 12), All Souls' Day (Nov.
2), Christmas (Dec. 25).

Chapter 48

Brazil

Federated Republic of Brazil *(República Federativa do Brasil)*

Area: 3,286,470 square miles The largest country in South America, comprising almost half of the continent.

Population: 157,800,000 (est. 1995)
Average annual rate of increase: 1.7%

Density per square mile: 48

Major Ethnic Groups: Decedents of Portuguese immigrants and African slaves make up the majority. Also Italians, Germans, Japanese, and native Americans (especially in the Amazon Basin). Brazil, more than any other country in the Americas, is highly mixed racially. Most Brazilians have some combination of European, African, Indian, Asian, and Middle Eastern ancestry. The number of pure Amerindians in Brazil is now estimated to be less than 200,000.

Languages: Portuguese (official), Spanish, English, French, and a number of indigenous languages. 174 different Indian languages and dialects have been documented.

Capital: Brasília

Largest Cities: (est. 1991) Sao Paulo (15,400,000);
  Rio de Janeiro (9,800,000); Salvador
  (2,100,000); Brasília (1,600,000)
Religion: Roman Catholic 70%
Literacy Rate: 81%

Geography

  Brazil occupies the eastern half of South America, and has an Atlantic coastline stretching 4,603 miles. The most striking features of Brazil are the Amazon River Basin and the Amazon River itself. The river and its tributaries have at any one time about 20% of the world's fresh water, and the basin contains some 30% of the world's remaining forest. The network of rivers has over 15,000 miles of waterway which is navigable by ocean-going freighters. The Amazon River itself is navigable by freighters all the way to Iquitos, Peru, some 2,300 miles inland.

  The northeastern part of Brazil is mainly high, relatively dry plateau, and is heavily settled and usually poverty stricken. The south central part of the country, which has good resources and a favorable climate, also has over half of the country's population. The narrow coastal belt contains most of the major cities.

Climate

  The Brazilian winter is from June to August, but it gets cold only south of Rio de Janeiro. The climate varies from hot and humid tropics to subtropical and temperate. In most of the country, short tropic rains occur year round. Only the plateau of the northeast has a pronounced rainy-dry cycle. The Amazon Basin is wet all year round.

Tourist Information

Visa: Visas are required for U.S. citizens, and
should be obtained before leaving, if possible,
from a Brazilian consulate in the United
States. It is also possible to obtain a visa from
a Brazilian consulate in another country. Passports are required, and must be valid for a
minimum of six months from the date of entry. An onward or return trip ticket is required. Visas are issued for 90 days and may
be extended for another 90 days.

U.S. Embassy: Brasília, Setor de Embaixadas Sul,
Avenida das Naçoes, Q 801, lote 3. Phone:
321-7272. There is also a U.S. consulate located in Rio de Janeiro.

Money: The monetary unit is the *cruzeiro real*.
Changing money is simple in the larger cities
at a *casa de câmbio*. Most large banks have a
foreign section at a slightly better rate, but
often involves some bureaucratic red tape.
Cash brings the best rate of exchange, but
traveler's checks can be exchanged in banks
and at most *casas de câmbio*. Credit cards are
readily accepted at better hotels, restaurants,
and shops.

Postal System: Postal services are reputed to be
good in Brazil. Most mail seems to get
through, and airmail letters to the U.S. usually arrive in a week or so. Rates are very
high, and an airmail letter costs about a dollar.

Telephone System: The Brazilian telephone company is EMBRATEL. Calls from Brazil to the
U.S. are expensive, and cost about $3 per
minute. Every town has a *posto telefônico*
(phone company office, from which international calls can be made, and which require a

313

large deposit. International collect calls (*a co-brar*) can be made from any telephone (dial 000-8010 for AT&T, 000-8012 for MCI, and 000-8016 for Sprint). Public telephones use *fichas* (tokens), which can be bought at news-stands, drugstores, etc. Phones are usually an-swered by the question, *"Quem fala?"*, which means "Who is speaking?"

Time Zones: Because of its immense size, Brazil has four time zones. Brazil currently uses daylight savings time, in which clocks are set ahead one hour in October, and back one hour in March or April.

Health: Generally there is no concern for serious diseases along the coastal strip from Rio de Ja-neiro and south. However in the Amazon Ba-sin and the northeastern plateau there is usually some malaria, yellow fever, dengue fe-ver, leprosy and leishmaniasis, and you should protect yourself against these. Occa-sionally health officials announce outbreaks of tuberculosis, polio, sexually transmitted dis-eases, hepatitis, and other endemic diseases. Sanitation is always a problem and you must be careful of what you eat and drink.

Risks: Robberies and theft on buses, city beaches, and tourist areas are common. Thieves work in gangs, are armed with knives and guns, and occasionally kill if resisted. Much of the street crime is directed against tourists. Don't carry more money than you can afford to lose and stay off the beaches at night. Use caution.

Cultural Specifics

Greetings: When a person is introduced to someone
of either sex, they shake hands. When two
men know each other well, they shake hands
and slap each other on the back, shoulders, or
stomach. When women friends meet, they kiss
on both cheeks. A married woman is likely to
kiss a single woman three times, the third one
a good-luck wish for marriage. In a group of
people, it is expected that you shake hands
hello and goodbye with each person. To fail to
do so is an insult.

First names are more commonly used than in the
other Latin American countries and are normally used in introductions (lists of names are
usually alphabetized by first name). Doctors,
professors, and priests usually go by their title
plus their first name. People with university
degrees are normally addressed as *Doutor*
(doctor). In business, men are addressed as
Senhor plus his family name, and a woman as
Senhora plus her family name.

Public Behavior: It is considered bad manners to
chew gum or eat while walking on the street.
Littering is accepted because city streets are
cleaned daily. Brazilians consider sending
greeting cards or flowers to be impersonal,
and prefer direct contact. Bargaining in markets and hotels for better prices is normal. Ask
people before taking their photograph. This is
a courtesy to follow anywhere.

In the Home: You are not likely to be invited to
someone's home, even after you have known
them for a long time (or unless it is specifically
to meet the family). Home is considered pri-

315

vate. Don't drop in without calling first, either. Should you, however, be invited to someone's home, arrive 15 to 30 minutes late.

Dress: If possible, it is best not to look like a tourist. You will be inviting robbery if you do. Shorts are not acceptable except at the beach, and most restaurants and offices will not permit them. Men should wear slacks or nice-looking jeans with leather shoes. Athletic shoes are more acceptable for the beach. When it comes to beachwear, it's your own choice. The beaches of Rio de Janeiro are known for their skimpy bikinis, both for men and women.

Meals: No matter where you eat, don't drink tap water or fruit juices to which tap water has been added. Don't use ice cubes made from tap water. Don't eat food from street vendors. Breakfasts are usually light and normally consists of coffee, fruit juice, bread and butter. Lunch is usually the main meal of the day and is served from 12:00 to 2:00. It usually begins with a soup followed by beef, chicken or fish, with rice and beans, and ends with coffee. At about 4:00 to 5:00 there is frequently an afternoon snack of cookies and a beverage. Dinner is usually served between 7:00 and 9:00, and is ordinarily a light meal. People usually expect guests to remain and talk for a long time, so don't plan on leaving right away.

Table Manners: Foods are always cut with a knife, no matter how soft, so don't use the edge of your fork for that purpose. The knife, when not in use is placed with the tip on your plate and the handle on the table. Do not eat anything with your hands, even chicken. It's considered both unsanitary and bad manners. If you must eat something with your hands, use

316

a napkin to hold it. Even sandwiches are eaten with knife and fork. Do not drink directly out of a bottle or can. Use a glass or a straw.

Dining out: In a casual restaurant it is normal to seat yourself, but in a more elegant restaurant, wait to be seated. Better restaurants frequently don't open for dinner until 9:00 PM. Don't ask for separate checks. The bill will not be itemized. If the service charge is not included, don't leave it on the table, but give it directly to the waiter.

Tipping: Restaurants normally add a 10% service charge. Give the waiter an extra 5%. Taxi drivers should be tipped 10%.

Gifts: Good gifts to take are small electronic items (expensive in Brazil), cassette tapes with music, perfume for women, cheap watches for children.

Holidays: New Year's Day (Jan. 1), Epiphany (Jan. 6), Feast of Saint Sebastian (Jan. 20), Carnival (from the Saturday before Lent through Ash Wednesday), Easter, Labor Day (May 1), Ascension Day (40 days after Easter), June Festival (June 24-29), Feast of the Assumption (Aug. 15), Independence Day (Sept. 7), Columbus Day (Oct. 12), All Saints' Day (Nov. 1), All Souls' Day (Nov. 2), Declaration of the Republic (Nov. 15), Flag Day (Nov. 19), Christmas (Dec. 24), New Year's Eve (Dec. 31). I challenge you to find a country with more official holidays. Find out about Carnival. It's special.

Chapter 49

Republic of Chile *(República de Chile)*
Area: 292,132 square miles,
    about twice the size of Montana
Population: 14,300,000 (est. mid-1995)
    Average annual rate of increase: 1.7%
    Density per square miles: 48.9
Labor Force: 19% agricultural, fishing, forestry;
    34% industry and commerce; 38% service
Capital: Santiago
Largest Cities: (est. 1992) Santiago (4,385,000);
    Concepción (331,000); Viña del Mar
    (303,000); Valparaiso (277,000); Talcahuano
    (247,000); Antofagasta (227,000)
Religion: Roman Catholic 89%, Protestant 11%.
    Some Muslim and Jewish
Literacy Rate: 94%
Language: Primarily Spanish, some Indian lan-
    guages in the north and the south
Ethnic Subgroups: Most Chileans are of mixed
    European/Indian descent, primarily from
    Spain, Germany, France, and Italy: 95%
    European and Mestizo, 3% Indian

Geography

Chile occupies the southern Pacific coast of South America, with a coastline of approximately 2,650 miles. Its northern neighbor is Peru, northeast is Bolivia, and to the east is Argentina. Its width varies between 100 and 250 miles. Along its eastern border is the Andes Mountain Range, with some of the highest peaks in the world. At its very south is the large island of Tierra del Fuego, shared with Argentina, (Argentina has the southernmost city in the world, Punta Arenas.) In the north central area is the Atacama Desert, the driest area in the world, where it frequently doesn't rain for years at a time. The central region consists of a fertile valley where most of the population resides, and farther south are forests and grazing land. Chile also claims Easter Island (part of Polynesia) and the Juan Fernández Islands, where the Robinson Crusoe story was set.

Climate

Chile has a temperate climate, very dry in the north, and cold and wet in the southern extremities, very cold and dry in the Andes Mountains. Because of the nature of the climate, very good wines are produced and there is a lot of beef.

Tourist Information

Visas: Not needed by U.S. citizens. A renewable 90 day tourist card is issued upon arrival. Passport required.

U.S. Embassy: Santiago, Agustinas 1343
U.S. Consulate, Merced 230
Phone: 671-0133

Customs: Inspections are usually routine.

Driving: An International Driving Permit is required, along with your regular driver's license.

Money: The unit of currency is the *peso*. U.S. dollars can be exchanged in banks and *casas de cambio*, the latter giving a rate of about 5% better. Travelers checks can also be exchanged, but at a slightly lower rate. Credit cards can be used for both purchases and cash advances, but are charged at the lower bank rate.

Postal System: Generally efficient, but mail sent out of the country should go *certificado* (certified).

Telephone System: ENTEL, the former state monopoly, and CTC (*Compañía de Teléfonos de Chile*) offer long-distance services throughout the country. Calls to the U.S. cost about $3 per minute. Both collect and credit card calls are possible. Some public phones accept coins, others require *fichas* (tokens).

Health: Chile has no particular health hazards, and the water is generally safe to drink. Be cautious of eating raw fruits and vegetables, though, because they are often washed in untreated water.

Risks: Chile is safer than most Latin American countries, and violent crime is rare. Petty crime, such as pickpocketing and purse snatching are not uncommon. Be careful, as always, with your valuables.

Cultural Specifics

Greetings: Men shake hands with other men when introduced, and if they know each other well, they shake hands and pat one another on the back. Women kiss one another on one cheek, but don't shake hands with either sex. Titles are not as commonly used as in most other Latin American countries. The only one regularly used is *doctor* for a medical doctor.

Public Behavior: Avoid aggressive behavior. Chileans emphasize personal respect, and aggressiveness is considered rude. Bargaining is not done, even in the street. Utility bills are paid in banks, and lines are frequently long. It is an insult in Chile to offer a bribe. Chileans tend to be very honest.

Dress: Good jeans are acceptable, but not shorts. Ties should be worn in the better restaurants, and women should wear dresses. Because of the climatic extremes of Chile, you should take some warm clothing along.

Meals: Breakfast is usually light and normally served with instant coffee (Chile is not a coffee producing country) or with tea. Lunch is usually served from 1:00 to 3:00, and is large, often with soup. The main course might be steak or seafood (abundant in Chile). There may be an afternoon snack at 5:00 or 6:00, and dinner is usually between 8:00 and 9:00, and is similar to lunch. Chileans tend to be open about inviting foreigners to their homes for a meal (as opposed to most Latin Americans). Plan on being about 15 minutes late.

Table Manners: Meals are normally served with food on the plate or is offered buffet style.

Food is not normally eaten with the fingers. Don't offer to help with the dishes, especially if there is a maid.

Dining out: Santiago, the capitol, has a large number of foreign and specialty restaurants, including Chinese, Italian, Mexican, Indian, and Brazilian. Hotels frequently have the best food in smaller towns. To get a waiter's attention, call out *garçon* (French for "boy"). Always one person should pay the bill. If you are with a group of Americans, you can split it later, but if with Chileans, reciprocity is expected at a later date.

Tipping: Service charges are usually included in the bill, but leave a little behind for good service. Don't tip taxi drivers. People frequently ask to wash your windshield, help you park, or guard your car. Give a small tip.

Holidays: New Year's Day (Jan. 1); Holy Thursday, Good Friday, and Easter Sunday; Battle of Iquique (May 21); Feast of the Assumption (Aug. 15); Independence Day (Sept. 18-19); Armed Forces Day (Sept. 19); Columbus Day (Oct. 12); All Saints' Day (Nov. 1) Feast of the Immaculate Conception (Dec. 8); Christmas (Dec. 25).

Chapter 50

Colombia

Republic of Colombia *(República de Colombia)*
Area: 439,735 square miles
Population: 37,700,000 (est. mid-1995)
    Average annual rate of increase, 1.8%
    Density per square mile: 85.7
Labor Force: 30% agricultural, 24% industrial,
    46% services
Capital: Bogotá
Largest Cities (1993 census): Bogotá, 6,500,000;
    Medellín, 1,800,000; Cali, 1,800,000; Bar-
    ranquilla, 1,400,000; Cartagena, 700,000
Religion: 95% Roman Catholic
Literacy Rate: 91.3%

Geography

Located in the northwestern part of South America,
it is the only country on the continent that borders on both
the Atlantic and Pacific Oceans. It is nearly equal to the
combined areas of California and Texas and is the fourth
largest country in South America.

Through the western half of the country, three Andean ranges run north and south, merging into one at the

Ecuadorian border. The eastern half is a low jungle-covered plain, drained by tributaries of the Orinoco and Amazon rivers. The fertile plateau and valley of the eastern range are the most densely populated parts of the country.

Climate

Because of its proximity to the equator, Colombia's temperature varies little throughout the year. However, the temperature does change dramatically with altitude, creating various climatic zones, from hot lowlands to permanent snow in the highest mountains. Colombia has two seasons: dry and wet. The pattern of seasons varies in different parts of the country. In the Andean regions there are two dry and two rainy seasons per year. This general pattern has wide variations throughout the Andean zone, with the seasons being wetter or drier, shorter or longer and occurring at different times. Weather in the high plateau has a more definite pattern. There is one dry season, between December and March, and the rest of the year is wet. The Amazon Basin does not have a uniform climate but, in general is wet all year round.

Tourist Information

Visa: Not required for U.S. citizens. Maximum stay, 90 days, extendible by additional 30 days

U.S. Embassy: Bogotá, Calle 38, No. 8-61. Tel. 285-1300.

Customs: You are allowed to bring in a camera, video camera, typewriter, radio, calculator, stereo, etc., as long as they show signs of use. Customs procedures are almost a formality on entering the country, but your luggage will be carefully searched for drugs upon leaving. On departure, you will need receipts for any emeralds, antiques, and articles of gold and platinum purchased in Colombia.

Money: The official Colombian currency is the *peso,* comprised of 100 *centavos.* There is no black market in Colombia, and the recommended places for exchange are banks or *"cajas de cambio."* Exchange rates vary from bank to bank, but the rate for travelers' checks will always be from 2% to 3% higher than for cash. Not all banks can change traveler's checks, but many *cajas de cambio* will, although the rate of exchange will not be as good. Credit cards can also be used to obtain cash advances. Using credit cards in hotels is a mistake, as is changing dollars or traveler's checks in hotels. Exchange rates in hotels will always be much less, and it will be to your advantage to get cash advances from banks against your card to pay hotel bills. Inquire in your hotel about which banks exchange dollars. It changes periodically. Ask the hotel to call the bank and ask during what hours they exchange money, because frequently it is only for one or two hours per day. Your passport is absolutely required to exchange money no matter where it is done.

Postal System: The Colombian postal service seems to be fairly efficient and reliable. Mail from the U.S. to most Colombian cities usually takes about 10 days. Mail is delivered directly to the home or office.

Telephone System: TELECOM (the national phone system) has offices located almost everywhere, even in the smallest villages. From there, you may make long distance calls nationally and internationally, and pay the cashier. The system is efficient and automated. International calls are expensive. Collect calls can be made to the U.S. You can also use telephone credit cards for calling to the United States.

Health: No vaccinations are required to enter Colombia. Colombia has excellent hospitals and well-trained physicians. Pharmacies are common, and most medicines are available in the larger ones. Many drugs which require a prescription in the U.S. are available over the counter. Tap water is said to be safe to drink in the larger cities, but I don't recommend it. Many Colombians prefer to use bottled water.

Risks: Colombia is not the safest of countries and you should be careful and on your guard at all times. Your biggest risks come from pickpockets and muggers. The problem is most serious in the large cities, with Bogotá, Medellín, and Cali being the worst. Bogotá, in fact, has a famous "university" where pickpockets from all over Latin America pay to be trained in the best methods.

Stay out of the slum areas and beware of downtown areas that have unsavory looking characters. Keep your passport and money well concealed (using one of the methods suggested earlier), your camera well secured, and don't wear jewelry or an expensive watch. Never leave luggage or packages for a moment. In restaurants, keep packages between your legs. Always carry your passport (or a copy) with you. Document checks on the streets are common. Be very careful about drugs...never carry them and never buy them. Colombia is very sensitive about this issue, and you'll be in for a long stay if you get caught. There have been reports of drugs being planted on travelers, so stay alert. Before traveling to remote areas, check to see whether there has been recent guerrilla activity.

Cultural Specifics

Greetings: Men shake hands with other men and with women. Women clasp one another's forearms. They don't shake hands. Among good friends, women and women, and men and women kiss on one cheek. Sometimes good men friends embrace and pat one another on the back.

Lines: Don't expect people to wait in line. You'll have to join the pushing match if you want a place.

Invitations: People will hardly ever respond negatively to an invitation. Only their degree of enthusiasm will tell you whether they will actually show up or not. Never pressure anyone for a firm commitment, though. Colombians consider directness by foreigners toward them as being insensitive.

Bargaining: It's fine to bargain in open markets, but not in stores. In a shop, if you're paying with cash, rather than with a credit card, you can ask for a 5% to 10% discount.

Toilets: Public toilets are scarce and usually not clean. Take your own toilet paper.

Dress: Colombians judge people by how they look and how well they are dressed. Don't wear shorts on the street, when visiting an office, or in a church. It's acceptable to wear shorts in coastal resort towns.

Meals: Lunch from 12:30 or 1:00 to 2:00 or 2:30. Stores and offices frequently close from 12:00 to 2:00. Dinner usually around 7:00. Colombian coffee is excellent and mild. Black coffee is called *"tinto,"* coffee with a little milk is called *"café périco,"* and milk with a little coffee is called *"café con leche."*

Tipping: Not necessary in taxis. Expect a 10% service charge to be added to your restaurant bill. If it isn't, leave 10%. Give porters 50 to 100 pesos for each piece of luggage.

Gifts: Don't give personal gifts (such as perfume) unless you know the person very well. Don't expect the gift to be opened in your presence. In fact, the gift may never even be mentioned.

Holidays: New Years Day (Jan. 1); Epiphany (Jan. 6); Saint Joseph's Day (March 19); Holy Thursday, Good Friday, Holy Saturday, and Easter Sunday; Labor day (May 1); Ascension Day (40 days after Easter); Feast of Saints Peter and Paul (June 29); Independence Day (July 20); Battle of Boyaca (Aug.7); Feast of the Assumption (Aug. 15); Columbus Day (Oct. 12); All Saints' Day (Nov. 1); Independence Day, Cartegena (Nov. 11); Feast of the Immaculate Conception (Dec. 8); Christmas (Dec. 25).

Chapter 51

Republic of Costa Rica *(República de Costa Rica)*

Area: 19,652 square miles. Second smallest country of Central America.

Population: 3,400,000 (est. 1995)
Average annual rate of increase, 2.2%
Density per square mile, 173

Capital: San José

Religion: Roman Catholic 95%

Literacy Rate: 93%

Languages: Primarily Spanish, but English is common

Racial Composition: Most of the population is descended from Spanish settlers. The Caribbean coastal area, especially Puerto Limón, consists primarily of descendants of black workers from the Caribbean islands. There is a very small population of Indians.

Immigrant Ethnic Subgroups: Many North Americans (est. 30,000) and Europeans reside in Costa Rica, primarily as retirees.

Geography

Costa Rica is bordered on the north by Nicaragua and on the south by Panama. It is roughly the size of West Virginia and almost as mountainous. A mountain chain, volcanic in origin, runs from the Nicaraguan border to Panama, dividing the country in two. In the central part of the country is a plateau with an elevation of approximately 3,500 feet to 4,000 feet, and about 60% of the population live in that area in four of the five largest towns of the country.

The Caribbean coastal area is characterized by frequent rainfall, virtually unbroken tropical lowland rain forest, swamps, mangroves, and sandy beaches. The Pacific coast is more rugged and rocky and is characterized by tropical dry forest. The Pacific coastal area has received a great deal of tourism development in recent years.

Because of Costa Rica's strategic location on the isthmus between North and South America and its climatic range, it has an unusually high number of species of both plants and animals. The country has made an effort to set aside a number nature preserves and national parks, but deforestation and encroachment upon both the parks and preserves remains at a high level.

Climate

Highland Costa Rica has two very distinct seasons based on rainfall. From late December through April (referred to as *verano*, summer) there is very little rainfall at all, and San José is likely to be cool and windy. The rest of the year (*invierno*, winter) is wet, normally with rain almost every day. Highland Costa Rica is cool, usually between 65 and 75 degrees fahrenheit, with coastal areas ranging from about 80 to 90 degrees. The constant spring-like weather has made the plateau area (*Meseta Central*) popular with tourists and foreign retirees.

Tourist Information

Visa: Not required for U.S. citizens. 90-day stay allowed, after which time one must leave the country and re-enter. A small fine is assessed for overstaying the entry permit. An onward or return ticket is required for entry.

U.S. Embassy: San José, Carretera Pavas
Phone: 220-3939

Money: The monetary unit is the *colón* (plural *colones*), divided into 100 *céntimos*. Dollars can be readily exchanged in banks, but there are frequently long lines because people pay their utility bills in banks (as well as in many supermarkets). There are a few *casas de cambio* in San José and they give a slightly better rate than banks. The best is *Helicópteros de Costa Rica,* located upstairs across from the Banco Central. They will also cash personal checks for Americans. Dollars can be readily changed on the street, but it is not recommended. Street money changers are very adept at short-changing customers, or simply running off with your money. Hotels offer very poor rates of exchange.

Postal System: Costa Rica has an atrocious mail system. Delivery is OK, but there is a big problem with mail theft, especially with letters arriving from the United States or Europe. Do not send money by mail. Houses do not have numbers and most streets do not have names, but home delivery is still accomplished by specifying a location for the house in terms of a certain number of meters in a certain direction from some popularly known location. Postal employees on motorcycles ask around until the house is found.

Telephone System: The telephone system is operated by *Radiográfica Costarricense* and ICE, and is modern and efficient. There are still not enough lines to go around for people who want them, and a black market for telephone lines exists. Telegrams and telexes can be sent from *Radiográfica Costarricense,* and international calls can be made and faxes sent from ICE offices. Public telephones are readily available downtown, in residential areas, and along major highways. They use the very practical system of coins put in a sloping slot, from which they drop into the phone as needed.

Health: There are no particular health hazards. There are two excellent private hospitals in San José, where Americans go frequently for surgery, especially plastic surgery, because of the lower cost. Public water throughout the *Meseta Central* is safe to drink, but it is unwise to trust public water supplies in the coastal areas.

Risks: San José has an increasing problem with street crime, usually non-violent. Because of heavy tourism and limited police interest, pickpockets and purse snatchers operate with virtual impunity in downtown San José. Be careful where you go, especially at night, and leave your valuables in the hotel. Puerto Limón is also dangerous, with physical assault being more common than in San José.

Be especially careful with traffic when walking in San José. The pedestrian does not have right-of-way, and it seems to be a game with how close a car can get to a pedestrian without killing him. It should be added that of all the countries in the world, Costa Rica is reported to have the highest rate of traffic deaths per mile driven (this, of course, includes pedestrian deaths).

Taxis are required to have meters, but watch carefully anyway. Some will not remove the previous fare and will overcharge you. Don't leave your luggage in the taxi and leave to do something. Sometimes they just drive off. Taxi drivers are devious in San José, especially with tourists.

Cultural Specifics

Greetings: Men always shake hands upon meeting and leaving. Women do not shake hands, but pat one another on the arm. Women kiss both male and female friends on the cheek. Titles are especially important in Costa Rica (Doctor, Engineer, etc.), so use them in conjunction with the surname. Costa Ricans have a strong sense of personal honor, and it is important to avoid criticism. Costa Ricans refer to themselves as *"ticos"* (for men) and *"ticas"* (for women).

Public Behavior: Unmarried Costa Rican couples are very affectionate in public, frequently holding hands and kissing.
Costa Rica is said to have a very egalitarian society with no economic or racial discrimination. There is, in fact, no legal discrimination, but there is social discrimination, both racial

and economic, but perhaps less than in most Latin American countries.

Bargaining while shopping is not expected, and rarely done, either in the street or in stores. People, in general, are friendly and accommodating (although tourism is changing this), but it is very difficult for foreigners to achieve real friendship, and especially difficult for foreigners to penetrate the upper-middle and upper classes.

Dress: Appropriate dress varies a great deal between hot coastal areas and the more formal, cooler central plateau. Shorts and sneakers are proper on the coast, but shorts are rarely seen in San José. Younger men usually wear jeans with athletic shoes, women usually wear skirts and high-heels. Women tend to dress carefully, with an eye to looking sexy.

Meals: Breakfast usually consists of coffee (which is excellent in Costa Rica), *gallo pinto* (means "painted rooster" and refers to a bean and rice dish with onions and coriander leaves), frequently with a soft fried egg on top. Lunch is usually between 12:00 and 2:00. Most offices and many stores close during this time. A common meal, at home and in restaurants, is the *casado* (which means "married"), usually rice, black beans, salad, meat, and vegetable. Dinner is usually a lighter meal, served around 7:00. It may consist of left- overs, but is frequently an *olla de carne* ("pot of beef," a soup made of beef chunks and various vegetables). Meals are frequently accompanied with *frescos*, tropical fruit juices mixed with water and sugar.

Table Manners: About the same as most other
Latin American countries. Many people eat
European style. Keep your hands above the
table.

Dining out: Costa Ricans enjoy a much wider variety of foods than most Latin Americans,
mainly because of the wide climatic range
(permitting the growth of both tropical and
many temperate plants) and the large numbers of foreign immigrants who have brought
specialties with them. Cheeses and seafood
are especially good. San José has Middle Eastern, German, French, Swiss, Italian, Chinese,
Japanese, Texan, and vegetarian restaurants.
Except for in the more expensive restaurants,
you can expect to receive indifferent service.
National law requires that restaurants add a
10% service charge (in addition to a 13%
tax), effectively eliminating motivation to earn
tips.

Although it is considered bad manners in most
of Latin America, Costa Ricans hiss between
tongue and teeth to get the attention of waiters and waitresses. It works, and may be the
only way to get their attention.

Tipping: Except for extraordinary service, there is
no need to tip in restaurants. Do not tip taxi
drivers. Hotel and airport porters should be
tipped about 25 cents per bag.

Holidays: New Year's Day (Jan. 1); Feast of St.
Joseph (Mar. 19); Holy Thursday through
Easter Sunday; Labor Day (May 1); Feast of
Corpus Christi (the Thursday after the eighth
Sunday after Easter); Feast of Sts. Peter and
Paul (June 29); Annexation of Guanacaste
Province (July 25); Feast of Our Lady of the
Angels (Aug. 2); Feast of the Assumption and
Mothers Day (Aug. 15); Independence Day

(Sept. 15); Columbus Day (Oct. 12); Feast of
the Immaculate Conception (Dec. 8); Christmas Eve (Dec. 24); Christmas (Dec. 25).

Chapter 52

Cuba

Republic of Cuba *(República de Cuba)*

Area: 44,218 square miles

Population: 11,200,000 (est. 1995).

Average annual rate of increase, 0.7%
    Density per square mile, 254

Labor Force: 30% services and government, 22% industry, 20% agriculture

Capital: Havana

Largest Cities: (est. 1990) Havana (2,100,000); Santiago de Cuba (406,000); Camagüey (283,000); Holguin (228,000); Guantánamo 200,400); Santa Clara (195,000)

Religion: 85% Roman Catholic before Castro, African derived religious forms persist

Literacy Rate: 94%

Language: Spanish; English, French, and Russian are common.

Racial Composition: 51% mulatto, 37% white, 11% black; some Mestizo, but no remaining Indian populations

Geography

Cuba is the largest island of the Caribbean, roughly equal in size to the state of Pennsylvania. It lies 90 miles south of Key West, Florida, 85 miles east of the Yucatan Peninsula of Mexico, 48 miles west of Haiti, and 90 miles north of Jamaica. Low hills and fertile valleys cover more than half the country, but it has three mountain ranges, the Cordillera de los Organos in the west, the Escambray Mountains in the central region, and the Sierra Maestra in the southeast. The highest point, 6,470 feet, is in the Sierra Maestra. The northern coast is rugged and rocky, the southern, low and marshy.

Climate

Cuba has a tropical climate, with rainy season from May to October and dry season from November to April. It is cooler during the dry season, though, and cold fronts pushing down from the United States can make it chilly. Cuba is in the hurricane corridor and is occasionally hit by one between June and October.

Tourist Information

Travel to Cuba: Travel to Cuba by citizens of countries other than the United States is simple, and no visa is needed. It is illegal (in the United States) for U.S. citizens to go to Cuba without a license to engage in transactions with Cuba, including going to and from Cuba, and spending money in Cuba. This includes travel which originates in a third country. Licenses are routinely granted to accredited journalists on assignment and representatives of international organizations of which the U.S. is a member, but under no circumstances are they given for tourism or business related travel.

This means that an American citizen who wants to go to Cuba must do so illegally. The most common method is to travel through a third country. The most popular cities for departure are Montreal, Mexico City, Cancun, and Nassau. American travelers are welcomed, either individually or as part of a tour group. A tourist card is necessary, and can be obtained from the Cuban embassies in the countries of departure. The simplest method is to get the card from an authorized tour agency. The cost is about $15. Passports are not stamped. Consequently there is no evidence that the tourist ever entered Cuba. The Cuban government does require that there be a confirmed hotel reservation for at least three nights. Additional information can be found on the internet at www.cubatravel.com.

Travel within Cuba: It is almost essential to rent a car. Bus service is patchy, and drivers frequently don't let foreigners board. Internal air travel is good, and relatively inexpensive. Cars rent for about $55 per day, but it is frequently very difficult to find gas.

Money: The monetary unit is the *peso,* divided into 100 *centavos.* Tourists cannot readily use them, however, because sellers prefer U.S. dollars. Street money changers are common, and will change dollars to *pesos* if you want to try to use them, but you cannot change *pesos* back into dollars. Credit cards are widely accepted, but only if they are not issued by a U.S. bank. Traveler's checks from Visa and Thomas Cook are accepted.

Telephone System: Antiquated and unreliable, very difficult to get international calls either in or out.

Health: There are few health hazards. Medical care for foreigners is available only at private clinics and hospitals and it is expensive.

Risks: Cuba is one of the safer countries for tourists in Latin America. It has a very low crime rate, but still you will need to protect yourself against pickpockets.

Dining out, Hotels, etc.: Be aware that you will be limited where you can spend your money as a tourist. Foreigners are not welcome in most stores, restaurants, and hotels. It is not that they do not like foreigners, but that they cannot accept *pesos* from foreigners, and are not authorized to accept dollars, although it is becoming increasingly common that they do so. You will have to buy in "dollar stores," eat in "dollar restaurants," and stay in "dollar hotels." Cuba wants your dollars, but restricts where you can spend them. The economy is such that there is frequently not enough of the basic goods to go around, including food, and this is one method for protecting citizens.

Chapter 53

Dominican Republic

Dominican Republic *(República Dominicana)*
Area: 18,704 square miles
Population: (est. 1995) 7,800,000)
    Average annual rate of increase, 2.1%
    Density per square mile, 417
Capital: Santo Domingo
Largest Cities: (1993) Santo Domingo
    (2,200,000); Santiago de los Caballeros
    (690,000)
Religion: Roman Catholic 90%
Literacy Rate: 83%
Languages: Spanish
Racial Composition: Mixed 73%, white 16%, Black
    11%

Geography

    The Dominican Republic shares the island of Hispaniola with Haiti, occupying the eastern two-thirds of the island. Its area equals that of Vermont and New Hampshire combined. It is crossed lengthwise by a mountain range with elevations as high as 10,400 feet, the highest in the Caribbean. It also has a saltwater lake whose surface is 144 feet below sea level.

Climate

The climate is tropical, usually with an easterly breeze. The Dominican Republic lies in the hurricane corridor and is occasionally hit between the months of June and October.

Tourist Information

Visa: Not required for U.S. citizens, entry is for 90 days

Money: The monetary unit is the *peso*, divided into 100 *centavos*. Dollars are accepted in many stores, restaurants, and hotels. Major credit cards and traveler's checks are also accepted.

Telephone System: Connections from the U.S. to the Dominican Republic are usually fast and clear, but in the reverse can be difficult. Direct dialing is possible.

Risks: The Dominican Republic is poor, and the greatest risks (other than falling into potholes in sidewalks) come from theft. Be especially careful with luggage at the airport and when exchanging money. The country is famous for people who offer to help you with belongings and then disappear into the crowd. Protect your cash and cameras.

Hotels and Tipping: The Dominican Republic is noted for its fine beaches and crystal clear water. Many excellent hotels exist in beach areas. Hotels and restaurants add a 21% tax, required by the government. 10% of this is service charge, so tipping is optional. Taxi drivers expect a 10% tip.

Chapter 54

Ecuador

Republic of Ecuador *(República del Ecuador)*
Area: 106,822 square miles
Population: 11,460,117 (est. 1995)
    Average annual rate of increase, 2.19%
    Density per square miles, 107
Capital: Quito
Largest Cities: (1992) Guayaquil (1,475,118);
    Quito (1,094,318); Cuenca (195,738)
Religion: Roman Catholic 95%
Literacy Rate: 88%
Languages: Spanish, Quechua, Jivaro
Ethnic Subgroups: Approximately 40% of the population is Indian, 40% Mestizo, and the remainder of European descent, Black, and Asian. The majority of the Mestizo and others live in the coastal areas, Quechua Indians (descendants of the Incas) live in the Andean region, and the Jivaro live in the Amazon Basin to the east.

Geography

Ecuador is one of the smaller countries of South America, but is one of the world's most geographically

345

diverse countries. It's western side borders on the Pacific Ocean (and also includes the Galapagos Islands), the high Andean mountains run north to south through the middle, and to the east the mountains slope into the great jungles of the Amazon Basin. Quito, the capitol, at nearly 9,300 feet elevation is the second highest capitol in the world (after La Paz, Bolivia). Because of the great environmental diversity, Ecuador is one of the most species-rich countries in the world for both plants and animals.

Climate

Ecuador has wet and dry seasons instead of the four seasons found in temperate zones. Rainy season is from January to April, dry season from June to September. On the slopes of the Amazon Basin rain can be expected almost daily all year long.

Tourist Information

Visa: Visas are not required for U.S. citizens, but a passport valid for at least six months is required. A "T-3" tourist card is necessary and may be obtained upon arrival. Keep the card handy because it is necessary for passport checks, extensions of stay, and for leaving the country. The maximum stay is 90 days, but not always given. Extensions can be obtained in Quito at the immigration office. The maximum stay of 90 days is cumulative during the course of a year, which means that you cannot spend more than 90 days per year in Ecuador. On the other hand, if you leave the country in less than 90 days, you can have the remainder should you return again during the same year.

Money: The currency in Ecuador is the *sucre*, frequently devalued, so that it is difficult to predict in advance what the rate of exchange will be at any particular time. There are two rates of exchange. The official rate of exchange, the lower of the two, is used in international business transactions. The higher free market rate is available at all exchange houses (*casas de cambio*). Exchange rates are best in the larger cities. Black market rates on the streets are slightly better, but there is some risk of receiving counterfeit money. Most major credit cards are accepted in restaurants, hotels, and for cash advances in banks.

Banks are open from 9 AM to 1 PM Monday through Friday. Some banks are open on Saturday mornings. *Casas de cambio* are usually open from 9 AM to 6 PM Monday through Friday, and until noon on Saturdays. Dollars can be bought back at airports and land borders when leaving the country.

Postal System: Outgoing mail is efficient and reliable, with letters often arriving within a week to the U.S. Incoming mail is not as efficient, sometimes taking as long as a couple of months to get there, and some letters never get there at all. For dependable communication it is best to use FAXs where possible.

Telephone System: IETEL provides long distance national and international telephone, FAX, telex, and telegram services. The offices are open from 6 AM to 10 PM daily. Waiting time for international long distance calls can vary from 10 minutes to an hour. AT&T operators in the U.S. can be reached in larger cities by dialing 119. Public phone booths are rare and require a special token (*ficha*) to use.

Health and Risks: Ecuador is generally a healthy country to visit. There is one iron-clad rule, however. Do not drink from public water sources. Restrict yourself to boiled or bottled water, and bottled or canned soft drinks or beer. Ecuador is safer for travel than the two adjoining countries, Colombia and Peru. Still, pick-pocketing is common in crowded areas. Assault and armed robbery are not common, but it is wise to stay out of obviously risky areas. If you are robbed, you have to get a police report within 48 hours because they will not process a report after that.

Cultural Specifics

Greetings: When introduced, when greeting, and when departing, Ecuadorians shake hands with people of both sexes. Between good friends, women and women as well as men and women kiss on one cheek when greeting and departing. Men shake hands with other men.

Dress: Jeans are common on the streets for both sexes. Shorts are appropriate in the coastal areas, but not downtown or in offices. Dress in the highlands is more formal. At the beach women should wear a one-piece bathing suit. Bikinis are not acceptable.

Meals: Breakfast is usually eaten between 7 and 8:30 AM. The meal is light: juice, coffee and rolls. Lunch is usually eaten from 1 to 2 PM, and is the main meal of the day. Dinner is usually eaten after 8 PM and is light, such as soup and coffee. On weekends and holidays meals are usually served later.

Dining out: Restaurants are usually open seven days per week, with dinner being served until 11 PM. Ecuadorians usually don't begin dinner until 8:30 or so. Only in the largest cities can you expect to find a variety of international restaurants or fast-food places for pizza, chicken and hamburgers. You do not need to wait to be seated in most restaurants. Only in the most expensive restaurants is that a practice. Don't ask for separate checks or suggest sharing the check. One person is supposed to pay for everyone.

Tipping: Restaurants add 15% to your bill for taxes and service, but you should add another 10% for the waiter.

Holidays: New Year's Day (Jan. 1); Epiphany (Jan. 6); Tuesday and Wednesday before Ash Wednesday, Holy Thursday; Good Friday; Labor Day (May 1); Pichincha Day (May 24); Bolivar's Birthday (July 24); Independence Day (Aug. 10); Columbus Day (Oct. 12); All Saints' Day (Nov. 1); All Souls' Day (Nov. 2); Christmas Eve and Christmas Day (Dec. 24 and 25).

Chapter 55

El Salvador

Republic of El Salvador *(República de El Salvador)*
Area: 8,260 square miles
    Smallest country in Central America.
Population: 5,900,000 (1995). Average annual rate
    of increase, 2.6%. Density per square miles,
    723. The most densely populated country in
    Latin America.
Capital: San Salvador
Largest Cities: (1993) San Salvador (972,810);
    Santa Ana (208,322); San Miguel (161,156)
Religion: Roman Catholic, 75%
Literacy Rate: 73%
Ethnic Groups: Mestizo 90%, Indian 5%, Other 5%

Geography

Bordered by Guatemala to the west, Honduras to the north and east, and the Pacific Ocean to the south. Most of the country is a fertile volcanic plateau studded with both active and dormant volcanoes and a number of crater lakes. Because of the high population density and intensive farming very little remains of indigenous forest.

Climate

The principal seasons, as in the rest of Central America, are the wet season (May to October) and the dry season (November to April). There is usually a heavy rain in late afternoon or early evening during the rainy season. The rest of the year is dry and dusty. Temperatures are pretty much the same throughout the year with coastal lowlands being hot and humid. San Salvador, at 2000 feet elevation, has a moderate climate.

Tourist Information

Politics & Economy: El Salvador recently (1982-1994) ended a 12-year civil war in which over 75,000 people were killed. As a result, the economy in general and tourism in particularly has suffered. I have driven through El Salvador twice in recent years and flown there on several occasions and have experienced no problems at all, but have in fact felt very welcomed. Although there still is a great deal of poverty, especially in San Salvador, the economy is beginning to boom, and both local businessmen and foreigners are taking advantage of the new opportunities.

Visa: Entry requirements are gradually being eased, but at the time of this writing a visa was required for American citizens to enter El Salvador. Check with an embassy or consulate before leaving. Driving through, I was able to obtain a visa at the border. The immigration official at the point of entry has the authority to decide whether to admit you, visa or not, so it is to your advantage to appear responsible. With a visa, the maximum stay is 30 days. This may be extended twice, for a maximum of 90 days. After that, visitors must apply for a temporary resident's permit.

Customs: Customs is generally lenient, especially if you present yourself as a respectable tourist, but the importation of fruit, vegetables, plant and animal products is restricted. Questionable articles can be confiscated.

Money: The currency of El Salvador is the *colón*. When leaving, change your extra *colones* before you go. Legally, the maximum amount that can be changed is US $40, but you can normally find money changers that will change however much you need.
It is difficult to change *colones* into other currencies once outside El Salvador. Major credit cards are readily accepted in hotels, restaurants, and banks.

Postal System: Fairly reliable. The country name in the address must be written as *"República de El Salvador, Central America"* to prevent the letter from being returned or sent to some other El Salvador in Latin America, a name held by many cities.

Telephone System: Public telephones are common. Local calls require a 10 *centavo* coin for 3 minutes. Long distance phone calls, telegraphs, telexes, and Faxs can be sent from any ANTEL office, which are located in every city, town, and village.

Health: Tap water is generally unsafe. Use alternatives. In general, El Salvador is a relatively healthy country to be in.

Risks: The 12-year civil war left a lot of firearms behind, and young armed gangs are a problem in many of the larger towns and cities. You are generally safe during the day, but don't go out at night without someone local with you. Normal city street crimes are common in San Salvador.

Holidays: New Year's Day (Jan. 1); Holy Thursday, Good Friday, Easter Saturday and Sunday; Labor Day (May 1), Festival of El Salvador del Mundo (August 3-6); Independence Day (Sept. 15); Columbus Day (Oct. 12); All Soul's Day (Nov. 2); Anniversary of First Call for Independence (Nov. 5); Christmas Holidays (Dec. 25-31).

Chapter 56

Guatemala

Republic of Guatemala *(República de Guatemala)*

Area: 42,042 square miles (Guatemala still claims ownership of Belize, but the area of that country is not included in the figure.)

Population: (1995) 10,600,000
Average annual rate of increase, 3.1%
Density per square miles, 252

Capital & Largest City: Guatemala City 2,000,000 (1993)

Religion: Mostly Roman Catholic

Literacy Rate: 55% This low literacy rate is largely accounted for by the large highland Mayan Indian population who do not have access to formal education.

Languages: Spanish, various Mayan Indian dialects

Ethnic Subgroups: Guatemala has a highly stratified society, with a relatively small number of Spanish descendants at the top. There is a larger number of Mestizos (Indian mixed with Spanish), and a majority population of Indians who maintain a traditional Mayan lifestyle.

Geography

Guatemala is bordered by Mexico, Belize, Honduras, and El Salvador, and has coasts on both the Pacific Ocean and the Caribbean Sea. High mountains run throughout western Guatemala, and there are numerous volcanoes, active and dormant. The bulk of the population lives in the highlands, and all of the larger cities are located there. Northeastern Guatemala, bordering on Mexico and Belize, is a vast jungle, littered with the ruins of formerly great Mayan cities, many of which are still unexcavated. The Pacific slope, with its rich volcanic soil, is heavily cultivated in coffee, cacao, fruit, and sugar cane.

Climate

Although Guatemala is in the tropics, temperatures can go below freezing in the mountains. Guatemala City and Antigua have temperate climates. Both the Caribbean and Pacific Coasts are hot and humid during the rainy season and hot and dry during the dry season.

Tourist Information

Visa: Visas are not required for U.S. citizens, and tourist cards can be obtain on entry. They are valid for 90 days.

U.S. Consulate: Guatemala City, Avenida La Reforma 7-01, Zona 10; Tel. (2) 311541.

Money: The basic unit of currency is the *Quetzal,* divided into 100 *centavos.* Many places accept U.S. dollars instead of *quetzales.* Dollars may be exchanged at banks and hotels, but there is also an active black market which pays slightly better than banks. Major credit cards are widely accepted. You can't legally change *quetzales* into dollars when leaving the country, so don't change more dollars than you need. Do not accept torn bills, because you may not be able to spend it. There is frequently a shortage of small change in smaller stores, and you might not be able to use a larger bill. Carry a supply of small denominations.

Telephone: Local phone calls can be made from coin phones. So can long distance, but take lots of coins. Long distance calls can also be made from national phone company (GUATEL) offices. You can also use MCI (189), AT&T (190), and Sprint (195) to call direct to the U.S. from coin phones. Public phones are most commonly found in pharmacies and hotel lobbies.

Transportation: Taxis don't have meters. Ask for the fare in advance. There are two kinds of buses for intercity travel, first and second class. First class tickets should be bought in advance to reserve a seat. The buses are usually retired Greyhound buses from the U.S. Normally they will not have people standing in the aisles, and do not stop before their destinations except to let individuals off along the way. Second class buses are retired school buses, do not have reserved seats, and squeeze aboard as many people as can fit. They normally stop at all the small towns along the way, as well as anywhere along the highway that someone wants to get off.

Health: There are no particular health risks in Guatemala. Do not, however, drink public water supplies. Milk and cheese in inexpensive restaurants may be home produced and not pasteurized. Peel fruits and vegetables unless they are well cooked.

Risks: There have been sporadic clashes between guerrillas and government troops for a number of years and death squads have occasionally wiped out Indian villages in the highlands. It is basically a fight between the haves and have-nots, who are seeking to have more control over their destinies. It is best not to travel at night in any part of the country because armed bandits occasionally rob travelers, and the highland areas are more risky than the Pacific lowlands. Guatemala City is especially noted for its pickpockets and the crowded urban buses have quite a few of them. Even with these problems, though, I have always felt safer after crossing the border from Mexico into Guatemala, where I no longer have to fear the Mexican police, who are themselves frequently crooks.

Cultural Specifics

Greetings: Handshakes are the rule upon being introduced or greeting a member of either sex. Expect a limp handshake, because that is what is normal. Men and women who are good friends and women who are good friends often kiss on one cheek in greeting. Men who are good friends often embrace and pat one another on the back.

Shopping: Bargaining is normal in markets and small shops. Generally offer half the asking price and go from there. When bargaining for the handicrafts made by Indians, please remember the very poor economic conditions under which they live and keep in mind that it may have taken months to have made by hand what they are offering for sale.

Dress: Don't wear shorts in the cities or in the highlands. Don't wear jeans in the cities. Women should wear skirt and blouse, not pants.

Meals: Breakfast is usually between 7:00 and 8:00 AM, and frequently consists of eggs, black beans, bread, orange juice and coffee. Lunch is usually around 12:30 or so, and may consist of soup, meat with boiled vegetables, fruit, black beans, tortillas, and fried plantains. Dinner is usually after 7:00 PM, and is much the same as lunch, except lighter.

Table Manners: Female guests usually sit to the right of the host, and male guests to the left. You are expected to eat everything on your plate, and they are happy if you want seconds.

Dining out: A *restaurante* is a high-class restaurant. A *comedor* is a small place serving typical Guatemalan food. There is a wide choice of restaurants in larger cities, especially Guatemala City, where there are many foreign and ethnic restaurants. Many of the better restaurants require coat and tie. To attract the waiter's attention, raise your hand. The check will not be brought automatically. You will have to ask for it. In Guatemala, unlike many other Latin American countries, there are no set rules about whether one person pays for the group or whether the check is split. Offer to pay your share.

Tipping: Service charges are not included in restaurant bills. Leave 10-15%. Tip others at your own discretion.

Driving: Traffic signals are turned off after 8:00 PM. Because of that and other risks, do not drive at night. Roads are generally good and well marked, and daytime driving is not a problem except in more remote areas. Always carry your passport. There are checkpoints along the main roads. Stay away from military convoys or vehicles.

Holidays: New Year's Day (Jan. 1), Easter week (Wed., Thur., & Friday before Easter), Labor Day (May 1), Army Day (June 30), Assumption Day (August 15), Independence Day (Sept. 15), Revolution Day (Oct. 20), All Saints' Day (Nov. 1), Christmas Eve and Christmas Day (Dec. 24 and 25), Old Year's Day (Dec. 31).

Chapter 57

Republic of Honduras *(República de Honduras)*

Area: 43,872 square miles

Population: 5,500,000 (1995)
> Average annual rate of increase 2.8%
> Density per square miles, 125.3

Capital: Tegucigalpa

Largest Cities: (1989) Tegucigalpa 608,000, San Pedro Sula 300,000

Religion: Roman Catholic, 94%

Literacy Rate: 73%

Languages: Spanish, several Indian languages, and English along the Caribbean coast. English is commonly used in business.

Ethnic Groups: Approximately 90% of the population is Mestizo, and roughly 7% are Indians living in various isolated areas around the country. Descendants of Caribbean Blacks who came to work the banana plantations in the 1800's live along the Caribbean coast and on the Bay Islands.

Geography

Honduras has coasts on both the Caribbean (about 380 miles) and the Pacific (about 75 miles). It is a mountainous country, rising to 9500 feet, with the highlands covered by pine forests. The highlands have a typically temperate climate. The Pacific coast is hot and mainly agricultural. The Caribbean lowlands are rainy, and the offshore islands are part of a barrier reef system extending down from Belize. It is popular for diving and is well known for its clear water. Large areas within Honduras still remain in a pristine condition, especially along the eastern Caribbean coast and in some mountain areas. Logging is rapidly deforesting the the country, however.

Climate

The Honduras climate is like that of other Central American countries, with a dry season and a wet season. The rainy season is roughly from May to October; dry season from November to April. Rain is common all year round along the Caribbean coast.

Tourist Information

Economy: Honduras is a poor country, with nearly 50% of the population either unemployed or under-employed. Agriculture accounts for 60% of the jobs. The main products are coffee and bananas.

Visa: Visas are not required for U.S. citizens. The initial entry is for 30 days, which can be extended another 60 days once in the country.

You may leave an re-enter the country for another 90 days and this process may be repeated as often as needed.

U.S. Embassy: Tegucigalpa. Edificio Embajada Americana, Avenida La Paz. Tel. 323120/4.

Money: The basic unit of currency is the *lempira,* which is divided into 100 *centavos.* The U.S. dollar is the only foreign currency which is easily exchanged. Cash is likely to get a slightly better rate than travelers checks. The black market usually offers a slightly better rate of exchange than the official bank rate. Major credit cards are widely accepted, especially Visa.

Postal System: Mail to the U.S. takes about seven to ten days. Mail from the U.S. to Honduras may never arrive if it looks like it could contain money. This problem is not uncommon in a number of Latin American countries, but is especially common in Central America.

Telephone: International telephone, telegraph, telex, and fax services are available at HONDUTEL offices throughout Honduras. International calls are expensive. AT&T USA Direct operators can be reached by dialing 123 from almost any telephone.

Health: The visitor's most common problem is likely to be intestinal. Do not drink untreated tap water anywhere in the country, and take precautions with raw vegetables and fruit. Malaria has been a problem along the eastern Caribbean coast, and anti-malarial medication should be taken in that area. AIDS occurs in the San Pedro Sula area in a much higher than normal frequency, mainly due to its proximity to a major port and the presence of large numbers of prostitutes. Cholera is a problem from time to time, but most Hondurans are aware of it and attempt to purify their water.

Risks: Honduras is a generally safe country, but petty crime is common in cities as it is in all Latin American cities. Take the usual precautions.

Transportation: Buses are the main mode of transportation, go almost everywhere, and are very inexpensive. Most are retired U.S. school buses, but are efficient. Bicycles are common, but only a small percentage of the population own cars.

Domestic air flights are inexpensive and are the only means of reaching some places on the eastern Caribbean coast.

Holidays: New Year's Day (Jan. 1), Day of the Americas (Apr. 14), Easter Week (Thurs., Fri., Sat. before Easter Sunday), Labor Day (May 1), Independence Day (Sept. 15), Francisco Morazan Day (Oct. 3), Columbus Day (Oct. 12), Army Day (Oct. 21), Christmas Day (Dec. 25).

Chapter 58

United Mexican States *(Estados Unidos Mexicanos)*
Area: 761,600 square miles
Population: 93,700,000 (1995)
    Average annual rate of increase, 2.2%
    Density per square miles, 123
Capital: Federal District (Mexico City)
Largest Cities: Federal District (Mexico City) (1989), 19,479,000 (Largest city in the world); Guadalajara, 3,186,500; Monterey, 2,858,800; Puebla, 1,707,000; Leon, 1,006,700
Religion: Roman Catholic, 89%
Literacy Rate: 88%
Languages: Spanish, plus approximately 50 different Indian languages
Ethnic Groups: 60% Mestizo, 30% Indian, 10% European descendants.

Diversity

Mexico is, without doubt, the most culturally and geographically diverse country in Latin America. There are deserts, high mountains, volcanoes, temperate areas, tropical scrub, and jungle. There are presently over 50 different native Indian groups with their distinct languages. It is estimated that over 150 languages have disappeared since the arrival of the Spaniards. Two of the most remarkably advanced early civilizations known, the Mayans and the Aztecs arose independently and coexisted for a while in Mexico. The country is rich in minerals, including gold, silver, and petroleum, and produces a wide range of agricultural products. Because of its magnificent diversity it is impossible to give thorough coverage of Mexico in this book, and it is recommended that you get one of the many travel books available, such as the one published by Lonely Planet.

Geography

Mexico shares borders with the United States in the north and Belize and Guatemala to the south. On the west it is bordered by the Pacific Ocean, to the east by the Gulf of Mexico, and south of Yucatan, by the Caribbean Sea. Northern and central Mexico (north of Mexico City) have coastal plains on the east and west and two north-south mountain ranges with broad central plateaus between them. Northwestern Mexico is dry, much of it desert. Northeastern Mexico is slightly wetter and becomes more so further south. Mexico City itself is situated in a high valley, and is temperate at about 5,000 ft. elevation. Once filled by a great lake with islands occupied by the center of Aztec government, it is now filled with unstable sediment occupied by a massive city surrounded by slums and constantly smothered by some of the world's worst air pollution. The elevation gradually drops south of Mexico City to the relatively narrow and flat Isthmus of Tehuantepec. South of this isthmus the land mass widens to the east out into the flat Yucatan Peninsula, and to the west, mountains gradually rise in elevation and continue into Guatemala.

Tourist Information

Visa: Not required of U.S. citizens. It is not recommended, but U.S. citizens can enter Mexico without a passport provided they have proof of citizenship such as a birth certificate of voter registration card. A tourist card, obtainable at the airport at time of departure, at a Mexican consulate, or at the border, is required to travel to the interior of Mexico. It is not required at U.S.-Mexico border towns for stays of less than 72 hours. You may specify the number of days you wish for the tourist card, up to a maximum of 180 days. If you do not ask for more time, it will normally be issued for 30 days.

Money: Mexico's basic unit of currency is the *peso,* divided into 100 *centavos.* There have been many changes in the relative value of pesos to dollars over the years, and it would be wise to check current values before you go. Dollars can be readily changed in banks (frequently time-consuming) or in *casas de cambio.* There is no black market (or at least I haven't been able to find it), but if you get stuck without *pesos* on a weekend you can usually change cash or traveler's checks at the larger hotels, although at a lower rate than banks. Major credit cards are widely accepted, and in many places can be used in ATM machines for cash.

Postal System: As in most of Latin America, mail is
unpredictable. It can take as long as two
weeks between the U.S. and Mexico, either direction. Letters should not appear to contain
money or checks.

Telephone: Local and national long distance calls
can be made from any telephone, including
public phone booths. International long distance calls are best made from special direct-
dial long distance phone booths called
"Latadel" or *"Larga Distancia."* These are located around the centers of most towns and
cities. AT&T and MCI operators can also be
reached through Latadel phones. Some will
have printed instructions; otherwise you can
get the information from an office of TEL-
MEX, the national telephone company. International calls can also be made from most
hotels, but many of them have large sur-
charges for the service.

Health: Health considerations depend mainly on
what part of Mexico you will be going to. It is
a good idea to be up-to-date on your immuni-
zation for tetanus. Some areas, but not many,
occasionally have problems with malaria and
cholera. Your main consideration should be
with sanitation of food and water. The often
joked about "Montezuma's Revenge" is no
joke when you have it and are trying to travel
at the same time. A good medicine to help
cure diarrhea should go along with you. Do
not drink unpurified tap water or any fruit
drinks made with water. Take along some io-
dine to purify water. It only takes a few drops
per gallon of water. Chlorine bleach will do
the same thing, though it takes a little more.
Stay away from salads or uncooked vegetables that may have been cleaned in tap water,

and don't use tap water to brush your teeth. Bottled water, canned or bottled soft drinks, and beer are safe, but the glass you pour it into may not be. Drink directly from the can or bottle. Some serious tropical diseases, such as malaria and dengue fever, are spread by mosquitoes (in all parts of tropical Latin America), especially during rainy seasons. I've found that the best repellents are mosquito coils, which when lit give out an incense-like smell, and when put in an enclosed area or upwind, will most definitely keep the mosquitoes away while sleeping. They are readily available throughout Latin America in grocery stores. When moving about where there are mosquitoes use a repellent.

Risks: Although Mexican males can get quite violent when they believe they are being insulted, violence is rarely a problem in Mexico if you steer clear of obviously dangerous areas and stay out of rowdy bars. Don't stare at anyone with your hands on your hips or give them the finger. Smile when possible. The largest risk is typical petty crime, such as pickpocketing in the cities. Mugging and armed robbery is becoming increasingly common, especially at night in the cities or in remote areas. Protect yourself. In the southern Mexican state of Chiapas there has been an occasional rebel conflict between Indians and the Mexican authorities. These seem to have diminished recently, but it would be a good idea to ask about safety before going into remote areas in Chiapas.

Bribery: A fact of life in Mexico is bribery and corruption. It is, to me, the greatest annoyance in Mexico, and unfortunately comes along with the very people you hope will be protecting

369

you—the police. Public employees throughout Mexico receive very poor salaries, often
not enough to even support their families, and
whatever income that can be gained through
bribes is seen as rightful income. Policemen
will not normally ask directly for a bribe
(called *mordida,* "the bite"), but will hint at
it. It will be up to you to make the offer. Unlike in the U.S., you will not get into trouble
for making the offer. I usually use an approach such as to pull out a few bills (representing a few dollars, depending on the
seriousness of the claimed offense) and ask
something like "Can we solve this problem in
a simple way?" Present the offer so that others cannot see it. Bribery is also commonly
used in public offices to get an application, petition, or whatever put on top of the pile instead of at the bottom. It can buy a driver's
license, an international ship's captain's license, or an extension to your tourist card,
provided that the offer is well presented. For
something serious, a lawyer can often be helpful in making the offer. I do not approve of
bribery or corruption in any form, but without it life can be difficult in Mexico.

Cultural Specifics

Greetings: Both men and women shake hands
when being introduced to someone of the
same sex. A man shakes hands with a woman
only when she initiates the gesture. Among
good friends women kiss on the cheek, and
men and women kiss on the cheek. Again wait

for the woman to initiate it before kissing her on the cheek. Mexican men who are good friends often embrace on greeting.

Interaction: Mexicans stand closer together when talking than do North Americans and they touch more frequently. Let them set the distance and physical interaction. To back off is an insult. Mexico is one of the two Latin American countries (the other is Puerto Rico) where you should not refer to yourself as an "American." In Mexico you should refer to yourself as a "North American." Because of their long history of close interaction with the United States, Mexicans are very sensitive about this issue. Best of all, simply say that you are from the United States when asked where you are from.

Another sensitive term is the word *"gringo."* Everywhere else in Latin America it simply refers to someone from Europe or North America and has no negative connotation. In Mexico it is a derogatory term and it is an insult if directed toward you. Although Mexican Mestizos themselves may look at Indians in a negative way, all realize that they, themselves, have some Indian ancestry, and will be offended if you speak negatively about Indians. Don't tell off-color jokes to a woman, and don't be sexually suggestive to one in public. This can get you into some serious trouble.

Shopping: Unlike many Latin American countries, bargaining is a way of life in Mexico. You are not going to be able to bargain in supermarkets, other food stores, or in up-scale shops where prices are marked, but in public markets, most stores, and on the street it is expected. Someone who doesn't bargain and

who pays the asking price is considered foolish. Offer about half, and negotiate from
there. Don't become angry or take it seriously
because it is like a game.

Dress: Dress in Mexico is more conservative than in
the U.S. and is influenced by European fashion. Jeans are OK, but slacks and shirts more
acceptable in the cities. Shorts are used only
in resort areas.

Meals: Mexicans usually eat later than North Americans or than Central Americans. Breakfast is
usually between 7:30 and 9:00, and may consist of coffee, sweet rolls, tortillas, refried
beans, eggs, and fruit. Lunch, usually the largest meal of the day, is eaten between 1:30
and 3:30. It may consist of soup, meat, rice,
beans, a dessert (frequently custard) or fruit,
and coffee. Tortillas are normally served.
There might be an afternoon snack, and dinner will usually be between 8:00 and 10:00.
There might be soup and tamales or beans,
cheese, fruit, coffee.

Dining out: Most better restaurants serve lunch
from 1:00 to 4:00, close and re-open for dinner at 9:00. Inexpensive restaurants are open
all day, breakfast through dinner. Dining out
in Mexico can be a fine culinary experience.
Unlike in most of the rest of Latin America,
where food tends to be on the bland side,
Mexicans take great delight in variety and in
spicy foods. There is a lot of regional variation. While some foods are present in all areas, such as tortillas and rice, every region has
its specialties and preferred foods, with even
more differences than in the U.S. with its Ca-
jun cooking, southern cooking, and New Eng-

land specialties. Although its occasionally a little on the hot side, I never get bored eating in Mexico.

Tipping: It has been my experience that table service in better Mexican restaurants is as good as, if not better than, in equivalent U.S. restaurants. It always seems a simple matter to catch the waiter's eye, because he's always watching. Some restaurants will add a service charge, but many don't. Don't hesitate to tip 10-20% for superior service. Tips are generally not expected in inexpensive restaurants. Porters, taxi drivers, chambermaids, and washroom attendants should also be tipped a small amount.

Holidays: New Year's Day (Jan. 1), Epiphany (Jan. 6), Constitution Day (Feb. 5), Flag Day (Feb. 24), Birthday of Benito Juárez (Mar. 21), Easter Week (Holy Thursday, Good Friday, Easter Sunday), Labor Day (May 1), Battle of Puebla (May 5), Anniversary of the Revolution (Sept. 16), Columbus Day (Oct. 12), Independence Day (Nov. 20), Christmas Day (Dec., 25).

Chapter 59

Nicaragua

Republic of Nicaragua *(República de Nicaragua)*
Area: 50,180 square miles
Population: (1995) 4,400,000
 Average annual rate of increase 2.7%
 Density per square miles, 87.6
Capital: Managua, population (1992) 974,000
Religion: Roman Catholic, 95%
Literacy Rate: 57%
Ethnic Groups: 77% of the population is Mestizo,
 10% of European descent, Blacks, 9%, and In-
 dians, 4%. The two latter groups live mainly
 along the Caribbean coast.

Geography

 Nicaragua is the largest, but most sparsely settled country in Central America. It has the largest lake in Latin America (Lake Nicaragua), which has the only fresh-water sharks in the world. It is bordered on the north by Honduras, on the south by Costa Rica, on the west by the Pacific Ocean, and on the east by the Caribbean Sea. The country has three distinct geographic regions. They are the Pacific lowlands, which are primarily in agricultural use, the north-central mountains, which are temperate, and the

Caribbean lowlands, mainly jungle, and aptly called the Mosquito Coast. There are many volcanoes in Nicaragua, a number of which are active. Nicaragua is also well known for its earthquakes, and a number of its cities have been badly damaged over the years.

Climate

There is climatic variation depending on elevation, but the greatest variation comes from rainfall patterns. December through April is the dry season and May through November is the wet season. The Pacific lowland area is very hot, but not especially rainy. The Caribbean lowland area is humid and rainy all year, but cooler than the Pacific lowlands.

Political Situation: After some 10 years of civil war between the "Sandinistas" (government) and "Contras" (rebels), free elections were held in 1990, and after some five years of delicate negotiations and political hostilities, the situation is fairly calm at this time. There is no more active fighting and the government has been making serious efforts to re-integrate the rebels into the mainstream.

Tourist Information

Visa: All visitors to Nicaragua must have a passport valid for at least six months. U.S. citizens are not required to have visas, but must obtain a tourist card, valid for 30 days, either from the airline when departing, or upon arrival. This can be extended twice, for a total of 90 days.

Theoretically, a tourist must have an onward
or return ticket, but this rule doesn't seem to
be regularly enforced.

U.S. Embassy: Managua, Km 4 1/2, Carretera Sur.
Tel. 66-601/3/5.

Money: The basic unit of currency is the *cordoba*
(also commonly referred to as *"peso"*), divided into 100 *centavos*. It generally cannot
be changed outside of Nicaragua, so it is a
good idea not to buy more *cordobas* than will
be spent. Dollars and travelers' checks can be
changed at any bank or *casa de cambio*. Major credit cards are widely accepted.

Telephone: Long distance domestic or international
calls can be made from TELCOR offices, but
direct dial, AT&T, MCI, and Sprint calls can
be made from private telephones. Fax services are available in photocopying and camera
shops, as well as in many TELCOR offices.
Keep in mind that each city in Nicaragua has
its own area code which must be used in addition to the international country code when
calling from another country.

Health: Surprisingly, tap water is usually safe to
drink in most of Nicaragua. One still has to be
alert for unsanitary conditions among street
vendors. Malaria is a problem during the
rainy season in the Caribbean lowlands area.
Chloroquinine is available in pharmacies and
should be taken as a preventative when in
lowland areas.

Risks: There is no longer any risk from warfare
now that the civil war is finished. However,
more than 50% of the adults in Nicaragua are
without employment, and street crime is common. Pickpocketing and bag slashing is common on city buses, so be aware and protect
yourself in advance.

The People

I have always been impressed with the Nicaraguan people, especially with their general sincerity and honesty. Many Nicaraguans fled the civil war and went south to their next door neighbor, Costa Rica. The middle and upper class people of Costa Rica frequently advertise specifically for Nicaraguan maids and gardeners because it is so widely believed that they work harder and are more honest than than their Costa Rican counterparts. I also found that to be true while living in Costa Rica. It is also commonly said that the increased problem with crime in Costa Rica is because of Nicaraguans. However, on those thirteen occasions in which I was robbed in Costa Rica, I know for a fact that it was Costa Ricans that did the deed.

Tipping: Most Nicaraguans do not tip. However there is nothing to keep you from doing it if you want. Some restaurants add a service charge.

Holidays: New Year's Day (Jan. 1), Holy Week (Thursday, Friday and Saturday before Easter Sunday), Labor Day (May 1), Battle of San Jacinto (Sept. 14), Independence Day (Sept. 15), All Souls' Day (Nov. 2), Immaculate Conception (Dec. 8), Christmas (Dec. 25).

Chapter 60

Panama

Republic of Panama *(República de Panamá)*
Area: 29,761 square miles
Population: 2,600,000 (1995)
    Average annual rate of increase, 2.1%
    Density per square miles, 87.3
Capital: Panama City, population 625,000 (1992)
Religion: Roman Catholic, 93%; Protestant, 6%;
    Other 1%
Literacy Rate: 88%
Languages: Spanish, English, several Indian lan-
    guages
Ethnic Groups: Mestizo, 62%; West Indian black,
    14%; European descent, 10%; mixed black,
    white, and Indian, 8%; Indian, 6% (six differ-
    ent tribal groups)

Geography

    Panama is a narrow isthmus connecting Central and
North America with South America. It runs West and East,
and is about 30 miles wide at its narrowest point. The
Panama Canal, with Colon to the north and Panama City
to the south, cuts across this narrowest point. Oddly
enough, because the country runs east and west, and the

Caribbean entrance to the canal is slightly west of the Pacific entrance, the sun rises above the Pacific Ocean at Panama City beaches. There is a ridge of mountains running down the center of the country, marked by a high point of over 12,000 feet near the Costa Rican border gradually dropping to almost sea level at the Panama Canal. A lower ridge of mountains picks up again and continues to the Darrein Gap area, connecting to Colombia. The Pan American highway, running continuously from the United States through Mexico and Central America terminates at the Darrein Gap because of its almost impenetrable jungles, swamps and rivers. It picks up again in Colombia and continues almost to the tip of South America. The western portion of Panama is primarily agricultural and pastoral, supplying the rest of Panama with plant and meat products. Volcán Baru, Panama's only volcano and highest point, has especially rich soil on its slopes, and because of its altitude, can produce crops normally found only in temperate regions. Both the Pacific and Caribbean coastal regions produce large quantities of bananas, most of which are exported to Europe. The ocean waters off Panama have not been over exploited (due to strict laws) and still offer abundant fishing. There are over 500 rivers in Panama and 1,600 islands off the long coastlines of the Pacific Ocean and Caribbean Sea.

Climate

As in the rest of Central America, Panama has two seasons, wet and dry. The Pacific coastal slope is much drier than the Caribbean, where it is likely to rain almost every day all year. The Pacific slope is mostly grassland and savannah, while the Caribbean slope is almost completely virgin rain forest and jungle. Temperatures are typically hot in the lowlands and cool in the highlands, and remain about the same all year round.

Politics and Economy

When many people think of Panama they think of ex-dictator General Manuel Noriega (currently in prison in Florida) and the drug traffic. As a consequence of Noriega, Panama, like Costa Rica, changed its constitution to eliminate the military. Although they do have a strong and well-trained police force, there is no more army and almost no possibility of a dictator in the future. It is true that Noriega and his organization was involved in shipping drugs, particularly cocaine, to the United States from Colombia and other countries in South America and in "laundering" money for drug organizations. However, there is not (and never has been), a great deal of drug use in Panama. There is also very little actual traffic in drugs through the country. Panama, however, has one of the strongest and most discreet banking systems in the world (considered by many to be better than Switzerland), and there are nearly 200 international banks with branches in Panama. As a result, Panama continues to be one of the major money laundering countries in the world, still serving the international drug traffic. Panama is much better off economically than most of the other countries in Latin America, partly because of the Panama Canal and its banking system, but also because its economy is based on the U.S. dollar, which tends to be very stable. Panama City, with its skyscrapers, international trade and shipping, is as modern as any capital city. Unemployment is estimated to be about 11%, but as it recovers from the Noriega era, it is probably a bit higher.

Tourist Information

Visa: A visa is not required for U.S. residents. A tourist card, valid for 30 days, and which can be extended for an additional 60 days is required and may be obtained from the airline upon departure. A passport is highly recommended, but a birth certificate will suffice to obtain a tourist card for U.S. citizens. A tourist card obtained with birth certificate cannot be extended. An onward or return ticket is required, and, on paper at least, you are required to have at least $300. Visitors are rarely requested to show either a ticket or money (a credit card will do).

U.S. Embassy: Panama City. The U.S. Embassy has recently moved into a new building, and I don't have the address. Ask a cab driver to take you. They know.

Money: Panama uses the U.S. dollar. Yes, the very same bills, although they are occasionally referred to as the *"Balboa,"* which is technically correct. Panamanian coins are the same denominations and sizes as U.S. coins, made of the same materials, interchangeable in coin operated machines, but have different face designs. All major credit cards are widely accepted, and ATM machines in all larger towns can provide you with cash from either credit cards or debit cards from your home town bank in the U.S.

Postal System: Mail service either to Panama or from Panama is reliable, and usually takes about a week to or from the U.S. Letters addressed to Panama must specify *"República de Panamá"* or they may be returned.

Telephone: INTEL offices throughout Panama offer international telephone, telegraph, and fax
services promptly. International operators for
collect calls (106), MCI (108), and AT&T
(109) can be reached through any public or
private telephone. Local calls and national
long-distance calls can be made through any
public coin phone, which are plentiful
throughout the country. Read the instructions: some you put the coins in first, some
you dial first and put coins in when the party
answers.

Health: Tap water is safe to drink throughout Panama as long as it is from a public source and
not a private well. Panamanians are very conscious of the importance of sanitary conditions
for food, and it is usually safe to eat in the
smallest and cheapest restaurants. There are
no particular disease problem in the country,
except for in the Darrein Gap area, where a
chloroquinine-resistant strain of malaria has
developed. Protect yourself from mosquitoes
in that area.

Risks: Crime, sometimes violent, is a problem in
certain parts of Panama City, and it makes
sense to listen to the residents and stay out of
those areas at night. The better areas are
much safer than most cities in the U.S. and
have restaurants and activities open all night.
In these areas armed security guards are sta-
tioned on every block. Panama City also has a
special police force, the *"Policía Turistica,"*
whose main purpose is to watch after and protect tourists. They are found in all tourist areas. Colon, on the other hand, and at the
other end of the canal, is probably the most
dangerous city in the western hemisphere. Do
not, under any conditions, walk on the streets

of Colon either during the day or at night. It is
not a question of maybe you'll have problems—you will have problems. Almost any
area in the interior of Panama is perfectly
safe, with normal precautions, either during
the day or at night.

Greetings: When people are introduced both men
and women shake hands. Good friends between women kiss on one cheek, both meeting and departing. Men and women who are
good friends also kiss on the cheek (women
are the recipients). Men shake hands, both
meeting and departing.

Interaction

Panamanians, like Costa Ricans, are among the
most friendly people of Latin America. Although people are
somewhat reserved in Panama City, if you walk around
with a smile on your face in the interior, look people in the
eye and say *"hola,"* you will make many acquaintances.
Unlike in much of Latin America, Panamanians will readily
invite foreigners into their homes and are open to genuine
friendships. Unlike persistent rumors to the contrary,
Panamanians, through their long exposure to Americans in
the Canal Zone, actually like and respect them. There is
some resentment about the invasion into Panama City, but
few people blame the individual American. While many
mothers in the U.S. hope that their daughters will marry
doctors, just as many in Panama hope that their daughters
will marry Americans. It is a good idea to avoid talking
about Manuel Noriega and the 1989 invasion. Quite a few
people lost jobs, and many families had relatives killed.
Panamanians have a great respect for education, so it's fine

to let them know that you are literate, but avoid discussing your possessions. Panamanians, in general, are not as interested in status and money as in most other countries.

When locals refer to "Panama," you can only tell through context whether they are referring to the country or the city. Panama City is always simply referred to as "Panama."

Cultural Specifics

Dress: Panamanians are not as concerned about clothing as in many other countries. Jeans, tee-shirts, and athletic shoes are acceptable for both sexes in most situations. Dresses and slacks are better for going out in the evening. Shorts are commonly worn by women throughout the country, but men run the risk of whistles and catcalls if they wear shorts. People in Panama tend to be more prompt for appointments than in most of Latin America, but 30 minutes late is not seen as being out-of-line.

Meals: Panamanians, as in the other Central American countries, eat their meals earlier than South Americans and Mexicans. Breakfast is usually around 7:00, and typically consists of sauteed liver and onions, thick deep-fried corn cakes or thin flour tortillas, white cheese, and coffee. In some parts of the country thick smoked beef jerky sauteed with onions substitutes for the liver. Lunch is usually served at noon. A simple lunch is usually *"sancocho,"* a chicken soup with potatoes and tropical root vegetables. A more elaborate meal might be steak or fried chicken, rice with chick peas and sauteed sweetened plantains. Dinner is usually around 7:00 and doesn't differ much from lunch, although it might include a salad, fruit, and dessert.

Table Manners: Just like in other Latin American countries. Keep both hands above the table, keep your napkin on the table. Just about as many Panamanians use the fork and knife European style as American style. Country people are apt to shovel everything up in a spoon grasped in the fist.

Dining out: Because of the international character of Panama City, restaurants with specialties from around the world are common. Excellent fresh seafood is readily available. Meals tend to be pretty ho-hum in the interior, with typically Panamanian food or Chinese food in most restaurants. Pizza and fried chicken places are enormously popular. Reservations are needed in very few restaurants, but dress up for the more expensive ones in the city. Very few restaurants add service charges and there are no add-on taxes. Everything is included in the menu price. It is appropriate to add a 10-15% tip, although many Panamanians don't bother.

Holidays: New Year's Day (Jan. 1), Day of National Mourning (Jan. 9), Carnival (four days preceding Ash Wednesday), Easter (Good Friday through Easter Sunday), Labor Day (May 1), Panama City Day (Aug. 15), National Anthem Day (Nov. 1), All Souls' Day (Nov. 2), Independence Day (Nov. 3), Flag Day (Nov. 4), First Call of Independence (Nov. 10), Independence from Spain (Nov. 28), Mother's Day (Dec. 8), Christmas Day (Dec. 25).

Note: Carnival in some towns of Panama rivals that of Rio de Janeiro, with wild dancing, tanker trucks spraying water, lots of drinking, and lots of fun. Everyone from the youngest children to tottering old folks participate during the four days of abandon.

Chapter 61

Paraguay

Republic of Paraguay *(República del Paraguay)*

Area: 157,047 square miles

Population: (1995) 5,000,000
    Natural rate of increase, 2.8%
    Density per square miles, 31.8

Capital: Asunción

Largest Cities: (1992) Asunción (800,000), Ciudad
    del Este (133,893), San Lorenzo (133,311)

Religion: Roman Catholic, 90%

Literacy Rate: 90%

Languages: Spanish, Guarani. Guarani is an Indian
    language, but is spoken by preference by
    many Mestizos who also speak Spanish. Gov-
    ernment officials are required to be able to
    speak Guarani. Many Indians speak German
    as a second language because the German
    Mennonite influence.

Ethnic Groups: 75% Mestizo, small minorities of In-
    dians (Guarani and others), Blacks, Asians,
    and about 10% of European descent.

Geography

Paraguay is one of the only two landlocked countries of South America (the other is Bolivia). Because of the size of South America, it appears small on the map, but it is almost exactly the same size as California. Most of the country is a plateau with rolling hills. Eastern Paraguay is well watered, and has the great bulk of the population and its agriculture. Western Paraguay has erratic rainfall, is not suitable for agriculture, and is used mainly for cattle ranching. Being located in the temperate zone of South America, and well south of the equator, its seasons are similar to North America, but reversed, and not so cold.

Tourist Information

Visa: U.S. citizens need a passport with visa, which should be obtained from a consulate. A tourist card, valid for 90 days is also needed, and can be obtained before leaving at the airport. By regulation, a statement from your local police or sheriff's department showing a clean record, along with a bank statement showing enough money, are needed to get the visa. Call a Paraguayan consulate to find out what current regulations are; they change.

Money: The basic unit of currency is the *guarani*. There are bank notes for up to 10,000 *guaranis,* and coins from 1 to 100 *guaranis*. Banks will exchange both dollars and traveler's checks. Street changers or hotels can change on weekends, but give lower rates. There is no black market. Major credit cards are accepted in the capital, but rarely elsewhere.

Telephone: ANTELCO, the national telephone
company, has offices in Asunción with direct
links to operators in the U.S. with which
credit card or collect calls can be made. You
can also pay cash at the offices. Public telephone booths are rare and accept tokens.

Health: Paraguay is a generally healthy country to
be in and the public water supplies are usually safe.

Risks: Crime is usually not much of a problem, but
use normal precautions. Be polite with the police and military, and always carry your passport in the event of a check.

Greetings: When introduced, men shake hands with
both men and women. Among friends women
kiss other women on the cheek and men and
women who are related kiss on the cheek (if
not related, they shake hands). Men shake
hands with other men. It is important to
shake hands both when meeting and when
parting.

Cultural Specifics

Paraguay has had a tumultuous political past, and
it is a good idea to avoid the subject. Even today, criticism
of the government can put you into jail. Be careful with
gestures. Crossing of fingers for luck is offensive in Paraguay. So is the OK sign, so common to North Americans.
Bargaining is acceptable in markets and street stands, but
not in established shops or stores.

Dress: Summer (December to March) is hot. The
rest of the year is mild, but with some cold
nights. Dress accordingly. Jeans are accept-

able for both men and women. Neither should wear shorts. Dresses and slacks should be worn for going out in the evening.

Meals: Breakfast is usually eaten around 7:00 and may consist of coffee or *yerba mate* (a kind of tea), and several kinds of bread. Lunch is around 12:30, and usually involves soup, meat, cassava (a tropical root), salad, and perhaps a dessert. Dinners are around 8:00, and frequently consist of a backyard barbecue, but may just be soup and bread. Vegetables are not popular in Paraguay.

Tipping: Restaurants do not add a service charge, so a tip of about 10-15% is appropriate. Taxi drivers should be tipped 10% of the fare.

Holidays: New Year's Day (Jan. 1), Feast of San Blas (Feb. 3), Heroes' Day (March 1), Holy Thursday, Good Friday, Easter Sunday, Labor Day (May 1), Independence Days (May 14 & 15), Corpus Christi (the Thursday after the eighth Sunday after Easter), Chaco Armistice (June 12), Founding of Asunción (Aug. 15), Constitution Day (Aug. 25), Victory of Boqueron Day (Sept. 29), Columbus Day (Oct. 12), All Saints' Day (Nov. 1), Feast of the Virgin of Caacupe (Dec. 8), Christmas (Dec. 25).

Chapter 62

Republic of Peru *(República del Perú)*
Area: 496,222 square miles
Population: (1995) 24,000,000
Capital: Lima
Largest Cities: (1990) Lima (5,826,000), Arequipa
    (634,500), Callao (589,000), Trujillo
    (532,000), Chiclayo (426,300)
Religion: Roman Catholic, 90%
Literacy Rate: 85%
Languages: Spanish, Quechua, Aymara, and other
    native languages
Ethnic Groups: Indian, 45%; Mestizo, 37%; Euro-
    pean descent, 15%, other, 3%

Geography

Peru extends for nearly 1500 miles along the Pacific Ocean. Colombia and Ecuador are to the north, Brazil and Bolivia to the east, and Chile to the south. Along the coastline is a strip about 50 to 100 miles wide which is very arid, desert in places. Running north and south are the Andes mountains, with peaks over 20,000 feet in elevation, high plateaus, and deep valleys. The western side of the Andes is relatively dry, but the eastern slope, which descends into the Amazon River basin, is very wet and covered with rain forest and jungle. Almost half the population lives in the highlands and a very high percentage of these people are Quechua Indians (Aymara around Lake Titicaca), direct descendants of the Inca. In the Amazon basin area there are around 70 distinct Indian groups, speaking some 70 different languages.

Tourist Information

Visa: U.S. citizens do not need visas, but your passport must be valid for a minimum of six months. Tourist cards are given upon arrival, and these must be carried at all times. They are valid for 90 days and may be extended for an additional 60 days.

U.S. Embassy: Lima. 1400 block of Garcilaso de la Vega. Tel. 28-6000 and 33-8000.

Money: Peru is presently using two currencies as a result of their rapid inflation. The old currency, the *inti*, is still in use, but being replaced by *sol nuevo*. The *sol nuevo* is worth one million *intis*. Dollars can be exchanged in banks, *casas de cambio*, or with street money changers. Some hotels will change dollars, but at lower rates. *Casas de cambio* have longer hours and shorter lines than banks, and the rates are about the same. Street changers are useful for after hours, but be very careful of being cheated and count your money carefully. Exchange rates are better for cash than for travelers' checks. Major credit cards are widely accepted.

Postal System: Mail is extraordinarily slow. Mail from the U.S. can take up to a month. Do not send cash.

Telephone: Throughout Peru, the phone company is ENTEL. The one exception is in Lima, where the company is *La Compañía Peruana de Teléfonos*. Both offer long distance national and international telephone, telex, and telegram services. They are expensive. To call, you leave a large deposit, are given a receipt, and the difference is refunded to you when finished. You may use telephone credit cards with AT&T (191), MCI (190), TRT (192), and Sprint (196). Very few public telephones exist, although they are available at ENTEL offices.

Health: Don't drink tap water or eat salads or vegetables and fruit that you cannot peel.

Risks: Peru has a well-deserved reputation for theft. There are pickpockets, bag-snatchers, razor blade slashers (pack and pocket) con artists and crooked police. The guerrilla organization *Sendero Luminoso* is still somewhat active, but much less so than before. Check with the locals before going into remote areas.

Cultural Specifics

Greetings: Men and women shake hands in greeting and parting. Men embrace close friends and pat them on the back. Women kiss one another on the cheek.

Interaction: Foreigners are especially welcome in Peru, more so than in most countries. People generally stand much closer together when talking than North Americans. It is an insult to back off. People will ask about marital status, family, and occupation right away.

Dress: In the cities, slacks and shirts are more appropriate than jeans. If you are going to the highlands bring a jacket. Don't wear Indian clothing; it will insult the Indians.

Meals: Breakfast is usually between 7:30 and 9:00, and is simple. It might be rolls with ham, cheese, or jam, along with coffee. Lunch is usually eaten between 12:30 and 3:00. It usually begins with a pasta course, followed by steak, chops, chicken or fish, with a salad and rice. Dinner is usually served around 8:30 or 9:00. There may be a soup with noodles, vegetables and rice. Generally light.

Dining out: Nice restaurants provide excellent service, with two or three waiters hovering around to take care of your needs. The person who makes the dinner invitation is expected to pay. Restaurants add a 10% service charge, so tipping is optional. If taxes are added, it will be another 21%.

Holidays: New Year's Day (Jan. 1), Easter Week, Labor Day (May 1), Sts. Peter and Paul (June 29), Independence Days (July 28-29), St. Rosa of the Americas (Aug. 30), National Heroes' Day (Oct. 8), All Saints Day (Nov. 1), Immaculate Conception (Dec. 8), Christmas (Dec. 25).

Chapter 63

Puerto Rico

Commonwealth of Puerto Rico.

Puerto Rico is a territory of the United States, its residents are U.S. citizens and are subject to federal laws of the United States. Residents do not have voting rights for presidential or congressional elections, nor do they pay federal income taxes. They have the right to vote themselves to become the 51st state, but have so far chosen to remain a territory.

Area: 3,459 square miles

Population: (1990) 3,522,037

Population density, 1,035 per square miles

Capital: San Juan (1990) 437,745

Religion: Roman Catholic

Literacy Rate: 90%

Languages: Both Spanish and English are official languages.

Ethnic: 99.9% Hispanic

Geography

Puerto Rico is an island with the Atlantic Ocean to the north and the Caribbean Sea to the south. Its climate is tropical, with a mean temperature of 77 degrees. Three-fourths of its area is mountainous. The remainder is coastal plain. Its highest point is Cerro Puntita at 4,389 ft.

Economy: Puerto Rico is a major hub of commerce, finance, and tourism. San Juan is one of the world's busiest cruise ship ports. The commonwealth has one of the highest standards in the western hemisphere.

Tourist Information

Visa: Neither visas nor passports are required for U.S. citizens. It is as simple as going from one state to another. Citizens of foreign countries are required to have a visa.

Money: U.S. currency. Major credit cards are widely accepted.

Transportation: Taxis, buses, and rental cars are available at the airport and major hotels.

Postal System and Telephone: Same as in the United States

Tipping: Service charges are not included in restaurants. 15% tips are expected.

Health: Puerto Rico has no special health hazards.

Risks: Risks in cities are essentially the same as in the United States. Beware of pickpockets in crowds.

Holidays: Same as in U.S.

Chapter 64

Uruguay

Oriental Republic of Uruguay *(República Oriental del Uruguay)*
Area: 68,040 square miles
Population: (1995) 3,200,000
    Average annual rate of increase, 0.7%
    Density per square miles, 47
    About 90% of the people live in cities; approximately half are in Montevideo.
Capital: Montevideo. Population (1992) 1,500,000
Religion: Roman Catholic, 66%; Other, 34%
Literacy Rate: 94%
Language: Spanish
Ethnic Groups: European descent, 88% (Spanish, Italian); Mestizo 8%; Black, 4%

Geography

Eastern Uruguay is comprised of rolling hills, while the west is more level. Its coast has fine beaches, large dunes and headlands. Much is grassland. Being in the southern hemisphere, seasons are opposite of North America. The climate is temperate, never very cold, and rainfall is evenly distributed throughout the year.

Tourist Information

U.S. Embassy: Montevideo. Lauro Miller 1776.
Tel. 40-9051.

Visas: U.S. citizens do not need visas, but are required to have a tourist card, valid for 90
days, and extendible for 90 more days.

Money: The basic unit, the *peso uruguayo*, replaced
the *peso nuevo* in 1993, but some of the old
money is still around. Inflation is very high.
Banks can change dollars, including travelers'
checks. *Cambios* are available in cities to exchange money. Major credit cards are widely
accepted. There is no black market.

Postal System: Mail service is poor. Important letters should be sent registered.

Telephone: ANTEL, the phone company, has long-
distance offices in most cities. Public phones
require tokens. AT&T operators can be
reached by dialing 000410.

Health: There are no particular health problems in
Uruguay. In the cities tap water is safe.

Risks: There are no particular risks in Uruguay.

Cultural Specifics

Greetings: Males and females shake hands. Good
friends, male and female, may kiss on the
cheek.

Dress: Casual wear for men is a sports jacket, shirt,
and pants. Women can wear pants. Neither
should wear jeans or shorts. If it is winter, remember to take a coat.

Meals: Breakfast is usually eaten around 7:00 to
7:30. It is light; usually toast, butter, and

cheese with coffee. Lunch is around 1:00, and
might consist of steak, potatoes, and salad.
Dinner, served around 10:00, is similar to
lunch, but lighter. Omelets are popular.

Dining out: Better restaurants usually serve dinner
from 9 PM to midnight. Informal restaurants
begin around 7:30. Among the middle and
upper classes, one person is expected to pay
for the entire group. People of the lower class
usually pay individually. Waiters should be
given a 10% tip.

Holidays: New Year's Day (Jan. 1), Epiphany (Jan.
6), Carnival (three days before Ash Wednes-
day), Holy Week, Day of the Landing of the
33 Easterners (April 19), Labor Day (May 1),
Anniversary of the Birth of Artigas (June 19),
Constitution Day (July 18), Independence
Day (Aug. 25), Columbus Day (Oct. 12), All
Souls' Day, (Nov. 2), Christmas (Dec. 25).

Chapter 65

Venezuela

Republic of Venezuela *(República de Venezuela)*
Area: 352,143 square miles
Population: 21,800,000 (1995)
>Average annual rate of increase, 2.6%
>Density per square miles, 61.9

Capital: Caracas
Largest Cities: (1990) Caracas (1,290,087), Maracaibo (1,206,726), Valencia (616,000), Barquisimento (723,587)
Religion: Roman Catholic, 96%
Languages: Spanish, several Indian languages
Ethnic Groups: Mestizo, 67%; European descent 21% (Spanish, Portuguese, Italian); Black, 10%, Indian, 2%, other, 1%. Indians live primarily in the Amazon River Basin. There are approximately 40 different Indian groups.

Geography

Venezuela occupies the northernmost part of South America. It has some 1800 miles of coastline along the Caribbean Sea, with clear water and beautiful beaches. Some of the more popular Caribbean islands, such as Aruba, Curacao, and Trinidad, lie just off its coast. Venezuela has a remarkably diversified topography. It includes part of the Andes mountains, more mountains along the coast, and the southern part of the country is taken up by the Amazon Basin.

Economy: Oil exportation is the heart of the economy for Venezuela. Until 1970 it was the world's largest exporter. As a result of oil revenues, Caracas is a very modern city.

Climate

Because of its proximity to the equator, the temperature is fairly constant all year long, varying mainly due to elevation. Rainfall is seasonal, with the dry season from December to April, and the rainy season from May through November. The Amazon River basin is rainy all year.

Tourist Information

Visa: Citizens of the United States do not need visas. Tourist cards, valid for 90 days, are issued by the airlines. They can be extended for another 90 days.

U.S. Embassy: Caracas. Avenida Francisco de Miranda and Avenida Principal de la Floresta, La Floresta. Tel. 285-2222.

Money: The unit of currency is the *bolivar,* divided into 100 *céntimos.* Banks and *casas de cambio* can change dollars. There is no black market, and banks offer the best rate of exchange both for cash and traveler's checks. Major credit cards are widely accepted.

Postal System: Mail service is slow and unreliable. Airmail letters to the U.S. can take up to a month.

Telephone: International calls can be made from CANTV office. There are plenty of public telephones available, but many don't work. The newer phones require phone cards, available at CANTV offices.

Health: There are no particular health problems in Venezuela, and tap water is generally safe to drink in the cities.

Risks: Venezuela is relatively safe, but street crime can be a problem in the cities, especially in Caracas. Carry your passport with you, and avoid the police if possible.

Cultural Specifics

Greetings: Shake hands with both sexes. Friends, both men and women or women and women, kiss on the cheek when greeting and parting.

Interaction: People stand very close to one another when talking. Don't back off. Unlike most of the Latin American countries, Venezuelans don't ask personal questions right away, such as marital status and about family.

Dress: People dress pretty formally in the cities, and only the more stylish jeans are acceptable. Shorts are acceptable only in resort areas. Ties should be worn in better restaurants.

Meals: Breakfasts, eaten early, are scrambled eggs with bread, rolls, and coffee. Lunch is eaten between noon and 2:00. It is the main meal of the day, usually consists of several courses, often including soup, salad, meat, vegetables, fruit, and dessert. Dinner is usually eaten around 9:00, and is normally light. Common is soup and sandwich.

Dining out: Reservations are needed for the better restaurants. Whoever invites for the meal is expected to pay. Frequently there are separate checks for drinks and food. Restaurants add 10% as a service charge. For good service, tip another 5%.

Holidays: New Year's Day (Jan. 1), Carnival (Monday and Tuesday before Lent), Holy Thursday, Good Friday, Labor Day (May 1), Battle of Carabobo (June 24), Columbus Day (Oct. 12), Christmas Eve and Christmas Day (Dec. 24 and 25).

To order these books, call 1-800-356-9315
(or 802-482-2988 from outside the U.S. and Canada).
The Romance Zone $29.95
Spanish Lingo for the Savvy Gringo 14.95
Mexican Slang plus Graffiti 9.95
Bilingual Cooking: La Cocina Bilingüe 5.00
Native Speaker: Teach English & See the World . . 5.00
Bookstores, call Sunbelt Publications 1-800-626-6579.

Index

Information & Orders

Thanks for reading our book; we hope it has helped you in your quest. Feel free to express your opinion regarding this book at any time by fax at 713-681-0950.

Visit our website at www.foreignromance.com

For information on T.L.C. Worldwide, Inc. services including tours; personal ads; their magazine, *The Latina Connection*; videos or membership, call 713-896-9993 or write to:
T.L.C. Worldwide, Inc.
P. O. Box 924994
Houston TX 77292-4994

To order books, call 1-800-356-9315.
The Romance Zone $29.95

Other books of interest: See your local bookstore or call 1-800-356-9315 (1-802-482-2988):
Spanish Lingo for the Savvy Gringo 14.95
Mexican Slang plus Graffiti 9.95
Bilingual Cooking: La Cocina Bilingue 5.00
Native Speaker: Teach English & See the World . . 5.00